GAMBLING IN THE
NINETEENTH-CENTURY
ENGLISH NOVEL

Gambling in the Nineteenth-Century English Novel

'A Leprosy is o'er the Land'

MICHAEL FLAVIN

sussex
ACADEMIC
PRESS

Brighton • Portland

#50693470

10-14-05

2 4 6 8 10 9 7 5 3 1

First published in 2003 in Great Britain by
SUSSEX ACADEMIC PRESS
PO Box 2950
Brighton BN2 5SP

and in the United States of America by
SUSSEX ACADEMIC PRESS
5824 N.E. Hassalo St.
Portland, Oregon 97213-3644

British Library Cataloguing in Publication Data
A CIP catalogue record for this book is available from the British Library.

Library of Congress Cataloging-in-Publication Data
Flavin, Michael.
Gambling in the nineteenth-century English novel : "a leprosy is o'er the land" / Michael Flavin.
p. cm.
Includes bibliographical references and index.
ISBN 1–903900–18–2
1. English fiction—19th century—History and criticism.
2. Gambling in literature. I. Title.
PR868.G32 F58   2003
823'.809355—dc21

2002014707

Typeset and designed by G&G Editorial, Brighton
Printed TJ International, Padstow, Cornwall
This book is printed on acid-free paper.

Contents

[v]

Contents

List of Illustrations

Acknowledgments

I would like to thank Geraldine Knights for proof-reading and heroic patience, in roughly equal measure. I am equally indebted to Ron Knights for meticulous technical support, and to Alise Knights for no less thorough hospitality. Finally, I would like to thank Liam and Rosemary, without whose help I managed perfectly well.

The author and publisher acknowledge Tate Picture Library for permission to reproduce *Derby Day* by William Powell Frith. *The Derby – At Lunch* is courtesy of Central Saint Martin's College of Art and Design, London, UK/Bridgeman.

Introduction

'The Most Prevalent Vice of the Age'

'Mix with the young nobility. There's many of 'em, who can't spend a dollar to your guinea, my boy. And as for the pink bonnets' (here from under the heavy eyebrows there came a knowing and not very pleasant leer) – 'why, boys will be boys. Only there's one thing I order you to avoid, which, if you do not, I'll cut you off with a shilling, by Jove, and that's gambling, sir.'

'Oh, of course, sir,' said George.

William Makepeace Thackeray, *Vanity Fair* (1847–8)

Why did gambling become such a pariah for the Victorians? After all, the gambling ethos was at the centre of Victorian society, as a number of its most successful subjects were gamblers in either financial or marital markets. Perhaps gambling was attacked *because* it exposed the principles of chance and speculation which lay at the heart of nineteenth-century English society, despite the best attempts of that society to present itself as rational and orderly.

This book explores gambling in nineteenth-century England through an examination of representations of gambling in the works of novelists. Literature's ability to construct overlapping discourses, in which representations of gambling also cast light on marriage, speculation, politics, morality and the impact of evolutionism, make it the ideal medium with which to assess gambling as a radically evolving cultural practice through the nineteenth century. My approach here will be to examine scenes of gambling from novels, to consider the role gambling played in the lives of the individual novelists and to place the overall findings in the wider context of the history of gambling in nineteenth-century England.

Chapter One, an historical overview, begins by first considering gambling from the early-nineteenth century up to the mid-1840s, focusing particularly on Crockford's club, 1828–44. Gambling in this period was associated with the excesses of a decadent élite. Theatrical representations of gambling in the first half of the nineteenth century abound. From about the 1840s, concern grew about the extent of working-class gambling, and this led to a Select Committee on Gaming in 1844 and a Gaming Act in 1845.[1] Parliamentary responses to gambling are discussed n the context of mid-century attitudes towards gambling. I will also look at non-fiction commentaries on gambling in the period 1844–1905, uncovering popular attitudes to gambling throughout the second half of the century. Although the final texts in this particular section date from the early-twentieth century they are included because they are an assault on gambling from the left wing of the political spectrum written by leading figures in the embryonic labour movement, and thus they offer a different perspective on the anti-gambling argument.

In order to explore fully the connection between gambling in nineteenth-century novels and gambling in nineteenth-century society, *Chapter One* focuses primarily on modes of gambling which are featured within the chapters on individual novelists. Hence the main forms of gambling featured in *Chapter One* are casino games and betting on horse racing. Card games for money also feature repeatedly and in reality such games were commonplace. However, their history is less well documented, mainly because card games most often took place in private homes rather than public spaces. George Cruikshank (1852) mentions the persistence of card playing in private clubs after the 1845 Gaming Act had ended the games of hazard with which club life was formerly synonymous, but, in general terms, there is no authoritative history of card playing in the nineteenth century.[2] Conversely, the history of horse racing is fully documented in Wray Vamplew's *The Turf* (1976).[3]

Existing histories of gambling do not deal extensively with all the modes of gambling foregrounded in this study and do not focus specifically on gambling in literature. Mark Clapson's *A Bit of a Flutter: Popular Gambling and English Society, 1823–1961* (1992) is the most substantial history of gambling covering the period in question, but has little to say about gambling in exclusive clubs in the first half of the century, and undertakes only a brief summary of legislation on gambling throughout the nineteenth century.[4] Furthermore, Clapson's study is not interested in gambling as a literary theme. Roger Munting's *A Social and Economic History of Gambling in Britain and the USA* (1996) is less useful. The first chapter covers the entire history of gambling up to 1914 in both Britain and America, but is too general to have much relevance to this study.[5] J. Jeffrey Franklin's *Serious Play: The Cultural Form of the Nineteenth-Century Realist Novel* (1999) devotes a chapter to a consideration of gambling in George Eliot's *Middlemarch* and Anthony Trollope's *The Duke's Children*, both of which feature in this study, but Franklin is more interested in the figure of chance (what he refers to as 'fortuna') than in gambling in nineteenth-century literature *per se*.[6] Nineteenth-century histories of gambling, such as Andrew Steinmetz's *The Gaming Table* (1870), and John Ashton's *The History of Gambling in England* (1899), are more anti-gambling polemics than historical surveys.[7] The discussion that follows of gambling and nineteenth-century England establishes a social context in which the individual texts may be considered.

Chapter Two looks at gambling in four novels by Benjamin Disraeli. His representations of gambling are considered in relation to the figure of the debauched aristocrat and to the contemporary political climate. Disraeli's representation of gambling is distinctive in that he often uses a horse race as an arena in which to play-out wider conflicts, a technique apparent in both *The Young Duke* (1831) and in the Young England trilogy (1844–7).

Chapter Three analyses gambling in four novels by Charles Dickens. In *Nicholas Nickleby* (1838–9) the gamblers are titled reprobates, with Dickens drawing upon an established image of the gambler in the first half of the century. In *The Old Curiosity Shop* (1840–1), one character lower down the social scale is plagued by a mania for gambling. In *Hard Times* (1854) Dickens associates gambling with outright villainy, as a gambler commits a robbery and ensures that the blame falls elsewhere. In *Little Dorrit* (1855–7) one of the main characters, Rigaud, is defined from the outset in relation to gambling and, in common with Thomas Gradgrind junior in *Hard Times*, he is villainous. *Little Dorrit* also features widespread, rampant and ill-judged speculation which has a ruinous effect, a theme previously explored by Dickens in *Martin Chuzzlewit* (1843–4).

Chapter Four considers the importance of gambling in William Makepeace Thackeray's early life and the extent to which this fed through into a concern with gambling in his writings. There is a significant autobiographical element in Thackeray's portrayal of gambling in both *The Paris Sketch-Book* (1840) and in *Pendennis* (1850–2). In Thackeray's writings, a gamble is often an unfair contest, a situation that may connect with Thackeray's own experience, as he was duped out of his inheritance in card games.

Chapter Five takes three novels by George Eliot in which an element of gambling is present. In *Silas Marner* (1861) gambling features in the character of Dunsey Cass in order to show his irresponsibility. In *Middlemarch* (1871–2) Eliot develops the theme of gambling to a greater extent, and in *Daniel Deronda* (1874) gambling, through the character of Gwendolen Harleth, becomes one of the most important elements in the novel, encapsulating fundamental aspects of Gwendolen's personality. Eliot's personal antipathy towards gambling is examined, and consideration given to how this feeds through into her writing in, for example, the character of Lapidoth in *Daniel Deronda*.

Chapter Six focuses primarily on Thomas Hardy's *The Return of the Native* (1878) and *A Laodicean* (1881), two novels which use gambling in different ways. In *The Return of the Native*, a gamble becomes the context in which a contest between two characters is played out, with Hardy using the medium of gambling to amplify an adversarial situation. In *A Laodicean* gambling is used to represent different aspects of two characters, George Somerset and Will Dare. In Somerset's case gambling reflects his situation at a specific juncture in the novel, but with Dare gambling is a more fundamental aspect of his nature.

Chapter Seven considers Anthony Trollope's use of gambling as a means of expressing the flaws in contemporary society as Trollope perceived it. In *The Way We Live Now* (1875) gambling is a form of recreation for the upper class, but it extends beyond this arena into the commercial world. Melmotte, the most spectacular financier in the novel, is shown to be a cross between a gambler and a confidence trickster. In *The Duke's Children* (1880), the gamblers are again upper class, but their recreation is thwarted by a character lower down the social scale.

Chapter Eight looks at three novels by George Moore, concentrating most on *Esther Waters* (1894). In earlier works such as *Spring Days* (1888) and *Mike Fletcher* (1889), Moore uses gambling as a signifier for irresponsibility and decadence, though he also (in *Spring Days*) employs the image of a race horse to comment about character and situation, a technique that is again apparent in *Esther Waters*, in which the world of gambling on horse racing is recorded in close detail. Moore adopts an anti-gambling position in *Esther Waters*, but this is modified by the extent to which he analyses the circumstances underpinning gambling. Moore had considerable knowledge of horse racing, knowledge which, on more than one occasion, becomes apparent in his writings.

It is not the intention of this study to be encyclopaedic. Rather, the purpose is to look at how gambling is represented in selected texts, and how this representation may be related to specific biographical and social contexts. An additional perspective takes place in relation to George Eliot, and particularly Thomas Hardy, as analysis suggests that these novelists' representations of gambling were influenced by evolutionism, with the chance element in gambling being used to reflect the important, deterministic effect of chance as suggested by Darwin. However, this issue is not examined in depth, partly because the present work does not seek to assess gambling in the context of the intellectual history of the nineteenth century (though it is acknowledged that the effects of Darwinian theory were social as well as intellectual and spiritual), and more pertinently because the impact of evolutionary theory on nineteenth-century literature has been explored thoroughly elsewhere, most notably by Gillian Beer.[8]

Contemporary accounts of nineteenth-century gambling use the word 'gaming' in relation to casino games; 'betting' is used to refer to gambling on horse racing. I shall use the most common present-day term, 'gambling', to refer generically to all betting and wagering activity, using more specific terms when this is relevant to the argument. The difference between various forms of gambling, and the effect that these distinctions have on the novels under consideration, will be discussed in the *Conclusion*, which ends the book by making some general observations on the literary, biographical and social significance of gambling in nineteenth-century English literature.

chapter one

Gambling in
Nineteenth-Century England

Gambling, Leisure and Crockford's Club, 1828–1844

♥

Before the industrial revolution, work and leisure were not demarcated clearly. Within a basically agrarian economy the framework for leisure was determined by the agricultural cycle and the ecclesiastical calendar. For most of the eighteenth century the ruling class tolerated the notion and practices of popular recreation. This was partly because both gentleman and commoner participated in similar forms of leisure, notably animal sports. Gambling was a key element in sporting and recreational activities, and indeed it was endemic in the leisure culture of eighteenth-century England.[1] Recreation was, in the main, sponsored by aristocratic patronage, and it was generally recognized that the populace needed the occasional opportunity to let off steam. In this respect leisure had a socially cohesive function, with aristocratic patronage tending to diminish any feelings of class animosity. One of the consequences of this form of social organization was that, as attitudes towards leisure changed through the nineteenth century, landed Tories were more amenable to the idea of a robust, popular culture than the liberal reformists who sought to advance the common people.[2] The aristocracy and the working class had a common link through leisure.

In chapter thirty-four of William Makepeace Thackeray's *Vanity Fair* (1847–8), a novel set around the Napoleonic Wars, a young man ruins his chances of gaining an inheritance when, in a drunken state, he attempts to entertain a wealthy, female relative with stories about prize-fighting, mentioning 'Dutch Sam' and the 'Tutbury Pet'. In so doing he highlights one of the most popular forms of sport and gambling in the early nineteenth century, as well as showing how certain areas of respectable society remained beyond its catchment area. Prize fighting, otherwise known as pugilism, was a central sport in the early part of the century.

The enthusiasm for pugilism was partly due to the national atmosphere around the time of the Napoleonic wars, as noted by Peter Bailey (1978): 'in the mythology of the Ring, the fist was England's national weapon and the skilful and courageous wielding of it in public kept alive the spirit of Waterloo.'[3] Officially, pugilism had been banned since 1750 but it had survived and indeed thrived because it benefited from aristocratic patronage, which was sufficient to keep the forces of law and order at a distance. However, pugilism declined in popularity from about the mid-1820s, attributable in part to the general change in manners and attitudes which signalled the onset of the Victorian era. Fighting was now thought to be vulgar, lacking in sobriety and respectability. Furthermore, more effective policing played a part in the sport's decline.[4] In addition, the very fact that pugilism was illegal created the conditions for its demise. As it existed technically outside the law it was vulnerable to the influence of criminal elements. More and more fights were fixed and the sport as a whole thereafter suffered a loss of integrity which, in turn, deterred large sections of the betting public.

J. C. Reid (1971) has described some of the features of the decline: 'decent boxers and impartial referees often went in fear of assault: indeed they were sometimes not only threatened, but beaten senseless for not falling in with the wishes of the gamblers.'[5] Pugilism was thus broken to a significant extent by corruption which, in turn, was the product of the potential profits to be had through gambling, although there was still sufficient interest in prize fighting for large crowds to travel by train to a fight between Ben Gaunt and Bendigo in 1845.[6] Later in this chapter, when we come to consider the development of horse racing in Victorian society, we shall see how a very different response from both the legislature and, even more crucially, the world of commerce, produced an entirely different situation in which gambling flourished.

Gambling in general was enormously popular during the Regency period, as explained by J. M. Golby and A. W. Purdue (1984): 'Regency England had an inordinate desire to wager, whether in the gilded surroundings of London clubs like Almack's or Whites, at the after-dinner card tables of genteel society or in the lowest of pubs or beer-houses'.[7] Almack's had opened in 1764. It later changed its name to Brooke's, and Charles Fox, Horace Walpole and William Pitt were all members. Gambling took place in all strata of society and was a national pastime. Significantly, Stock Exchange transactions in the Regency period and indeed throughout the first half of the nineteenth century were thought to be far closer to gambling than they are today, partly because they were very poorly regulated until the mid-century.[8]

However, the gradual shift in perception of the Stock Exchange also reflects wider class stratification. The predominantly upper-class Exchange distanced itself from gambling as gambling began to develop a set of unwholesome connotations. The close relationship between Stock Exchange dealing and gambling in the early nineteenth century may be gauged by the fact that stockbrokers sold national lottery tickets as well as shares.[9]

One of the principal reasons for the shift in the perception of gambling was the emergence of the concept of rational recreation, a movement that owed its origin to a more general drive to reform the habits and ways of the working population. Recreation acquired considerable momentum from the 1780s to the 1830s, and was an inevitable result of the developing pace of industrialization. As there arose an economic necessity for an orderly and regulated workforce, so anything which had the potential to compromise labour discipline became a matter for concern. The rise in population was also a factor. The population doubled between 1801 and 1851 and, as employment opportunities multiplied in large towns and cities, people became more mobile. This prompted government anxiety, with a growing and shifting working population having the capacity to create social disorder.[10] In August 1814, during celebrations for the centenary of the Hanoverian accession, gambling booths in Hyde Park formed part of the merriment. However, after the festivities had finished the crowd carried on gambling for another week until the Home Secretary intervened and the gambling booths were closed down. Gambling was thus associated all too easily with working-class indiscipline.[11] Furthermore, specific economic pressures were generated in the aftermath of the Napoleonic wars. Although this period was, for the rich and privileged, both prosperous and hedonistic, the wider social picture was unsettled. Demobilization within the military swelled the workforce and thereby unemployment, and the nation as a whole incurred a significant financial burden as a result of the conflict with France. There was no direct impact on the wealthiest people in society but it did cause both hardship and resentment in the remainder of the population. The degree of alarm felt by the ruling class about the disorderly potential of the populace was considerable, as John Belchem (1991) asserts:

> In the troubled period after the Napoleonic wars, labour discipline and public order appeared everywhere in crisis. The casualization of the agricultural proletariat in the south-eastern counties was followed by rapidly rising rates of vagrancy, pauperism and petty crime. In the factory towns of the north, peace and order were seemingly unenforceable at times of

cyclical downturn and mass unemployment. In London there was an urgent need for a professional police force both to control politically motivated crowd disturbance and to contain juvenile delinquency – masterless apprentices, orphans, under-employed youths, child prostitutes, all seemed to symbolize a breakdown in the order of the family, the parish and the workshop. Hence there arose the fear of what was soon to be called the 'dangerous classes' – a term borrowed from the French – an alliance of vagrants, criminals, political agitators and the unemployed, an ominous collective presence which threatened to corrupt and contaminate the entire working class.[12]

One of the themes of Benjamin Disraeli's *Sybil* (1845), examined in chapter two, is the destructive potential of the working classes, although the gamblers in *Sybil* are not the riotous proletariat but the indolent and socially ignorant aristocracy. Disraeli uses gambling in *Sybil* to signify the aristocracy's abrogation of its responsibility to lead, but wanton violence is the preserve of the masses. The novel illustrates how fear of the working class and its potential for unrest persisted for a considerable time after the Napoleonic Wars.

The desire to contain the working class in the early nineteenth century was acute and extended into the leisure arena. A change in attitude amongst the ruling class was taking place. The notion of leisure for the populace as a social safety valve was giving way to a desire to control a potentially unruly workforce. Arenas for general social congregation began to be regarded as morally corrosive. In 1830, an evangelical preacher, R. C. Dillon, illustrated graphically the hazards of unfettered recreation in a sermon about the evils of fairs:

> But again and again is the question put to us, – 'What harm can there be on once complying with the wishes of our children, and letting them go, at least once, to a place of public amusement? We take them merely to gratify a natural and innocent curiosity.' Brethren, the curiosity is too natural to be innocent.[13]

Leisure was now equated with exposure to temptation, leaving individuals prey to their innate depravity. The ruling class now tended to regard leisure as a 'dangerous frontier zone', requiring state vigilance and control.[14]

Against this social change, Crockford's Club stands out as a boisterous expression of confidence amongst the élite. William Crockford, the son of a fishmonger, was born in 1775. He appears always to have derived the bulk of his income from gambling, having been both a bookmaker and a racehorse owner. Henry Blyth (1969) compared Crockford to a famous character from Charles Dickens's *David Copperfield*:

At heart he was of the same breed as Uriah Heep; outwardly servile and humble in the presence of the rich, but inwardly plotting their downfall. And in the years to come William Crockford, like Uriah Heep, was to spend much of his time rubbing his fat white hands together in the background whilst the young blades who despised him were losing their patrimony to him by their extravagance and senseless folly.[15]

The building of Crockford's gaming club in St. James's Street, in the West End of London, commenced in 1826. According to Captain R. H. Gronow, in his *Reminiscences and Recollections*, the club was built partly on the proceeds of one twenty-four hour gambling session, in which Crockford won over one hundred thousand pounds from a party including Lord Thanet and Lord Granville.[16] Aristocrats gamble for equally staggering sums, and with similarly dramatic consequences, in Benjamin Disraeli's *The Young Duke* (1831). In the light of Gronow's testimony, Disraeli's fictional account of a card game between aristocrats for phenomenal sums appears to have had some actual precedent.

The social climate within which Crockford became renowned was, for a select few, decidedly hedonistic. In the aftermath of the Napoleonic wars, peace brought a more carefree disposition amongst those wealthy enough to enjoy it. A. L. Humphreys (1953) notes: 'after the peace there came a reaction, and life became a pursuit of pleasure. Crockford's was opened, and in full swing, between the years 1828 and 1844'. Crockford's benefited from a period of peace and prosperity, a period when the governing philosophy appears to have been, 'live well, drink hard, and laugh immoderately'.[17]

There was a voyeuristic admiration for the splendour and opulence of the post-Napoleonic wars high-life. *Bentley's Miscellany*, in an article from 1844, describes the opening of Crockfords:

> On the opening of this superb mansion in 1828 the whole fashionable world, male and female, crowded with eager curiosity, under cards of admission from the great proprietor and the old and privileged members of the Club, to view it. The newspapers were lavish of praise, and elaborate in description of its splendour and magnificence, and the population of London thronged to its exterior survey under much greater excitement than was apparent on the late opening of the splendid and stupendous national structure, The Royal Exchange.[18]

The opening of Crockford's was a fashionable event, featuring a congregation of the highest and most splendid tier of society. The club was renowned, according to Gronow, for 'the gentlemanly bearing and calm and unmoved demeanour, under losses or gains, of all the men of that generation.'[19] Gronow's observation has been underlined recently by J. Jeffrey Franklin (1999): 'gaming was a defining part of the traditional aristocratic ethos; the ability to win with magnanimity, to lose with dignity, and to honour gambling debts without question became one mark of a true gentleman'.[20] Under these conditions it is not hard to see how Crockford's acquired near-mythical status. It was patronized by the élite and made an ostentatious display of wealth; it was far removed from the ordinary lives of the vast majority of the population. Whether or not the stories that came out of it are true is not important. Crockford's provoked voyeuristic fascination. Part of its appeal lay in the fact that clubs were long-established in England and carried strong connotations of exclusivity. White's, also in St James's Street, was the oldest club in London, having been established in 1697. According to Gronow, 'its list of members comprised nearly all the noble names of Great Britain.'[21] White's famous gamblers included Lord Melbourne, Queen Victoria's first Prime Minister. In the early nineteenth century White's was renowned, as was the most exclusive club, Brooke's, for its games of whist for extraordinarily high stakes.[22] Gronow states that Whigs 'won and lost hundreds of thousands' playing faro and macao at Brooke's.[23] Wattier's Club, in Piccadilly, boasted the membership of the Duke of York and it was the favourite haunt of Beau Brummell. Heavy gambling also featured at clubs such as the Union and the Cocoa Tree, further down the social scale at Arthur's and Graham's. The Guard's club, of which Gronow, as a military man, was a member, only allowed billiards and whist for low stakes and thus safeguarded itself against heavy gambling. In fiction, the incorrigible gambling and military man, Rawdon Crawley (*Vanity Fair*) finds his most profitable victims in private parties at his house, rather than amongst his military comrades. The severe membership restrictions operating within many of the clubs reinforced class distinctions and bestowed a definite aura of superiority upon club members. Crockford's exclusive membership only served to enhance its reputation.

A number of famous personalities were associated with Crockford's. The Duke of Wellington was chairman of the management committee.[24] Edward Bulwer-Lytton and Benjamin Disraeli were both members, although Disraeli was not able to achieve membership until 1841, probably because of his Jewish origins.[25] When, in chapter two, we come to examine Disraeli's perspective on gambling in his novels in more detail, we will see, for example, how he set the opening chapter of *Sybil* in a fashionable gaming-house on the eve of the Epsom Derby. Disraeli understood the imaginative potential of the exclusive gaming-house as a signifier for wealth, nobility and opulence. While Queen Victoria and her husband did not gamble, it is worth noting that George Anson, Prince Albert's private secretary, was himself a gambler at Crockford's and thus the royal household was not entirely impervious to the appeal of the club.[26] The standing of the patrons of Crockford's reshaped, to an extent, the perception of gambling as 'it was now done openly, and it had the support of the principal men in London, socially and politically'.[27] The legislators who might have attacked Crockford's frequently enjoyed its hospitality. This fact was not wholly overlooked by the population at large. At a trial, in 1833, of six people accused of keeping and maintaining a common gaming-house, Mr Phillips, for the defence, 'advised the parish officers to go to Crockford's, not far distant from the house in question, where they would find lords and peers of the realm at play'.[28] Gambling was associated with the ruling class, but as the nature of the ruling class changed through the century so did the perception of gambling and it came to be associated with a decadent and irresponsible elite who found their working-class corollary in a debauched proletariat, leaving only a conscientious middle class to uphold decency.

There was contemporary opposition to Crockford's. An article in *The Times* of 1 January 1828, reporting on the opening the club, appeared under the headline, 'Crockford's Hell':[29]

> The establishment of the Pandemonium in St James's under the entire superintendence of the fishmonger and his unblushing patronizers, lately called forth the opinion of the highest personage in the kingdom, who expressed himself in a manner which reflected the utmost credit on his head and heart. A nobleman of some standing at Court, in answer to a question from his Royal master denied, in the most unequivocal way, having become a subscriber.

Clearly, King George IV wholly disapproved of Crockford's. He was reported as stating, in the same article, that it and similar establishments, were 'not only a disgrace to the country at large, but the age in which we live'.[30] Curiously, however, he had been significantly less hostile to gambling only a few years earlier, when he was a notable patron of pugilism, as Reid points out.

> The Prince of Wales, who became Prince Regent and later King George IV, his brothers, the Duke of York and the Duke of Clarence, later King William IV, were supporters, patrons, bettors; the presence of one or other of these at an 'illegal' contest at Moulsey Hurst or Crawley Downs was sufficient to deter even the most zealous of magistrates from issuing a warrant. Not only did the Prince of Wales attend fights, at least until 1788, and visit the training-rooms in London, but he cultivated the society of

boxers and received them at Court. On 24 July 1821, when he was crowned King, eighteen of the leading pugilists of England, including Cribb, Spring, Belcher, Richmond, Owen, Hudson and Oliver, under the direction of 'Gentleman' John Jackson, were chosen by the King to act as ushers at Westminster Hall.[31]

It is possible that, by 1828, the monarch sensed, or had been made aware of, the changing atmosphere of the times and therefore adopted an anti-gambling stance. His condemnation, however, does not appear to have had any effect on the patrons of Crockford's. Rhetorical disapproval and selective tolerance existed alongside each other. This paradoxical feature of orthodox views about gambling runs right through the nineteenth century, with, for example, the suppression of off-course betting on horseracing for the bulk of the population being accompanied by the untroubled survival of Tattersall's, the off-course betting arena for the upper class. Towards the end of the Victorian period, George Moore's *Esther Waters* (1894) highlights explicitly the class bias inherent in the treatment of gambling by both the legislature and the judiciary (see chapter eight). George IV condemned gambling though he had participated in it himself. The judge in chapter thirty-nine of *Esther Waters* hands down a custodial sentence to a woman reduced to criminality because of gambling, yet his own gambling, which is well known, is condoned or at least ignored.

William Crockford derived considerable wealth and influence from his club, and capitalized on a favourite hobby of the moneyed upper class. His career reflects wider social and economic changes, involving friction between the professional businessman and the gentleman amateur:

> One may safely say, without exaggeration, that Crockford won the whole
> of the ready money of the then existing generation. As is often the case at
> Lord's Cricket-ground, the great match of the gentlemen of England
> against the professional players was won by the latter.[32]

Crockford prospered as money began to rival connections and breeding as a route to power and influence. He held a very real economic power over many of his clients. He resigned in 1840 but Crockford's the club continued to trade, though the loss of its founder signalled the end of an era. Its demise was heralded by the 1844 Select Committee on Gaming, which will be examined shortly, at which Crockford himself was called as a witness, but he was (from the Committee point of view) vague and unhelpful in his evidence. The Committee presented its report on 20 May 1844; Crockford died five days later. The subsequent Gaming Act of 1845 introduced a harsher legal climate in respect of gambling. The decline of Crockford's as a point of assembly for the wealthy and fashionable was, according to Humphreys, typified by its tolerance of public smoking, a practice which hitherto had been frowned upon by the club.

> At Crockford's there was in 1844 no smoking-room, and it is surprising to hear that in the summer evenings members used to stand at a late hour outside in the porch drinking champagne, smoking cigars, and looking at people going home from parties and the opera. This sounds a rapid descent from the good manners of an earlier date. It may sound a strange saying, but it is nevertheless true that Crockford's without Crockford rapidly became demoralized and of no account.[33]

For Blyth, the demise of William Crockford symbolized the end of the early nineteenth-century hedonistic spirit and the beginning of 'the new Victorianism'.[34] The legislators in the House of Commons and, even more significantly, the interest groups and individuals propelling the economy responded more urgently to concerns which were recognized increasingly as middle-class. Significantly, in 1836 the Reform Club published its first list of members, including Gronow. Rule twenty-four prohibited hazard, the most popular game at Crockford's. Rule twenty-five stated: 'no higher stakes than half-a-guinea points shall ever be played for, nor shall any card or billiard playing be permitted in the Club after 2 a.m.'[35] The exclusive gambling club of the early nineteenth century was on the way out, as new, more sedate forms of recreation took their place, thereby signalling a change in the mood of the upper classes. Crockford's was the swansong of an outmoded age, characterized by self-indulgence among a confident, upper-class elite.

One of the main reasons why gaming houses were outlawed in the Gaming Act of 1845 was because they had begun to cater for an increasing number of working-class gamblers, which prompted anxiety in the wider context of concern about the ways in which working people amused themselves. The gaming houses that the working class frequented were a far cry from Crockford's in terms of decor, clientele and atmosphere. Primary source information concerning them is, to say the least, thin on the ground. One article which does deal with them, however, is 'Hells in London', published in *Fraser's Magazine* in 1833.[36] It begins by surveying the up-market clubs and their visible prosperity in the face of nominal prohibition: 'their enormous wealth is applied to the corruption of evidence, always unwilling, because the witnesses expose their own habits and culpablity in attending these nefarious dens of infamy' (p. 193). The author moves on to focus on the lower class clubs: 'on an average during the last twenty years, about thirty hells have been regularly open in London for the accommodation of the lowest and most vile set of hazard players' (p. 194). The figures are not substantiated by any further comment, but even if they are only very broadly accurate they suggest that the facilities for working-class gambling in gaming houses were extensive. The most telling distinction between these clubs and Crockford's (aside from the social class of the clientele) lies, according to the author, in the nature of the proprietors, the pressure applied to exact payment and the refreshments on offer.

> The generality of the minor gambling-houses are kept by prize-fighters, and other desperate characters, who bully and hector the more timid out of their money, by deciding that bets have been lost when in fact they have won. Bread, cheese, and beer, is supplied to the players, and a glass of gin is handed, when called for, gratis. To these places thieves resort, and such other loose characters as are lost to every feeling of honesty and shame: a table of this nature in full operation is a terrific sight; all the bad passions appertaining to the vicious propensities of mankind are portrayed on the countenances of the players. An assembly of the most horrible demons could not exhibit a more appalling effect; recklessness and desperation overshadow every noble trait which should enlighten the countenance of a human being. (p. 195)

The tone of hysteria to which the author rises exposes fully the vitriolic anti-gambling argument inscribed in the text. We may thus approach the report with a certain degree of scepticism yet, on the other hand, the article is intended to be an account of working-class gambling in London based on factual observation. The author may bring his own attitudes to the text but, given the intricacy and accuracy with which he describes the game of hazard (p. 194), it seems most likely that the article veers more towards fact than fiction.

There appeared to be a limited prospect of social mobility between the various kinds of gaming-houses. A successful gambler at a low gaming-house could, through his newly acquired wealth, gain entry to 'houses of higher play' and thereafter to 'crown houses, and associate with gamblers of respectable exterior' (p. 196). The author is keen to maintain distinctions between the various kinds of houses, detailing the 'third-rate houses' (above the lowest ones), of which he counts approximately twenty-five, and the 'middle class of gambling-houses' (p. 197), which are distinct from the lowest houses not only by virtue of the stakes played for but also because they open at three in the afternoon, rather than eleven at night. We can therefore see that the forms of social stratification perpetrated by so-called respectable society were repli-cated within the demi-monde of gambling.

While the odd individual might enjoy a gambling success and thus elevate himself, if only temporarily, in society, the only sure winners in the gaming-houses were the proprietors. Crockford was the most notable example of this principle, but the author of 'Hells in London' focuses upon an unnamed gaming-house keeper who prospers to the extent that he is able to fraternise with the aristocracy in horse racing circles. Racing is thereby identified as the most superior mode of gambling, a belief challenged in practice by the increased participation of working-class people in gambling on horse racing from around the mid-century onwards. The idea that gambling on horse racing was qualitatively distinct from and superior to other forms of gambling remained attractive, as evidenced in, for example, Anthony Trollope's contribution to *British Sports and Pastimes* in 1868 (see chapter seven). The value of 'Hells in London' is that it gives some indication of the scale of working-class gambling in gaming-houses in the period after the opening of Crockford's and before legislation suppressed the houses. While facilities for gambling were plentiful they do not appear to have reached epidemic proportions. Furthermore, while the working-class houses seemed to have been rather dangerous places they did not bear witness to the spectacular gains and losses which charac-terized play at the grandest houses. At the end of the article the author of 'Hells in London' appears to accept aristocratic profligacy as an endemic feature of the upper classes, and he is only concerned with its effects on the rest of society: 'The rich have a right to gamble – it is a privilege the law may give them; but let there be a barrier fixed, let them keep the vice to themselves, and let the cordon be effective, that it may not through them, as it has done, again inundate the country, vitiating and producing consequences of an alarming nature to the general inter-ests of the community' (p. 206). The idea of setting a bad example reflects a middle-class perspective which imbues 'Hells in London' as a whole.

The shift in the perception of gambling was, in part, a reaction against the excesses of the previous age.

> The reaction against the aristocratic style in gaming, as in dress, leisure and morality, headed by Wilberforce, the Clapham Sect and ultimately by Utilitarianism and moral evangelism, was accompanied in the 1830s and 1840s by the political threat to the aristocracy by the new middle class. (. . .) The very raising of the issue (of gaming) drove home the extent to which the upper classes and royalty had not only put their fortunes at risk

and set a bad 'example' – their excesses also gave radicalism its nearest equivalent to the pre-revolutionary *ancien régime*.[37]

Gambling was a feature of an aristocratic and hedonistic lifestyle, rejected by the subsequent generation which was propelled ideologically by capitalist economic theory and evangelical Christianity. A new moral climate emerged, characterized by restraint and sobriety. Nineteenth-century orthodoxy increasingly associated gambling with recklessness and self-abandonment, developments which we will see in practice when we come to examine novelists' perceptions (for example, Disraeli's *The Young Duke*, Charles Dickens's *Nicholas Nickleby* and *The Old Curiosity Shop*, and Thackeray's *Vanity Fair*), in which the characters who gamble are irresponsible, parasitic and duplicitous. In society as a whole, an ambitious middle class with a strong entrepreneurial streak became synonymous with the creation and not the dissipation of wealth. The new society was also highly industrious. Gambling epitomized the pleasure-seeking and irresponsible nature of the late eighteenth and early nineteenth-century aristocracy. They squandered wealth, they were unproductive, they were ostentatious.

Gambling and Melodrama

The plays chosen for examination arise from a period in which gambling was perceived as an upper-class pastime which was evolving into a lower-class vice. Some observations on the representations of gambling in nineteenth-century theatre are relevant because of both the cultural significance of popular theatre in the Victorian era and the frequency with which literary works were adapted for stage production (this point is particularly pertinent in relation to Charles Dickens). My approach here will be to offer some general observations on nineteenth-century theatre and melodrama, and then to consider three plays, one from 1827 and two from 1840, in which gambling is a point of significant interest. My choices are rooted in the general methodology of this study, the next section of which will identify 1844 as a significant year in the history of gambling in Victorian England.

Strictly speaking, melodrama refers to a mode of theatrical representation using highly stylized gestures and speech, absolute moral categories, and music to identify and intensify the emotions, that emerged in France and Germany towards the end of the eighteenth century. The first piece known to be called a melodrama was Jean-Jacques Rousseau's *Pygmalion* (1770), and the first English performance to be designated a melodrama was Thomas Holcroft's *A Tale of Mystery*, loosely based on a piece by Pixerécourt, staged at Covent Garden in 1801. English melodrama emerged in the early nineteenth century to answer the popular demand for mass entertainment in the expanding towns. The basic energy of melodrama was essentially proletarian, though audiences at melodramas were far from being exclusively working-class.[38] Melodrama is constructed fundamentally on a dualism of values centred on the notion of good versus evil. This dualistic perspective, however, spills beyond the boundaries of both stage melodrama and prose fiction. On the largest scale of all, the most far-reaching issue which came to face the Victorians was itself both dualistic and extreme: did humankind descend from Adam or from ape?[39] Acknowledging the pervasiveness of the melodramatic imagination in the nineteenth-century psyche, we may thus, by considering what happens to gambling when it is seen through melodrama, better understand common perceptions of gambling. It is further clear that the success of stage melodrama, which went through a constant metamorphosis as the century progressed, was implicated in a range of other factors: moral, aesthetic and social.

Gambling, as we shall see, did occur as a theme in melodrama, but this in itself was not an innovation. In 1753, Edward Moore's play, *The Gamester*, used gambling to signify the villainy of one character, Stukely, and the weakness of another, Beverly.[40] Stukely uses a crooked gambling game to swindle Beverly, with the final aim of seducing Beverly's wife. At the end of the action, following the death by self-poisoning of Beverly and the arrest of Stukely, it is left to another character, Lewson, to deliver the explicit moral message in the concluding words of the play: 'let frailer minds take warning; and, from example, learn that want of prudence is want of virtue'. *The Gamester* did not disappear from the public consciousness after the mid-eighteenth century: it was still sufficiently well-known for the author of 'Hells in London' in *Fraser's Magazine* (1833) to state, in relation to a perceived reluctance of the press to notify the public of the dangers of gambling, 'the press has not performed its duty, or it would have more exposed the Stukeleys of society, and thereby have lessened the Beverleys in it'.[41] The association between financial restraint and moral probity helped to create the conditions in which gambling could be seen as a threat to society.

H. M. Milner's *The Hut of the Red Mountain: or, Thirty Years from a Gambler's Life* (1827), utilized fully the melodramatic potential of gambling.[42] Milner's play is a translation of a French melodrama, *Trente Ans, ou La Vie d'un Joueur*, by Ducange and Dinaux.[43] On page 7 of the preface to *The Hut of the Red Mountain*, it is pointed out that the translation is, at times, rather loose, especially in Act Two. This is because the second act of the French play is directly modelled on *The Gamester*, and the translator may have made reference to Moore's English text as well as the authentic French version. The plundering of *The Gamester* typifies a common practice within melodrama, with plots being recycled in a number of plays. *The Hut of the Red Mountain* is divided into three acts, with the first set in 1790, the second in 1805 and the third in 1820. It follows the career of Augustus Derancé, a helpless gambling addict who, through his weakness and corruption, causes the death of his father and murders two men, including his wife's uncle: his violation of family ties is his greatest crime. He is helped on his road to ruin by Warner, a wily and ruthless gambler. As the play opens, the stage directions indicate that gambling is to be associated with the upper classes, as the surroundings are bright and sumptuous.

> A suite of apartments in a Gaming-House, communicating by open doors with one another, brilliantly lighted and elegantly furnished – The middle one is the entrance – In the furthest Room the table is set out for the game of Rouge et Noir – In the front Chamber, chairs, sofas, &c.

The scene is witnessed by the morally upright Dermont who, soliloquizing on the conduct of Augustus, asks, 'is it possible that Augustus Derancé (. . .) can nightly resort here to squander his fortune and to lose his character?' thereby equating loss of money with loss of reputation, while implicitly associating financial prudence with moral righteousness. The ideology of *The Gamester* was clearly still alive and well some seventy-five years later.

Augustus's father dies when he realizes the scale and consequences of his son's gambling. His dying words utilize the melodramatic convention of extreme language, as he vehemently condemns Augustus.

> The destiny of the gamester is inscribed on the gates of hell. Ungrateful son! remorseless parricide! you will be a brutal husband and an unnatural father. Play will open to you the abyss of guilt, into which you will madly plunge. Your days will be recorded but by your crimes; and your life will end in poverty and despair.

The father's words foreshadow much of the rest of the action. Augustus and his family become increasingly impoverished until they are reduced to destitution. They have a son, Albert, who has been lost to them for many years. As the play draws to a close Albert reappears, although

Augustus does not realize that the stranger is his offspring. Warner hatches a plot, into which Augustus is drawn, to murder Albert. In the concluding scene Augustus is told that his intended victim is his son. At this point he turns against Warner and kills him, stating 'the father will protect the son'. The sanctity of family ties eventually prevails against vice. Augustus speaks the final words of *The Hut of the Red Mountain* and then kills himself. His final speech emphasizes the didactic aspect of the play, as he passes a final instruction to Albert: 'my son, as you would avoid my crimes, my dismal fate, shun gaming'. Gambling in *The Hut of the Red Mountain* is nefarious in the extreme, producing shame, ruin and death. In the year before the opening of Crockford's, gambling was stripped of its glamorous veneer by Milner and presented as a threat to family life. Judging by the thematic continuity from *The Gamester* to *The Hut of the Red Mountain*, the fear of gambling's destructive potential was deeply rooted in the popular imagination and, as the century progressed, this anxiety was increasingly drawn into the open by a variety of commentators.

On 8 December 1840, Edward Bulwer-Lytton's play *Money* was premiered at the Theatre Royal, Haymarket.[44] Although it is not a melodrama, *Money* is of interest because it uses gambling to make points about the direction in which society was moving. *Money* follows the fortunes of Alfred Evelyn, a man of considerable ability and insight but limited means. He receives a large inheritance unexpectedly, whereafter he is fawned upon by people who had previously treated him with condescension. His support is pursued by rival political factions. Their conduct causes Evelyn to compare politics to a game of battledore (a form of badminton), in which a useless object is simply knocked back and forth in the air by the protagonists. Disillusioned by the hypocrisy and sycophancy which follows wealth, Evelyn loses money deliberately to the wily professional gambler, Captain Dudley Smooth, otherwise known as 'Deadly Smooth'. Smooth is cool, calm and calculated, 'the finest player at whist, écarté, billiards, chess, and piquet between this and the Pyramids'. He favours modes of gambling in which he faces a human opponent and thus he is intensely combative beneath his impassive veneer. As he is seemingly devoid of emotion he can be seen as the personification of gambling as he is not burdened by considerations of right and wrong and is solely interested in economic exchange. In a culture obsessed with surface gentility, Smooth deliberately addresses each character by their first name. He refuses to obey social decorum by being deferential and instead deals with each person according to their merits and talents.

Throughout the play the aristocracy is satirized. Sir Frederick

Blount is foppish and unmanly and cannot pronounce the letter 'r', as in 'stwange person, Mr Evelyn! – quite a chawacter!'. He is comparable to Charles Dickens's feckless aristocrat in *Nicholas Nickleby* (1838–9), Lord Frederick Verisopht, who finally displays strength of character when he is involved in a confrontation at a gambling table (see chapter three). The representation of the aristocracy in *Money* can be related to the dominance of domestic melodrama in the mid nineteenth-century theatre, which focused on the trials and tribulations of female rather than male characters, but its ethos was strongly anti-aristocratic.[45] In *Money*, Evelyn, having experienced life both as a rich man and a poor man, is profoundly conscious of the hypocrisy pervading society, stating, 'that is the difference between rich and poor: it takes a whirlwind to move the one – a breath may uproot the other!'. The characters in *Money* interact in a social environment in which esteem is determined by material wealth and inherited privilege. The feckless aristocrat in *Money* is tolerated by most of the other characters precisely because he is an aristocrat. Money will also do this job in *Money*, demonstrating how capital was coming to rival lineage as a means of getting ahead.

Following a romantic misunderstanding between Evelyn and Clara Douglas, the woman he loves, Evelyn enters into a loveless betrothal with Georgina Vesey, the daughter of the avaricious Sir John Vesey. This is the point at which Evelyn's gambling begins, not as the pursuit of wealth but, paradoxically, as an act of defiance against greed. His wilful defeat in the marriage foreshadows his deliberate gambling loss. When challenged about his new hobby, Evelyn states, 'a cheap opiate – anything that can lay the memory to sleep. The poor man drinks, and the rich man gambles – the same motive to both!' Here, gambling is a form of escapism, allowing the gambler to withdraw temporarily from his problems. Evelyn's phrase is also resentful of the line of demarcation between rich and poor with regard to their preferred modes of recreation, and he sees them united by a common denominator and purpose.

The gambling theme in *Money* comes to the fore in act three, scene three, which is set in a club. The stage directions at the beginning of the scene emphasize the indolence of the club members and, in so doing, foreshadow the beginning of Benjamin Disraeli's novel, *Sybil* (1845):

The interior of ———'s Club; night; lights, &c. Small sofa-tables, with books, papers, tea, coffee, &c. Several members grouped by the fireplace; one member with his legs over the back of his chair; another with his legs over his table; a third with his legs on the chimney-piece. To the left, and in front of the stage, an old member reading the newspaper, seated by small round table; to the right a card table, before which *CAPTAIN DUDLEY SMOOTH* is seated and sipping lemonade; at the bottom of the stage another card table.

Smooth is alert where the other characters are inert. He is not at the club for pleasure and relaxation: he is there to work. In the ensuing action Evelyn appears to lose his fortune to Smooth, whereafter Smooth is much sought after by his social superiors in a process that parallels Evelyn's transformation in the wake of receiving his inheritance. The irony of the situation is not lost on Smooth, who remarks to Sir John Vesey, 'the more a man's worth, John, the worthier man he must be!'. Smooth is acutely conscious of the power of capital in a changing society, where social mobility was on offer to those with the requisite entrepreneurial skills.

The social world in *Money* is an environment in which, as Evelyn comments, 'it was not criminal to gamble – it was criminal to lose'. The objection to gambling is not on moral grounds, rather it is a case of money being the only value system recognized by the majority of the characters: success equals virtue and failure equals vice. As the play heads towards its conclusion, Evelyn and Clara Douglas renounce each other for truly moral reasons, even though this action requires considerable self-sacrifice; they act with a sense of purpose not determined by the pursuit of wealth. This is apparent in Evelyn's protestation of love:

> Could you but see my heart at this moment, with what love, what veneration, what anguish it is filled, you would know how little, in the great calamities of life, fortune is really worth.

Evelyn, the character at the moral centre of *Money*, espouses a value system of greater integrity and depth than most of his fellow characters can attain. In the wider context it is an over-simplistic position because, in a society in which an increasingly large number of people were engaged in wage-labour, money was critically important. However, *Money* is a pertinent satire on avarice in the context of a society in which strategies for gaining wealth were a matter of concern. By condemning avarice it could be argued that *Money* espouses an older value system but this is undercut by Bulwer-Lytton's representation of the aristocracy. Gambling in *Money* is more than simply a vice as it also provides an implicit commentary on the mercenary nature of contemporary politics and the marriage market.

In the nineteenth century it was commonplace for popular contemporary works of fiction to be adapted for the stage. Given the sizeable volume of serial publication in the Victorian era, this created the peculiar situation whereby works frequently appeared on stage before they were completed in print, as commercially-minded theatres were eager to be the first to stage a production. Given Charles Dickens's popularity as a serial novelist, his works were adapted for the nineteenth-century stage probably with greater frequency than those of any other Victorian writer. Dickens's love of the theatre is well known and, prior to the commencement of his career as a novelist, between 1836 and 1837, he wrote three works for the stage. His work is particularly well-suited to stage adaptation as it often employs the language and plot structure of melodrama. In considering Dickens and melodrama, however, two points are noteworthy. The first relates to the problems involved in making cross-generic comparisons. The stage and the novel are separate forms, their pace and extent of development in the nineteenth century is substantially different and it is therefore unfair to regard a Dickens novel as a displaced melodrama, or to draw over-simplistic conclusions regarding the presence of melodrama in Dickens. It is, however, reasonable to assert that certain aspects of melodrama percolated through into Dickens's fiction given his theatrical background and the pervasive nature of the melodramatic imagination, and the influence of melodrama on Dickens's novels is well documented.[46] The second problem relates to the nature of the audience. There is a significant difference between the readership of Dickens's novels, which was drawn substantially from the middle class and the skilled working class, and the average crowd at a melodrama which, for much of the century, featured a majority of people from the unskilled and uneducated proletariat (though, as noted earlier, the audiences at melodramas were not exclusively working class). The practical upshot of this difference was that, when the novels were adapted for the stage, the more subtle themes were often sacrificed in the pursuit of action, adventure and spectacle. Melodrama, centring on performance and instantaneous effect, did not have the luxury of gradual development. There was also a substantial difference in audience expectation. People attended the theatre to be entertained and thrilled. The context of reception for prose fiction allowed for a more ruminative and exploratory procedure. Melodrama was bound generically to impact immediately upon the eyes and ears: the action of a novel is conducted in the mind.

In common with many other works by Dickens, *The Old Curiosity Shop* was the subject of stage adaptation. On 9 November 1840, Edward Stirling's melodrama, *The Old Curiosity Shop; or, One Hour from Humphrey's Clock*, was premiered at the Adelphi theatre.[47] At the time when Stirling's *The Old Curiosity Shop* was produced, Dickens's serialized novel was appearing in the periodical, *Master Humphrey's Clock*. Stirling's stage version appeared when the novel had reached chapter forty-nine. There are very significant differences between the two works. Stirling's version opens with Nell's grandfather as the sole occupant of the stage. He is in the grip of his gambling mania from the outset.

> I'll do it yet – I will – I will – it's all within my grasp – gold – glittering – shining – heaps – heaps (*stretching out his hand convulsively, grasping*) mine – mine – hers – ha, ha!

The grandfather's character is exposed rather than constructed and, similarly, shifts in the plot of Stirling's melodrama are sudden, being foreshadowed only by the overt signposting of forthcoming developments. Thus Master Humphrey, the visible narrator in Stirling's *The Old Curiosity Shop*, alerts the audience to the significance of Nell's grandfather leaving his home at night, in act one, scene two.

> There must be some hidden mystery in this, or he surely would not leave that dear child shut up in yonder gloomy dwelling, without a human being to comfort or advise her during the solitary hours of night. (. . .) His wandering manner and restless looks speak volumes – his seeming affection for his granddaughter may not be inconsistent with villainy of the worst kind.

The playwright is creating the conditions for the subsequent exposure of the grandfather's gambling mania.

The fact that Nell's grandfather is a gambler is revealed by Daniel Quilp who taunts him by referring to 'the gaming table, your nightly haunt'. However, the main gambling episode in Stirling's melodrama occurs in act two, scene three, when Nell's grandfather plays cards with the operators of a Punch and Judy show, Codlin and Short Trotters. In the novel this happens much later and the gamblers are List and Jowl, whom Nell and her grandfather encounter on their travels (ch. 29). In terms of melodramatic continuity and logistics this alteration seems reasonable enough as it would be difficult to introduce two new characters at an advanced stage in the narrative. Furthermore, List and Jowl are merely more evil versions of Codlin and Trotters, and therefore the words and deeds of the former dovetail comfortably with the personalities of the latter. The scene is set at Southampton races, thereby implicitly establishing gambling as a theme from the outset. Nell, occupying the foreground, informs her grandfather and the audience simultaneously that she is suspicious of Codlin and Short Trotters. Her grandfather's response demonstrates his imbecilic nature:

> No, dear Nelly; no, they will shut me up in a stone room, dark and cold, and chain me up to the wall – flog me with whips – never let me see thee more.

Trotters suggests a game of cards, the remark is overheard by Nell's grandfather, and the stage directions indicate that he reacts 'with wild energy'. However, Nell is reluctant to give her grandfather their money. The stage directions surrounding this process signify both her dutiful nature and his demonic energy:

> You hear, I must – I will have it – I will – I will – I'll right thee, child, never fear! (*she gives him her little purse – he snatches it and runs to the table eagerly*.)

The audience is informed that the grandfather is being duped by the other players. This is made clear when he presents the purse in order to gain entry to the game, eliciting the following reaction from Codlin which is, in turn, lifted directly from the mouth of Isaac List in the novel:

> Rather a light purse, but it may be enough to amuse a gentleman for half an hour. (*whispers to Trotters*) Right as ninepence.

His aside to Trotters does not appear in the novel. Stirling is informing his audience clearly and unambiguously that Nell's grandfather is about to lose. As her grandfather enters the game, Nell weeps, the context of the stage enabling her to represent her dismay explicitly. She thereafter provides the game with a running commentary:

> How he exults in this wretched sin, sitting there so wild and restless, so terribly eager, so ravenous for the paltry money! Oh! I could almost better borne to have seen him dead – this must be madness.

Presumably, the audience would be unable to see the cards being played. They therefore needed to be kept informed of the progress of the contest by the one character not involved directly. Although she does not describe each card and its significance, nor the ensuing (and fairly predictable) outcome, she directs the crowd's attention to her grandfather's irrational and immoral desire to gamble. The game concludes abruptly in abject defeat for Nell's grandfather, and the scene concludes with him making one last lunge towards the cards:

These! these! to make you rich! (*they exit R. through tent – Punch going on – Mob laughing.*)

His parting shot emphasizes the mania to which he has succumbed. The drama is suitably amplified by the background noise, indicating tumult and mockery.

The remainder of Stirling's melodrama consists of a series of implausible encounters as it rushes towards its conclusion. Firstly, Nell accidentally meets Quilp and then, as she and her grandfather take flight, they seek refuge at a cottage which turns out to be the home of their friend Kit Nubbles and his benevolent employers, Mr and Mrs Garland. Quilp devises a scheme to kidnap Nell, whereafter his nominal accomplices, Fred Trent and Dick Swiveller, begin to withdraw their allegiance from him. This confirms Quilp as the unchallenged villain of the melodrama. As the kidnap attempt takes place Fred refuses to take part, an act which facilitates a family reunion at the end of the action. Quilp is thwarted and ejected by a combination of Kit and Mr and Mrs Garland. The speed with which the plot concludes is, from a literary point of view, unsatisfactory but the fundamental criterion for successful melodrama is fulfilled. Virtue emerges triumphant, the villain is overthrown. In common with *The Hut of the Red Mountain*, vice is conquered with the aid of the strength of family ties.

Many features of Dickens's novel are overlooked in Stirling's play. The most interesting omission, with specific regard to gambling, is the episode in which Nell's grandfather enters her bedroom and steals money from her purse in order to play cards with List and Jowl. This, at first sight, seems strange, simply because of the high dramatic potential of that scene. However, in terms of melodramatic classification it is pertinent to recall that the villain of *The Old Curiosity Shop* is clearly Quilp, not Nell's grandfather. A representation on stage of the grandfather's theft of the money would involve the breaking of an established convention of melodrama, namely that the villain is the perpetrator of all wrongdoing in the play. Furthermore, in a genre in which the family was represented as a formidable bulwark against corruption, this act of betrayal would be particularly difficult to accomplish.

Dickens was aware of Stirling's production of *The Old Curiosity Shop*, and it is known that he assisted at a rehearsal. It therefore appears that the liberties taken with his creation did not disconcert him to any great extent. Furthermore, Dickens mentions the production in a letter, dating from November 1840, to William Charles Macready, a leading contemporary figure in drama.

My dear Macready,
I have been detained this week by some new arrangements with Chapman and Hall, and shall have to break tomorrow (which I had set aside for ten hours work) by going down to Yates and preventing his making a greater atrocity than can be helped of my poor Curiosity Shop, which is 'done' there on Monday night.[48]

The tone here is of good-humoured resignation, although it is also clear that Dickens does not expect much of the production. The actor Frederick Yates's portrayal of Quilp was, contrary to Dickens's reservations, received enthusiastically by *The Times*, which stated that Yates 'seemed on this occasion to have completely stepped out of himself and taken possession of the body and limbs of Quilp'. The production as a whole, according to the same correspondent, was 'dramatised with great skill and effect'.[49] Commercially, Stirling's play was moderately successful, and it ran for one and a half months.

In total, there were four stage productions of *The Old Curiosity Shop* that appeared around the time of the novel or in its immediate aftermath (1840–2). Further versions continued to make substantial alterations from Dickens's original. Probably the first to feature the theft of Nell's money by her grandfather was *The Old Curiosity Shop*, by George Lander, which premiered at the Theatre Royal, York, in May 1877.[50] However, the scene was reworked substantially as it occurs before Nell and her grandfather are forced to leave their shop and, furthermore, Nell prevents the theft. Melodrama and the plot of the novel are thus more or less satisfied simultaneously. Lander's inclusion of the theft scene may also reflect a wider, emerging tendency in the final quarter of the nineteenth century to view gambling, in the words of a commentator from 1889, as 'the most prevalent vice of the age'.[51]

It can be seen, from *The Gamester*, that the stage had long recognized gambling as a signifier for villainy. This was useful subsequently for a melodramatist such as Milner, who was able to employ gambling's signifying potential in order to identify a villain and to provide him with a means of working through his duplicitous and morally weak nature until he commits suicide. The presence of gambling in *Money* is a form of social commentary, highlighting the hypocrisies arising out of the unprincipled pursuit of money. With regard to *The Old Curiosity Shop*, the issue of the representation of gambling in melodrama becomes complicated by the fact that Nell's grandfather's gambling blurs the absolute moral categories inherent in the genre. In order to have Quilp stand alone as the undisputed villain of the piece, the worst of the grandfather's gambling excesses in Dickens's text are weakened in Stirling's melodrama, and thus he is no serious rival to Quilp in the villain stakes. Gambling is a useful theme in melodrama, but a gambler devoid of villainy can become an unwanted enigma in a mode of representation which relies upon rapid decoding.

The 1844 Select Committee on Gaming, and the Development of Horse Racing

Throughout the ages, legislation concerning gambling has been characterized by concern over the consequences of the practice and by a recognition (however tacit) of the preferences and requirements of the ruling class. Under Richard II, legislation enacted in 1388 forced people to spend money on military items rather than on gambling. In 1477, a statute of Edward decreed that houses could not be used for games of chance, as they were thought to have caused riots among demobilized members of the army. Popular gambling was condemned by Henry VIII in 1541 on the grounds that it weakened military ability and disrupted social order. In Cromwell's time, short-lived legislation passed in 1657 allowed the loser of a bet to sue for twice the amount lost. It also made debts incurred through gambling irrecoverable in the courts, unique legislation in the sense that it sought to combat all gambling rather than gambling within a specific social group. In 1664, under Charles II, a law was passed which targeted cheating and excessive gambling. Debts of one hundred pounds or more were unenforceable if incurred at any one time or meeting. This legislation defended the excesses of the very rich who, perhaps under the influence of drink, were known to gamble with large amounts. It also allowed losers to sue in the event of cheating or fraud. The 1664 Act was tightened under Queen Anne in 1710, with increased penalties for cheats.[52]

The more immediate legal framework for gambling in the nineteenth century may be summarized as follows: in 1739, 'an Act for the more efficient preventing of excessive and deceitful gaming' was passed which imposed penalties for keeping a gaming-house. However, this law appears not to have been enforced with any efficiency or zeal, at least as far as the upper classes were concerned. John Ashton (1899) lists several successful prosecutions against gamblers in the mid-eighteenth century, none of which were directed against people of high social standing.[53] Acts of 1822 and 1839 were concerned with strengthening police powers, but they affected gaming as they decreed that a gaming-house keeper could be imprisoned with hard labour, and gave the police powers, albeit limited, to raid suspected gaming premises.[54] There was, however, significant resistance to these measures and, at a horse race meeting at Lancaster in 1840, violence erupted when the police attempted to dismantle gaming tables.[55] Given the legislation prevailing at the time, it is clear that the gambling undertaken at Crockford's and other clubs was technically illegal yet, at the same time, the club flourished. Crockford's was able to escape prosecution because of the high social standing of its clientele, and, according to Roger Munting (1996), because it paid bribes to law enforcers.[56] Furthermore, Crockford's and other exclusive clubs occupied an anomalous position in relation to the law. As Crockford's was a private members club it was not a common gaming house to which anyone could gain entry and therefore, it was argued, it was not outside the law as wagering itself was not illegal. Contradiction in the legislation was one of the matters addressed by the 1844 Select Committee on Gaming.

Before the spread of gaming-houses, concern had been expressed about the state lottery, which had been run intermittently between 1569 and 1826. The 1808 Select Committee on Lotteries listed some of its alleged consequences: 'truth betrayed, domestic comfort destroyed, madness often created, crimes are committed and even suicide itself is produced.'[57] The state lottery was aimed at the property-owning classes, with less well-off people being largely excluded by the high price of the tickets (£13 from 1760 to 1826). Furthermore, lottery prizes took the form of plate and tapestry as well as money, thus encouraging and privileging upper-class participation. However, the working classes did take part in the lottery, by buying a fraction of a ticket in return for a fraction of any corresponding prize (a practice known as 'insurance'). The middle-men who co-ordinated this activity took their own cut and thus working-class people had to pay a premium to participate.[58] Over time the lottery significantly diminished in importance as a source of revenue for the government. The last draw was scheduled for 18 July 1826 but, owing to a slow public response and a consequent dearth of ticket sales, it was postponed until 18 October. Despite the end of the state lottery, individuals who wished to use them continued to do so. This was achieved by the organization of unofficial lotteries, some (if not most) of which were bogus, by entrepreneurs or within communities, and through the purchase of stakes in foreign lotteries. The state responded by banning the advertising of foreign lotteries in 1836. In George Moore's *Esther Waters*, the servants at Woodview organize a lottery amongst themselves in the form of a sweepstake, which is a successful enterprise to the extent that it is fairly conducted.[59] This was a form of autonomous, working-class gambling.

The Gaming Act of 1845, 'An Act to amend the Law against Games and Wagers', the end product of the 1844 Select Committee, failed as a piece of legislation. Whilst it curtailed the gaming houses it failed to recognize the growth and commercialization of horse racing. Furthermore, by removing the role of the courts in settling gambling disputes, the 1845 Act increased the volume of cash betting in the nation as a whole. As the courts could no longer be called upon to settle a dispute, more stakes tended to be placed up-front. The failure of the 1845 Act and the subsequent proliferation of the system of off-course betting on horse races known variously as betting-houses, list-houses, betting shops or betting-offices, resulted directly in the Gaming Act of 1853, 'An Act for the suppression of Betting Houses'. This Act was introduced to the House of Commons by the Attorney-General on 11 July 1853. Its clear-cut intention was, 'the suppression of betting houses (. . .) as the evils which had arisen from the introduction of these establishments were perfectly notorious, and acknowledged upon all hands'.[60] The consensus of parliamentary opinion in support of this legislation was such that it received Royal Assent little more than a month later, on 20 August 1853. However, the 1853 Act did not seek to interfere 'with that description of betting which had so long existed at Tattersall's and elsewhere'.[61] Tattersall's, originally horse auction rooms at Hyde Park, was an exclusive venue. The Act of 1853 betrayed overt class prejudice. The rich could gamble with impunity, unlike the working class. As events transpired, the 1853 Act merely forced gambling out of the list-houses and into the streets, as the working class simply adapted to prohibition in order to continue with their preferred forms of leisure. The state responded with local by-laws against obstruction and a parliamentary Act of 1874, both of which were designed to prevent street bookmaking.[62] In the anti-gambling crusade which gathered momentum in the second half of the century, both middle-class reformers and leaders of the embryonic labour movement (who saw gambling as being parasitic upon the poor) consistently failed to appreciate that for a majority of working-class people betting on a sporting event was simply a part of leisure. It was self-controlled and affordable entertainment.[63]

Victorian England saw a great mass of Parliamentary Reports and Investigative Papers on every subject from drama to drains. There were four parliamentary enquiries on gambling between 1808 and 1902.[64] The 1844 Select Committee on Gaming highlights particularly well mainstream perceptions of gambling around the mid-century. The 1844 Committee, established in response to growing concern about gambling, did not regard it as a chronic social problem. Instead, they saw it as having diminished from the excesses of the eighteenth century.[65]

> In the last century the practice of Betting was much more common in this country than it is now. (. . .) At present Wagers are chiefly confined to sporting events, but the practice of Wagering is still deeply rooted in the habits of the nation, and the practical imposition of pecuniary Penalties for Wagers would be so repugnant to the general feelings of the people, that such Penalties would scarcely ever be enforced, or, if enforced, would be looked upon as an arbitrary interference with the freedom of private life. (p. v)

The Committee's sentiments were typified by the evidence of Captain the Honourable H. John Rous, a magistrate and a Member of Parliament in the House of Commons: 'if you legislate against betting you would make this country not fit for a gentleman to live in' (p. 204). He saw the issue of gambling, for the upper class at least, as a question of freedom of choice: 'I think the great pleasure of living in a free country is, the being allowed to bet upon any subject you please' (p. 208). However, an alternative view is to be found in an exchange between the Chair of the Committee and The Honourable Frederick Byng, Chairman of the Petty Sessions and former churchwarden in St James.

> 1006. Chairman – Are you aware that the increase of gambling has tended to demoralize society in any manner not directly connected with the gambling itself? – Very considerably so; it has tended, as I am informed, to robberies in shops where they cannot take stock. I know several instances where shopkeepers have been robbed to a great extent. Some of my brother parishioners tell me that they suspect they have robberies in their shops now, and that the money thus acquired from the robbery goes into gambling-houses.1007. Are these robberies committed by forcible entrance, or by the shopmen? – By the shopmen.1008. Who have lost their money at play? – That is the supposition in the mind of the shopkeepers, that they are constantly robbed, and that to a great extent. I should also state, that in speaking both to Mr Chesterton and Mr Tracy, the governors of the largest prisons we have in London, it appeared, that with respect to all the cases of better instructed people that have gone through those gaols, whenever they have questioned them as to the commencement of their crimes, it has been from gambling. (p. 83)

This link between gambling and criminality is later given literary form in *Esther Waters*, in the sub-plot in which a female servant steals from her employers in order to raise money for a bet. In the above extract from the Committee's proceedings, the view put forward is that gambling leads to corruption and damages commerce. If we ascribe to gambling this potential to undermine and disrupt respectable living, then any perceived growth in gambling is threatening to society. Consequently, when Vincent Dowling, then the editor of *Bell's Life in London*, the leading sporting newspaper of the Victorian era, informed the Committee that, in addition to the large volume of gambling on horse racing, boat races on the Thames were a focal point for betting, it appeared that few if any areas of sporting life were immune from the practice. Gambling seemingly pervaded all areas of recreation.

The most significant new measure proposed by the Committee, and subsequently enshrined in the Gaming Act of 1845, was the removal of the role of the courts in settling gambling disputes. This was a practical response to the problem of adjudicating in private disagreements. Gambling disputes were deemed to be a waste of the court's time. The measure was based on laissez-faire principles, as shown in the following section of the Committee's report.

> In earlier periods of European civilization it was thought to be the duty of Governments to exercise a minute superintendence and control over all those private actions of the members of the community, which, through their operation upon the individuals concerned, could be supposed to bear indirectly upon the general interests of the community at large; and for this purpose Governments thought themselves not only entitled but bound to restrain the imprudence of private persons, and to protect them against the consequences of their own improvidence.
>
> The notion was not confined to despotic Governments, but was shared by representative Legislatures; and thence arose the Laws on our Statute Book which described to the different classes of our people what apparel they should wear, what Games they should play at, what amount of money they might win or lose, how their tables should be served; and which established many other interferences with the free action of individuals in the management of their private concerns.
>
> Such Regulations are out of date; and nobody now disputes the opinion of Adam Smith, that Governments ought not to pretend to watch over the economy of private people, and to restrain their expense by Sumptuary Laws; but that if they look well over their own expenses, they may safely trust private people with theirs. (p. iv)

The Committee's recommendation also removed any implied state support for the practice of gambling. As long as a gambling dispute could be resolved in court, gambling in general could be perceived to be a legitimate activity. The removal of the court's role, whilst it did not criminalize gambling, distanced it from the state.

A moral crusade against gambling emerged and became increasingly vocal as the century progressed. Mr John Adams, Serjeant at-Law and Chairman of the Middlesex Quarter Sessions, told the Committee about the difficulties of prosecuting people suspected of running gaming-houses, as two testimonies were required to enable the police to raid a house. Adams, in response to a question from a Committee member, set out his idealistic solution.

> 555. You say, one of the great difficulties in prosecuting is, that there are no persons who will set the law in motion; can you recommend any provision to remedy that? – It is extremely difficult; I know not how that can be done; I believe the most effectual means will be the increase of religious and moral feelings in mankind in general. (pp. 43–4)

The actual measures proposed as a result of the Committee did endeavour to combat the gaming-houses. Clause two of the 1845 Gaming Act was directed against games where a bank was kept by the proprietor and where there was 'a dead pull against the player'.[66] The legislative clause appeared to be an egalitarian gesture as it effectively criminalized socially exclusive clubs such as Crockford's. However, common gaming-houses open to all-comers had emerged, mainly (though not exclusively) in the East End, where they were known as 'copper hells', and they had begun to cater for working-class customers. They are described in the 'Hells in London' article from *Fraser's Magazine* (1833).[67] The Committee, as other parts of its findings showed, was not too concerned by upper-class gambling, but was troubled greatly by its perceived rise amongst the working classes. The 1845 Act and subsequent legislation was concerned primarily with the suppression of working-class modes of gambling.

Whilst the Committee adopted a broadly tolerant attitude towards gambling in general, they were unreservedly hostile towards the gaming-houses:

> common Gaming-houses (. . .) are founded on fraud, are maintained by fraud, and, as has been stated in Evidence, frequently lead by their results to the commission of fraud by persons who, in such places, have begun by being only dupes. (. . .) Your Committee cannot too strongly recommend that these nuisances should be effectually put down. (p. vi)

Condemnation of the gaming-houses came forcibly from the police. Richard Mayne, a Commissioner of the Metropolitan Police, cited a report from one Superintendent Baker, who had raided suspected gaming-houses. He stated he was 'extremely anxious that something more should be done respecting the gaming-houses, to put them down, which are the cause of so many young men's ruin' (p. 15). The existing law, according to Mayne in an answer to a Committee member, was unworkable because it inconvenienced the two individuals who submitted information and cast them in the role of police informers (p. 14), hence the reason why gaming-houses continued to exist despite official disapproval. Furthermore, if the police raided a building which turned out not to be a gaming-house (and it was alleged that some buildings were presented, with mock secrecy, as gaming-houses in order to lure the police into precisely this error) they would make themselves vulnerable to legal action for trespass. Mayne stressed this possibility:

> 104. Mr *V. Smith* – Supposing, in some of those places where you say lights have been held out as a lure, the police had gone in, they would have got into a scrape? – I have no doubt an action would have been brought; we have reason to believe that the gamblers have a fund for that purpose. (p. 11)

If Mayne was correct, then there was a significant conspiracy amongst gaming-house proprietors to entrap the police. However, there is no evidence to suggest that the proprietors had any kind of organization, however informal. A communal legal fund implies an unlikely degree of co-operation amongst commercial rivals who were all operating outside the law. The police, however, finally gave the Committee considerable pleasure, as evidenced in the following observation from the Committee's report:

> Your Committee, however, learned, with great satisfaction, on the last day of their Inquiry, that a few nights previously the Police had, by a simultaneous movement of several parties of their Force, entered at one and the same time, all the common Gambling-houses, seventeen in number, which were then known to exist within the Metropolitan Police District. (p. vii)

The police are seen to be effective law-enforcement officers at an apposite time, yet it is noteworthy that the action was targeted against 'common' houses, not the private (and exclusive) clubs.

The best-known gaming-houses were concentrated in the West End. The district of St James's in the West End was particularly notorious and it was not coincidental that Crockford's was located in St James's Street. Mr. Thomas Baker, Superintendent of Police for St James's, was able to give the Committee some idea of the scale of the problem:

> 348. Can you state how many, to your knowledge, there is reason to suppose are still going on in your district? – I have entirely broken up seven, either by force or strategem, since the passing of the Act in 1839, and I think

there are about 15 or 16 now in existence; some are low gambling-houses, where the lowest of the low resort. (p. 30)

Gaming-houses were also to be found away from the metropolis. One witness, Robert Baxter, testified to the Committee that in 1824 there were '40 or 50 houses' in Doncaster (p. 85). This sounds an unreasonably high number, expectedly since Baxter was particularly hostile towards gambling. On the other hand, the fact that Doncaster had a well-known racecourse may well be significant, as a horse racing meeting encouraged other facilities for gambling.

The Committee, in their questions to Thomas Hall (a magistrate), endeavoured to clarify Crockford's legal status.

242. Viscount *Jocelyn* – It is generally understood that gambling goes on to a great extent at Crockford's; under this Act, do you consider that, upon the information of two householders, the police could enter into Crockford's in the same way as any common gaming-house? – I cannot answer that question without knowing the peculiar circumstances under which they play there: I know nothing of the system pursued at Crockford's.

243. Mr *V. Smith* – How do you define a gaming-house? – A house kept for the purposes of gaming for lucre or gain.

244. Does it depend upon every person having a right to enter it, or if it is limited to certain persons, can it be considered a common gaming-house; for instance, could a club be considered a common gaming-house? – It would depend upon circumstances; generally speaking, a club would not be considered a common gaming-house. (p. 21)

Exclusivity did not give private clubs immunity from prosecution. The police had the same powers in law to raid a private club as they did a common gaming-house, as long as the necessary criteria were fulfilled. Thomas Baker confirmed this to the Committee.

446. Supposing you had information given you as to gambling going on in a club-house, should you feel yourself justified in acting as you would do in the case of a common gaming-house? – Certainly; if any gentleman was to come forward with the necessary affidavits (...) then I should apply to the Commissioners of Police for their order and warrant, and upon obtaining it, I should feel myself justified in acting. (p. 37)

Although this sounded fair and equitable, in practice it made the position of a private club secure because it was unlikely to suffer complaints from its own members, as it tended to be upper-class and therefore less vulnerable to police attention. Conversely, a common gaming-house, as it admitted just about anybody, was vulnerable to denunciations from aggrieved clients. However, in the final analysis it was the anomalous legal position of the private clubs that allowed them to function. Adams reaffirmed to the Committee the qualitative difference between a common and a private house.

> 591. Mr *Hawes* – What, in your opinion, constitutes a common gaming-house? – A common gaming house is a house to which any persons may have access, with the permission of the owner of it, for the purpose of playing at unlawful games, and for the lucre and gain of such owner; it does not extend to subscription houses, or to a private house.
>
> 592. You think a club-house, however great its numbers, would not come within the definition of a common gaming-house, though it might be proved that gaming was carried on? – Certainly not, for it must be for lucre and gain; (. . .) a club-house is merely the joint occupancy of a thousand people. (p. 46)

Practices at the Stock Exchange were another anomaly for the Committee to consider. D W Harvey stated that a gambler 'would be more likely to be detected in the City, except at the Stock Exchange, where gentlemen of all pursuits are known to speculate extensively' (p. 69). Commercial, capital speculation is undoubtedly a form of gambling, to the extent that a stake is risked in the hope of gain. However, Harvey went on to say that the Stock Exchange 'is a voluntary association, governed by its own rules' (p. 75). The Exchange, like the clubs, had a certain exclusivity. This fact purchased a considerable degree of respectability. The working classes could not gain entry and therefore could not be corrupted by exposure to temptation.

The 1844 Committee was concerned about upper-class gambling setting a bad example to the rest of society. Thomas Hall expressed the view that gambling was mainly an upper-class pursuit which had potentially dangerous reverberations.

> 234. Mr *M. Gibson* – You stated that from your experience you believed that there was little or no gaming amongst the labouring class, and that you thought there was some gaming amongst servants, and persons of that description; did you mean that, in your opinion, the greater part of the gaming in existence was amongst the upper class of society? – Gaming prevails to the greatest extent, I am inclined to think, in the upper class.
>
> 235. Do you think that the example of the upper class has the effect of inducing servants, and persons in other classes, to form a taste for gambling? – It is very likely that inferiors take a lesson from their superiors. (p. 21)

Hall's view was echoed by D. W. Harvey.

> 858. Mr M. Gibson.) Do you not think that the example of persons of fortune is likely to influence the conduct of persons in humbler stations in life, and to cause gambling to pervade society much more than it otherwise would do?- I consider that the more generally moral obligations are observed, the better for the whole community, and that a bad example among the higher classes operates injuriously upon the lower. (p. 74)

From this perspective the private gambling clubs were vulnerable to attack. Frederick Byng, in his evidence to the Committee, condemned the very existence of Crockford's, stating, 'I think the increase of gambling-houses is entirely the offspring of Crockford's' (p. 76). He was insistent upon the connection between private gambling clubs and common gaming-houses.

> 991. Would you not make a distinction between a club, such as Crockford's, and a common gaming-house, into which every person that pleases may enter? – But the one is the offspring of the other. The taste acquired at the table of the club gives a desire for gambling to all manner of persons that enter into that club, who never dreamed of gambling before. (p. 82)

This point was not lost on Baxter who reported that, in Doncaster, 'a very strong feeling exists in the place, that if the lower gambling-houses are suppressed, it is unfair to the common people that the higher gambling-houses should be permitted to continue' (p. 88). The Committee was therefore obliged to consider gambling as such, whether in private clubs or common houses. In point of fact, their proposals did exhibit a class bias, as betting on horse racing, long associated with the upper classes, was left untouched by the Act of 1845. The attempted suppression of other forms of gambling resulted in more working people betting on horse races, as this clearly enjoyed the sanction of the state. Having said this, it should be noted that the growth in horse racing was not only a result of the 1845 Act but also of technological developments such as the growth of the railway and the electric telegraph system which, respectively, allowed more people to attend races and facilitated the rapid transmission of results to off-course gamblers.

Working-class gambling remained a source of anxiety to the Committee. Adams stated that: 'mischievous as gaming is in all classes, its evils are greater in the lower ranks than the higher, from the ruin it necessarily brings on wives and children' (p. 15). Working people had significantly less disposable income and therefore, if they gambled, they squandered a sizeable portion of their wages. Adams did not consider that working people might be able to afford moderate gambling. The idea that working-class gambling was particularly problematic created the conditions in which individuals promoted the idea of separate legislative provision depending upon the social class of the gambler, a suggestion put forward by Harvey: 'I think that a penalty may be usefully enforced against certain classes, where others might be unmolested; because it is decidedly, I think, an evil for a spirit of gambling to prevail among the working and industrious community, while I should have no desire to interfere with that class of persons who, having ample funds and leisure, desire so to dispose of their property.' Even working-class children playing pitch-and-toss in the streets with small coins was a problem because this form of gambling could lead the unwary into a life of crime.

> 835. Mr *M. Sutton* – Taking it for granted in the first instance, that the playing at pitch-and-toss in the streets is a harmless amusement, is there not very considerable risk, that if a boy is in the habit of playing at pitch-and-toss in the streets he will fall in with very bad characters, who will seduce him to acts much less harmless, and inveigle him into crimes of a serious description? – Amusements of that description are a step towards crime, inasmuch as they bring him among a class of persons who may entice him to do worse. (p. 73)

However, the actual extent of working-class gambling was a matter for debate. Baker took the view that it was considerable.

> 406. Mr *M. Gibson* – Is there much gaming amongst the lower classes?-No doubt there is; I have convicted keepers of coffee-shops for allowing card-playing and bagatelle; in Blenheim-street I convicted a landlord for gambling with a boy for *2d.* (p. 34)

Conversely, Hall took a more sanguine view: 'I do not think that amongst the labouring classes much gambling does go on in London' (p. 19). Nor did he believe that much illegal gambling occurred within pubs, the principal place of social congregation for working people (p. 18).

The concern over working-class gambling was contradicted by the desire to make a profit from it. The Committee received evidence indicating that horse racing derived considerable financial support from gambling enterprises on racecourses. Certain individuals were allowed to erect gambling booths on site during race meetings, for which they paid exorbitant rent to the course owners. The existence of these booths was largely accepted without complaint. Furthermore, the revenue from the gambling-booths ensured sufficient prize money for the races. The main gambling scene in Charles Dickens's *Nicholas Nickleby* (1838–9) takes place in one of these booths. Horse racing itself, and the betting that accompanied it, enjoyed a greater degree of respectability than any other form of gambling. Hall made this point to the Committee.

> 270. Mr *V. Smith* – You were asked whether you were aware that horse-racing stood in a different position from other games, to which you answered in the affirmative; will you explain that answer? – I think the Legislature seems to have regarded it in a more favourable light than ordinary gaming.
> 271. Mr *M. Sutton* – Are you aware that plates are given by the House of Commons? – Yes. (p. 23)

No other form of gambling could boast official parliamentary support. Of course, it could be argued that the House of Commons was supporting the sport rather than the gambling, but the two were so extensively connected as to be practically interwoven. Robert Baxter, however, argued that, in Doncaster, gamblers were keeping respectable people away from the racecourse (p. 91). This may be so, but it appeared that, in general, the proprietors of racecourses did not have the economic luxury of excluding gambling and gamblers from race meetings. Significantly, as mentioned, the Committee proposed no new legislation in respect of horse racing. Their report outlined their position, as follows: 'your Committee have some Evidence to show that frauds are occasionally committed in Horse-racing and in Betting on the turf; but they feel difficulty in suggesting any remedies for this evil more stringent, or more likely to be effectual, than those already in existence' (p. viii).

Overall, the 1844 Committee, notwithstanding its uncompromising hostility towards gaming-houses, adopted a practical stance to a problem which still appeared to be fairly manageable. The fact that another, more stringent Gaming Act was deemed necessary a mere eight years later, and that yet another Act was passed in 1874, suggests that gambling increased as a source of alarm as the Victorian era developed. It is further clear that the most consistent element in legislation concerning gambling in the Victorian era was class prejudice. Upper-class forms of recreation tended to be protected while the working classes could expect their relatively modest gambling to be suppressed by an unsympathetic legislature.

Away from Parliament, the second half of the nineteenth century witnessed a significant increase in commercialization. In parliament the most obvious example of this was legislation in 1855–6 allowing limited liability.[68] The Limited Liability Act stimulated economic activity (though not all commerce was entirely responsible) and commercial expansion also created new job opportunities in the expanding urban conurbations. As the urban population gained in size over the rural, leisure time for working-class people, limited though it was, needed to be catered for in some way. This became more important from the third quarter of the century onwards, with the introduction of the Saturday half-holiday. The Bank Holidays Act of 1871 also increased working-class opportunities for leisure.[69]

One of the main beneficiaries of commercialization was horse racing. Gambling and horse racing have always existed in a symbiotic relationship, and racing underwent a massive boom in the Victorian era. Between 1837 and 1869 the number of racehorses in England more than doubled. Horse racing, like pugilism, had benefited from aristocratic patronage but in the case of racing this arrangement was institutionally based from a relatively early stage in the development of the sport. The Jockey Club, the governing body of flat racing, had existed from around the mid-eighteenth century and in 1803 it published a set of rules for racing. Pugilism, by contrast, did not introduce the Marquis of Queensbury rules until 1860. The Jockey Club did not publish an official list of members until 1835 but, according to Wray Vamplew (1976), 'it seems clear that from the beginning the membership was predominantly aristocratic'.[70] The view that horse racing was associated closely with the upper classes is certainly given credence in *The Greville Memoirs*.[71] Charles Greville (1794–1865, Clerk of the Council in Ordinary 1821–59, an office which brought him into close contact with the leading figures of his day) was a race horse owner and a gambler, and he was involved regularly with upper-class gambling at race meetings. In 1830, King William IV gave Greville three hundred pounds in order to pay off debts incurred by the Duke of York. The following year at Ascot, Greville records the arrival of William IV and the indifferent reaction of the crowd.[72] Later, in 1848, Greville describes Lord Stanley being made Steward of the Jockey Club. Stanley became Prime Minister in 1852, but Greville draws attention to an incident in the previous year, when Stanley attended the races at Newmarket.

> There he [Stanley] was in the midst of a crowd of blacklegs, betting men, and loose characters of every description, in uproarious spirits, chaffing, rowing, and shouting with laughter and joking. His amusement was to lay Lord Glasgow a wager that he did not sneeze in a given time, for which purpose he took pinch after pinch of snuff, while Stanley jeered him and

quizzed him with such noise that he drew the whole mob around him to partake of the coarse merriment he excited.[73]

The incident highlights one of the features of gambling on horse racing that came to cause concern. Horse racing brought the different social classes together in close association. Eventually, the solution to this perceived problem arose in the shape of enclosures, exclusive stands for which an admittance fee could be charged. Races, held traditionally on public land, had always been disorderly events but enclosure, by (in effect) segregating the crowd, changed the entire atmosphere of racing and imposed social stratification. From this innovation it was but a modest step to charging an entrance fee for everyone, the first successful attempt at this taking place at Sandown Park racecourse in 1875. At their most subtle level, enclosures and admission charges dampened the holiday feeling which had characterized racing previously. When it was undertaken on common land in holiday time, the entire event was removed from the ordinary world, thereby turning it into a festive occasion outside social conventions. Admission charges turned horse racing into commerce and incorporated it into ordinary social life.

Horse racing drew great benefit from legislative protection. Just as pugilism suffered by being prohibited, horse racing prospered by being sanctioned. Nevertheless, the turf was, in the early and mid-century, riddled with corruption culminating in the Derby of 1844 which featured horses above the age limit, not to mention a jockey who pulled up in favour of the horse he had backed to win. A court trial ensued, and the concluding remarks of the judge, Baron Alderson, are worth quoting:

> Since the opening of this case a most atrocious fraud has been proved to have been practised: and I have seen with great regret, gentlemen associating themselves with persons much below them in station. If gentlemen would associate with gentlemen and race with gentlemen, we should have no such practices. But if gentlemen will condescend to race with black-guards, they must expect to be cheated.[74]

The integrity of horse racing improved as the Victorian era wore on. This may be due partly to more effective leadership within the Jockey Club, and to the emergence of a similar governing body for steeple-chasing, the National Hunt Committee, in 1866. Equally, however, it may well be argued that commercialization itself was chiefly responsible for the improved state of affairs. The customer was increasingly paying for the privilege of watching races and was thus injecting capital into racing. In order to rely on his continued patronage the managers of the races were obliged to provide an honest product. Vamplew sums up the state of affairs in late-nineteenth century racing thus: 'the paying customer had become the focal point of racing and the honesty of turf affairs was seen as a key feature in attracting large crowds'.[75] Commercialization, having triumphed over ethical objections to gambling, brought greater integrity to horse racing. The conflict between the desire to control working-class recreation and the desire to make a profit from it was won by the entrepreneurs over the moralists. The moral crusade against gambling most certainly did not cease (hence the emergence of the National Anti-Gambling League, see below) but it did not triumph. Gambling continued and was drawn increasingly into a regular commercial framework.

Non-Fiction Commentaries on Gambling, 1844–1905

Although horse racing flourished in the second half of the nineteenth century, hostility to gambling grew, as evidenced in a number of commentaries from a variety of sources. Non-fiction offers an interesting contrast to the representation of gambling in Victorian novels, though there are also points of comparison between the two forms. In the non-fiction articles considered in this study, gambling is the central focus of the authors' interest, whereas, in fiction, gambling is one of a number of related themes and thus its presentation is modified. An article in *Bentley's Miscellany* from 1844, 'A Fashionable Gaming-House – Confessions of a Croupier', was opposed to gambling, but was also conscious on a voyeuristic level of the opulence of the surroundings.[76] The establishment is shown to be particularly splendid:

> It was a large room, richly carpeted. Two rich and massive chandeliers suspended from the ceiling showed the dazzling gilt and colour of the empanelled walls; from which, at alternate distances, extended elegant mirror-branches, with lights. The chimney-piece was furnished with a plate of glass, which reached the ceiling, the sides were concealed by falling drapery of crimson and gold, and supported by two gilt full-length figures bearing lights. (p. 553)

Ostentatious wealth is enhanced by the description of the money put on display by the bank:

> ONE THOUSAND SOVEREIGNS! a shining golden heap! and TEN THOUSAND POUNDS in notes! the reader may imagine the scene which every evening met the eye. Yes, every evening, into a silver vase,

which stood on the hazard-table, were emptied ten bags, each containing one hundred sovereigns. (p. 554)

The scene could hardly be more spectacular. This gaming-house is clearly associated with the highest tiers of society. However, there is something very un-Victorian about it. In its self-conscious splendour it is more akin to the excesses of the late-eighteenth century than the sobriety of the mid-nineteenth. It is possible that the description is intended as much to alienate as to entice the reader.

The narrator speaks of 'a tall, good-looking, prepossessing young man' who loses all of his money. This is not the end of his woes because 'not long afterwards he became insane!' (p. 557). The narrator obligingly reinforces the polemic:

> I have shown the unavoidable results of this vice; the reader has seen, as from a tower, its downward progress to poverty and crime, and I may add, premature death! (p. 563)

Gambling, we are told in the conclusion, 'is the certain road to infamy and ruin' (p. 564). The message in 'Confessions of a Croupier' is clear-cut: gambling destroys. 'Confessions,' published around the time when the 1844 Select Committee was in session, highlights some of the contemporary anxieties about gaming-houses although, unlike the committee, it has no pretensions to objectivity.

One pamphlet and two articles from 1852, all of which are concerned with betting-shops, give some indication of the contemporary social debate about off-course betting on horse racing in the period immediately prior to the passing of the 1853 Act. *The Betting-Book*, by George Cruikshank, is a thirty-two page pamphlet highlighting the social effects of gambling, particularly betting on horse racing.[77] Cruikshank declares his position on betting-shops in the opening paragraph, stating 'I despise them' (p. 3). He discusses the proprietors and the punters at a betting-shop, comparing both to different members of the animal kingdom in order to express the relationship that exists between them:

> Observe the two sly foxes in confab leaning on the counter, they are watching and weighing a fat green goose, who is feeding on the lists, (the majority of birds that come here are geese, but there are some hawks amongst them,) they are evidently saying what 'a fine bird' he is, and calculating, as he seems 'in fine feather,' how and when they may best pluck him – their eyes glisten and their mouths water (gin and water) as they think how he will 'cut up,' – and what 'pretty pickings' there will be – ah! (p. 6)

Cruikshank shows a relationship of wily, predatory hunter and ignorant prey. The narrator then considers the means by which betting-shops might be suppressed. He is suspicious of parliamentarians, whom he suspects of being hypocrites, stating 'how, then, is it possible for Parliament, with any show of decency, to pass a law to shut up those offices, *they being opened expressly for the purpose of betting upon the horses kept and run, and betted upon, by the very men (or by their friends and connexions,) who will have to make the law?*' (p. 9, Cruikshank's italics). Cruikshank is concerned about the extent to which gambling is still prevalent amongst the upper classes, notwith-standing the fact that most of the anxieties concerning the betting-shops pertained to their patronage by working-class people. However, whilst he has little confidence in Parliament he acknowledges a more general improvement in behavioural standards: 'there is undoubtedly a change for the better, in the habits and manners of the people; education, and the good example set by the higher orders, have done much towards this' (p. 11). In common with the 1844 Committee, Cruikshank perceives an improvement in contemporary morals which, paradoxi-cally, underlines the threat posed by gambling as it represents the shadow of an earlier, less wholesome time that still loomed threaten-ingly over an infant culture and society.

Cruikshank's anger, along with his acute awareness of hypocrisy, is directed not only towards common betting-shops, but also towards Tattersall's:

> But here we are at 'Tattersall's' which I suppose we must not designate as the great 'Betting Office,' of the great sporting world, although I cannot help thinking that the difference between the common Betting-shop and Tattersall's is not very great. (. . .) Here we see the Duke, the Marquis, the Lord, the Baronet, the Squire, the M.P., yes, the lawmaker, all engaged in what? – why GAMBLING. (pp. 17–18)

From Tattersall's the narrator moves directly to gambling at the lowest level of the social scale and highlights 'a miserable, half starved urchin' (p. 18) with halfpence as his stake. He thus draws a direct connection between upper-class and lower-class gambling, a connection which was repeatedly denied by the legislature as, in the terms of parliamentary acts in the nineteenth century, it discriminated between gamblers along class lines. However, for Cruikshank, gambling is ubiquitous, occur-ring throughout society in many different forms.

'Betting-Offices' in *Chambers Edinburgh Journal* analyses the different kinds of establishments and betting-shop patrons that are found in contemporary society.[78] It commences by citing, with ironic approval, a sample of names under which the businesses trade: '"Betting-Shop" is vulgar, and we dislike vulgarity. "Commission Office," "Racing Bank," "Mr Hopposite Green's Office," "Betting-Office," are the styles of announcement adopted by speculators who open what low people call Betting-shops' (p. 57). It further describes the evolution of the establishments, stating 'many offices have risen out of simple cigar-shops' (p. 57). This experience is echoed in George Moore's *Confessions of a Young Man* (1888) in which Moore recalls frequenting betting-shops in his youth, drawing attention to 'the spitting and betting of the tobacco shop' (p. 4).[79]

'Betting-Offices' divides gamblers into various types, most of whom are either working-class people or disreputable characters. However, it also mentions gamblers higher up the social scale, showing how the betting-shop reaches out to incorporate and contaminate nominally respectable people.

> We must not pass over a class of speculators who bet, and yet who are not true betting-men: they do not wish to be seen in the betting-shops, yet cannot keep away. They are not loungers, for they may be observed passing along the thoroughfare seemingly with all desirable intentness upon their daily business; but they suddenly disappear as they arrive at the door of the betting-shop. These are your respectable men; worthy, solid, family men. But it is not easy to enter a betting-shop, and avoid rubbing against some clinging matter. Betting-men generally are not nice in their sensibilities; and perhaps on a fine Sunday morning, proceeding with his family to the parish church, our Pharisee may receive a tip from some unshaven, strong-countenanced *sans culotte*, which may cause his nerves to tingle for the rest of the day. (p. 58)

The article goes on to discuss race fixing, thereby emphasizing the criminality of the betting-shops, and shows how the patrons end up being driven to insanity, theft and even suicide. The final sentence drives home the narrator's polemic: 'the insane are shut up – the desperate transported – the dead buried – the deserted families carted off to the workhouse; and the betting-office goes on as before' (p. 58). 'Betting-Offices' highlights the villainy of the betting-shops, focusing upon their destructiveness and their pervasiveness. Its description of the consequences of gambling are similar to those outlined in 'Confessions of a Croupier', although the earlier article had looked at club gamblers rather than gambling on horse racing. It can thus be suggested that orthodox society accepted a close association between gambling, irrationality, crime and premature death. Few if any other modes of recreation held such infamous connotations.

Charles Dickens's response to the problem of off-course betting, 'Betting-Shops', was published in *Household Words*.[80] The article opens by satirizing the self-appointed wisdom of horse racing tips in newspapers. Dickens refers to the tipsters as 'Prophets' and cites one whose motives are, allegedly, philanthropic:

> One sage announces that when he casts his practised eye on the broad sur-
> face of struggling society, and witnesses the slow and enduring perseverance
> of some, and the infatuous rush of the many who are grappling with a cloud,
> he is led with more intense desire to hold up the lamp of light to all.' (p. 333)

The tipster encourages avoidance of work and offers illusory pros-perity. Dickens is conscious of the appeal of this proposition to 'fast young gentlemen' (p. 333), who are taken in by such advertisements. The tipsters existed in a symbiotic relationship with the betting-shops, promoting interest in the races, the growth of which created, in turn, a larger market for the tipsters.

The establishment focused upon in 'Betting-Shops' is run by Mr Cheerful. The name indicates that it is almost certainly fictitious but the account given is by no means incredible. A bet is placed and the ritual attached thereto is described:

> So, we stepped across the road into Mr Cheerful's Betting-Shop, and,
> having glanced at the lists hanging up therein, while another noble
> sportsman (a boy with a blue bag) laid another bet with Mr Cheerful, we
> expressed our desire to back Tophana for the Western Handicap, to the
> spirited amount of half a crown. (. . .) It being Mr Cheerful's business to
> be grave and ask no questions, he accepted our wager, booked it, and
> handed us over his railed desk the dirty scrap of pasteboard, in right of
> which we were to claim – the day after the race; we were to be very partic-
> ular about that – seven-and-sixpence sterling, if Tophana won. (p. 334)

Mr Cheerful's clients are young, working men, reflecting the perceived growth in working-class gambling in the mid-century. The correspon-dent returns the day after the race to find the shop populated by 'a crowd of boys, mostly greasy, dirty, and dissipated' (p. 334). Mr Cheerful has departed without paying-up on any of the winning bets, a practice known as 'welching'. The explanation for his absence offered by his clerk, '"coz it's Sunday, and he always goes to church, a 'Sunday"' (p. 335), is as transparently ironic as is the name of the establishment, although the proprietor clearly has good reason to be cheerful.

Throughout 'Betting-Shops', Dickens treats gambling with hostility and he views its influence as pernicious. However, the conclusion he comes to is more considered and less reactionary:

Now, it is unquestionable that this evil has risen to a very great height, and that it involves some very serious social considerations. But, with all respect for opinions which we do not hold, we think it a mistake to cry for legislative interference in such a case. (p. 335)

Dickens's objection to the legislative abolition of the betting-houses is based on two counts. Firstly, the government had neglected to provide for the recreation of the people. If it were to ban gambling it would, not unreasonably, be seen to be unduly repressive. Secondly, Dickens doubted whether parliamentarians had sufficient moral authority to make such a decision. He stated that 'the Elections before us, and the whole Government of the country, are at present a great reckless Betting-shop' (p. 336). He had no confidence in legislators, seeing the principles of gambling inherent in the wider political system. Morals had been replaced, in Dickens's view, by reckless speculation.

Gambling in 'Betting-Shops' is still seen primarily as a personal character flaw. The economic forces underpinning gambling are not subjected to detailed examination and there is little concern with gambling as a legitimate form of recreation. Dickens's argument against prohibition in 'Betting-Shops' was not libertarian because he wanted the community, rather than politicians, to control gambling: he presupposed that gambling was hazardous. Control, however, is not the same as repression; Dickens is looking to containment rather than abolition. All three of the 1852 commentaries on betting-shops cited in this discussion are hostile to gambling. However, neither Dickens nor Cruikshank rely on Parliament to solve the problem. The subsequent 1853 Act justified their doubts as it left Tattersall's intact and, far from ending working-class gambling, simply forced it into the streets.

Between November 1857 and February 1858, a series of lectures were delivered in Exeter Hall before the Young Men's Christian Association.[81] Two of the lectures, both delivered by churchmen, touched on the subject of gambling and are thus useful in illustrating religion's perspective on gambling in the 1850s. 'Manliness', by the Rev. Hugh Stowell Brown, uses the adverb 'manly' as an umbrella term under which he draws together a host of virtues. Conversely, he also identifies what he perceives as unmanly behaviour:

Sir, you think that there is something manly in vice, in prize-fighting, in horse-racing, in gambling, in profane swearing, in obscene language, in revelry, in profligacy; yes, and to be plain and honest with you, you think that there is something manly even in that most damning of all crimes, seduction. I tell you, Sir, that there is no manliness in sin of any kind. (p. 34)

Gambling is seen as one of a set of vices. It is associated with fast living, immorality and a lack of decorum. In due course, however, the speaker moves on to consider gambling in isolation, focusing on horse race meetings.

> On the one hand, there are brutal pastimes; on the other, recreations of a silly and effeminate character; and besides these, there are many which, while neither brutal nor effeminate, are extremely demoralizing. All forms of gambling belong to this class, if, indeed, gambling be not a far too terribly earnest thing to be catalogued among amusements at all. The sporting world! In truth, there is no world in which there is less sport than that which arrogates this title to itself. There is not much sport perhaps on the area of the Exchange, but there is far more there, even on the dullest day of mercantile depression – more real cheerfulness and pleasure than among the bookmakers at Newmarket and at Epsom; and if on the Exchange there be much gloom, anxiety, and despair, they are mainly traceable to the fact, that the men on 'Change have introduced into their speculations so much of the spirit of Newmarket and Epsom. (p. 45)

He goes on to contrast 'the high morality of genuine commerce with the accursed immorality of the turf and the betting-room' (p. 45). Here, if Brown's position is representative of his time, we have evidence of the shift in perception of the Stock Exchange and its successful distancing of itself from gambling. The extent to which businessmen were motivated by high morals rather than the pursuit of profit is, to say the least, debatable, but the successful reinvention of the Stock Exchange speculator reflects the social class from which they came and the increasingly nefarious perception of gambling as working-class gamblers became highly visible in towns and cities. In 'The Lessons of the Street', the Rev. William Landels describes horse racing as 'a disgrace to the aristocracy of England' (p. 203). Here at least it is not the working classes who are bearing the brunt of the attack. However, his observation on horse racing forms simply a part of his overarching theory of recreation: 'that, while we have not been sent into the world to amuse ourselves, but to do God's work and prepare for the enjoyment of a better world, pleasurable recreation, being not unlawful in itself, is admissible when consistent with the end of life, and should be wisely and conscientiously sought after, inasmuch and in so far as it tends to increase and prolong our capability of exertion' (p. 203). Leisure exists to serve the ends of work: the idea that recreation might have intrinsic value does not figure.

Both speakers, echoing the concerns of the rational recreation movement, see leisure as a potentially dangerous practice, in need of control.

All the Year Round, edited by Charles Dickens until his death in 1870, featured a number of articles on gambling. *All the Year Round* was aimed broadly at the lower-middle classes and, infused with Dickens's reforming zeal, it was intended to inform, persuade and galvanize its readership. In 'The Demon of Homburg' (*AYR* 1860), the narrator takes a critical position, referring to 'the glaring splendour' of the surroundings.[82] The article also focuses upon the clientele, highlighting 'an old French marquis' and 'a ruined major' (p. 521), living relics of a bygone age. In 1874, they find an echo in the opening chapter of George Eliot's *Daniel Deronda*, where an ageing and emaciated gambler is addicted to gambling in a continental casino, and thus gambling is identified as a vice for the preceding generation. Violence and intimidation is practised upon winning gamblers in The Demon of Homburg by 'the bullies of the bank' (p. 521), demonstrating that to gamble is to leave the safety of society.

In 'You Must Drink!' by Andrew Halliday (*AYR*, 1864), the target, as the title suggests, is alcohol, which is seen as a greater hazard than gambling.[83] Halliday argues that anti-gambling legislation has merely fostered excessive drinking: 'fully sensible of the evils of gambling, I must, nevertheless, question the wisdom of the law, which is so careful to prevent a man losing small sums at a game of chance, while it takes pains to compel him to spend his money in drink' (p. 439). The tightening of the law with regard to gambling has not resulted in an improved standard of conduct in working people, rather they have simply switched to the other form of recreation most readily available. In point of fact there is not much evidence to suggest that the 1853 Act reduced the amount of gambling. It seems more likely that gambling continued, notwithstanding the climate of prohibition. Halliday also wrote 'My Two Derbies' (1865), an article which reflects the growing commercialization of horse racing.[84] Halliday describes two Derbies he attended at Epsom racecourse, the visits being several years apart (the year of his first race is not mentioned, but it seems likely that his second visit was in 1865, as he refers to it being 'the other day', p. 493). With regard to the first visit, Halliday states, 'we did not pay anything to go on the course (. . .). We guessed which thimble the pea was under, and guessed wrong' (p. 492). However, on the more recent visit, 'we paid a guinea to go upon the course'. Furthermore, gambling is now viewed differently, as a proposal to have a sweepstake among the party 'was indignantly rejected' (p. 493). Therefore, in the gap between the two visits horse racing has become incorporated into a capitalist framework of leisure; gambling, even on a modest scale, is condemned.

'Against the Grain' (*AYR*, 1865), one of several articles on horse racing and gambling in *All the Year Round* by Joseph Charles Parkinson, is characterized by hostility: 'it is time that the miserable nonsense about "upholding English sports," and "interfering with the pastimes of the people," was exploded and put down' (p. 445).[85] Such hostility reflects frustration with the association of gambling with tradition; it also assumes that leisure should not be immune to overt political control. 'Against the Grain' associates gambling with 'the disreputable crew of small book-makers, touts, thieves, and tipsters' (p. 442), mostly seen as criminals: 'in other words, nearly all the vociferous blackguards I see pocketing shillings, and half-crowns, and sovereigns, are thieves, or skittle-sharpers, or three-card men, or their associates' (p. 443). The article concludes in an aggrieved tone, resentful of the public presence of a criminal fraternity and the apparent disinclination of the authorities to intercede. It asks, 'whether a purely suppositious connexion with the race-course is held to entitle detected swindlers and convicted felons to prey upon the credulous and ignorant, without dread of punishment or prospect of interference?' (p. 445). It appears that the narrator is especially troubled by the dishonest conduct of gambling entrepreneurs. The Victorian population needed to have faith in their capitalists and therefore the presence of blatant conmen was awkward and most undesirable. 'Against the Grain' is particularly concerned by the re-emergence of gambling in the aftermath of two prohibitive Gaming Acts.

> The nuisance as it exists now is a far worse pest and a deeper disgrace than the petty tavern sweepstakes and small list-houses, which were, amid a chorus of national self-praise, put down by an act of parliament a few years ago. (p. 445)

Parkinson is aware of the failure of the 1853 Act, and he anticipates the resentment which resulted in the 1874 Act, directed against street gambling.

Disquiet and anger is also evident in Parkinson's, 'The Roughs' Guide' (*AYR*, 1865), an ironic parody of sporting publications.[86] It focuses on dishonest transactions within gambling, such as fraudulent sweepstakes in which the prizes are never awarded, and a series of letters in the sporting press pertaining to bookmakers who have welched on a bet. This indicates the large number of crooked bookmakers who cheat the betting public but, equally, it may constitute a form of internal policing. Gamblers addressing gamblers through the press creates a network of information separating the honest from the dishonest bookmakers. However, of the letters referred to in 'The Roughs' Guide', not one is actually referenced or attributed. Thus, there may be a measure of artistic licence on the part of the narrator. The tone of the article shifts as it reaches its conclusion:

> Such is my guide to the turf. It appeals alike to roughs and gentles, and is surely a marvellous illustration of the tastes, habits, and amusements of a large section of the people. We sneer at the nations who encourage gambling in their capitals, and brag of having put down lotteries; while shilling sweepstakes are openly advertised. (p. 496)

Parkinson is at his most bitter in 'Derby Dregs' (*AYR*, 1866), where he challenges the view that the Derby is a great occasion, 'when peer and peasant, shopkeeper and artisan, mingle together on equal terms'.[87] Instead he focuses on the 'depravity and riot' he witnessed:

> Take the famous hill, an hour after the racing of the day is over, and when the grand stand and its adjacent tributaries look ghastly and tomb-like in their emptiness. Foul language, drunken shrieks, fights, blasphemy and theft, seem things of course, and are rampant on all sides. (p. 487)

Parkinson is not looking at the glamour of the enclosures but the less controlled activities occurring on the periphery of the horse racing itself. Another spectator makes him aware that 'a little game o' roulette may be had behind the long booth yonder, all quiet and comfortable, and with no chance of the Bobbies spiling sport' (p. 488). Gambling clearly survives in a climate of prohibition. However, despite Parkinson's disdain for what he sees, there is a note of compassion when he describes a fraudulent bookmaker attacked by his aggrieved clients:

> An utterly worthless scamp, who made bets and received stakes without the most remote intention of paying his losses, his chastisement was of course merited. Yet, as he limped painfully along, and every now and then putting his hand to his bandaged head, looked vacantly around, it was impossible to withhold commiseration. To be publicly thrashed by many infuriated men, to have one's garments torn and one's body bruised; to be marked as a swindler by professional visitors of every race-course in England, and to be now making for home branded, penniless, forlorn, and writhing at every step, seemed a heavier punishment for swindling than even the law awards, and suggests some curious reflections as to the various degrees of moral turpitude and the penalties attached to them by the world. (p. 489)

Parkinson and others draw attention to fraudulent gambling, but it appears more likely that the majority of gambling in the nineteenth century was conducted honestly. People will not continue to patronise an arena where they are being cheated, unless there is some credibility in the idea that gambling is addictive. Parkinson despises the gamblers at Epsom: 'they were below the level of animals the foulest and most obscene' (p. 489), and he is never able to see gambling as legitimate recreation. He also wrote two articles on prize fighting, 'Genii of the Ring' (*AYR*, 1866) and 'The Eve of the Battle' (*AYR*, 1866).[88] These reflect the continued existence of prize fighting, although the practice was outlawed. That it had also fallen into disrepute is reflected in 'Genii of the Ring' where the followers of pugilism are 'thieves and card-sharpers on the look-out for prey' (p. 232). 'The Eve of the Battle' visits the lower-class pubs where the supporters congregate. The fall of pugilism from its early-nineteenth-century heights is starkly apparent: this is no longer a sport that attracts the aristocracy who, by the 1860s, headed the coterie in the exclusive stands at horse race meetings. The clear sense of anger in Parkinson's *All the Year Round* articles is directed frequently against the legislature. The fact that illegal gambling persisted undermined authority and therefore was a potential threat to social stability.

Other *All the Year Round* articles are interested in aspects of gambling from an historical perspective. In 'Clubs and Club-Men' (*AYR*, 1866) the author looks back on the eighteenth century as 'the golden age of clubs'.[89] There is a nostalgic fondness here, indicating a frustrated and corroded sympathy for the leisure pursuits of the upper classes, their gentility rather than their recklessness. The article provides a history of clubs in England, seeing them as a laudable aspect of English cultural history despite, or more probably because of, their exclusivity. We are told that gambling 'went on to a fearful extent at the Cocoa-Tree' (p. 286). Similarly, there was colossal gambling at Almack's:

> In the club-book of Almack's there is this note – 'Mr Thynne, having won only twelve thousand guineas during the last two months, retired in disgust, March 21st, 1772.' (p. 286)

Clearly, this kind of profligacy could not expect anything other than condemnation from Victorian society, but there is a kind of voyeuristic delectation in the narration of late-eighteenth-century excess. Condemnation is muted, slightly fond reminiscence is more pronounced. In another *All the Year Round* article from 1866, the author looks at 'Horse-Racing in India', in which English practices have been exported and the individual races are known as the Derby and the St Leger, all governed by the 'Calcutta Turf Club' (p. 250).[90] The association between horse racing and English culture appears legitimate, although the focus of the article is more on the horse racing itself than the gambling (described in the article as 'lotteries', p. 249) which arises therefrom.

In 'Royal Ascot' (*AYR*, 1867), the narrator is keen to stress the historical context of the event.[91] The Victorians could legitimately enjoy a horse race if it was freed from the taint of gambling. The presence of working-class spectators in 'Royal Ascot', however, is a problem:

> Great Gainsborough hats, and cutaway coats of the genuine Regency pattern, suggest many points of resemblance with the old racecourse, but the influx of the general public is so great that the once distinctive feature of aristocratic Ascot is gone. (p. 380)

There is nostalgia for the Ascot of old. Criticism is here levelled not at debauched aristocrats but at the impertinent masses. History is also a point of interest in 'Old Stories Re-told: A Gambler's Life in the Last Century' (*AYR*, 1867) which tells a story from 1725, when 'the green cloth these men played upon soon led to the green fields of Tyburn and the leafless tree' (p. 324).[92] There is no nostalgia for gambling here, but, then again, the gamblers are not aristocrats.

Foreign gambling, specifically in America, is the subject of 'Far-Western Gamblers' (*AYR*, 1868).[93] The author believes that 'closely allied to the spirit of gambling is the reckless and mercurial temperament of the Western man' (p. 491). Gambling is held to express an aspect of national character, just as pugilism may have captured something of the bullish and indomitable essence of Britain after the Napoleonic wars. *All the Year Round* takes a fairly consistent position on gambling and, through its numerous articles in the 1860s, it attains a panoramic perspective, from the Royal Enclosure at Ascot to back-street list-houses. From its informed middle-class position it repeatedly expresses anxiety pertaining to the persistence of gambling and its wider social impact. At a time when its writers could expose gambling's defiance of prohibition, *All the Year Round* is rarely anything other than wholly critical of gambling and gamblers.

In *The Seven Curses of London* (1869), James Greenwood (the 'Amateur Casual'), undertook social commentary on gambling in a chapter entitled 'Betting Gamblers'.[94] His general position is apparent from the outset: 'there can be no doubt that the vice of gambling is on the increase amongst the English working classes' (p. 377). Set alongside this warning, however, is a generous dose of self-satisfaction:

> It is a comforting reflection, however, that in their sports and pastimes
> Englishmen, and especially Londoners, of the present generation are less
> barbarous than those of the past. (. . .) In the present enlightened age we
> do not fight cocks and 'shy' at hens tied to a stake at the Shrove-Tuesday
> fair; neither do we fight dogs, or pit those sagacious creatures to bait bulls.
> (p. 378)

As well as making historical distinctions, Greenwood also makes divisions along class lines, placing his middle-class readership above the gambling prevalent amongst working-class people. Greenwood concludes with a lengthy cautionary tale, concerning a ruined young man, 'with his pale haggard face and his dull eyes' (p. 412). The victim narrates his own story:

> Eighteen months ago I was well-dressed and prosperous. I was second clerk
> to ———, the provision merchants, in St Mary Axe, on a salary of a
> hundred and forty pounds – rising twenty each year. Now look at me!
>
> You need not ask me how it came about. You say that you have seen
> me often in Farringdon-street with the betting-men, so you can give a good
> guess as to how I came to ruin, I'll be bound. Yes, sir, it was horse-betting
> that did my business. (p. 414)

The young man goes on to tell how he was duped by a horse-racing tipster in the press, and how he had been sending money to the tipster who was supposedly wagering it on the young man's account. After a few very modest successes, the tipster requested a series of much larger amounts, which were never returned. The story highlights the slippery slope leading to absolute degradation. Greenwood ends with a call for action, a call for the suppression of gambling, and an insistence that this standpoint 'should be the earnest wish of all right-thinking men, who would break down this barrier of modern and monstrous growth, that blocks the advancement of social purity' (p. 419).[95]

In 1870, Andrew Steinmetz, a barrister, published *The Gaming Table: Its Votaries and Victims, In all Times and Countries, especially in England and in France*.[96] As its grandiloquent title suggests, it endeavours to be a comprehensive history of gambling, from 'the ancient Hindoos' to the present day. In common with other writers, Steinmetz is eager to point out the excesses of the previous generation:

> No nation has exceeded ours in the pursuit of gaming. In former times –
> and yet not more than 30 or 40 years ago – the passion for play was predominant among the higher classes.

Genius and abilities of the highest order became its votaries; and the very framers of the laws against gambling were the first to fall under the temptation of their breach! The spirit of gambling pervaded every inferior order of society. The gentleman was a slave to its indulgence; the merchant and the mechanic were the dupes of its imaginary prospects; it engrossed the citizen and occupied the rustic. Town and country became a prey to its despotism. There was scarcely an obscure village to be found wherein this bewitching basilisk did not exercise its powers of fascination and destruction. (p. 24)

Later, he analyses how this state of affairs came about. The aftermath of the French Revolution was a particularly significant phase:

Then came upon the nation the muddy flood of French emigrants, poured forth by the Great Revolution – a set of men, speaking generally, whose vices contaminated the very atmosphere.

Before the advent of these worthies the number of gambling houses in the metropolis, exclusive of those so long established by subscription, was not more than half-a-dozen; but by the year 1820 they had increased to nearly fifty. Besides *Faro* and *Hazard*, the foreign games of *Macao*, *Roulette*, *Rouge et Noir*, etc., were introduced, and there was a graduated accommodation for all ranks, from the Peer of the Realm to the Highwayman, the Burglar, and the Pick-pocket. (p. 122)

Steinmetz seeks a scapegoat for the development and enduring presence of gambling in English society. Objective analysis is sacrificed in the face of a reactionary need to find an evil-doer. He excludes private members' clubs, as they had pretensions to respectability arising out of their clientele. He further neglects to note that the gradual economic migration from country to city created a desire for recreation in an urban context and thus working-class gambling in cities increased.

Steinmetz repeatedly castigates foreign locations. In Baden-Baden, a German spa town with a number of gambling halls, 'Princes and their subjects, fathers and sons, and even, horrible to say, mothers and daughters, are hanging, side by side, for half the night over the green table; and, with trembling hands and anxious eyes, watching their chance-cards, or thrusting francs and Napoleons with their rakes to the red or the black cloth' (p. 157). The gambling towns of Europe become the focal point for vice of every hue, an argument which the narrator, quoting an article from *The Daily Telegraph* of 15 August 1868, is eager to pursue:

It would seem that all the aged, broken-down courtesans of Paris, Vienna, and Berlin have agreed to make Wiesbaden their autumn rendezvous.

[55]

Arrayed in all the colours of the rainbow, painted up to the roots of their dyed hair, shamelessly décolletées, prodigal of 'free' talk and unseemly gesture, these ghastly creatures, hideous caricatures of youth and beauty, flaunt about the play-rooms and gardens, levying black-mail upon those who are imprudent enough to engage them in 'chaff' or badinage, and desperately endeavouring to hook themselves on to the wealthier and younger members of the male community. They poison the air round them with sickly perfumes; they assume titles, and speak of one another as 'cette chère comtesse;' their walk is something between a prance and a wriggle; they prowl about the terrace whilst the music is playing, seeking whom they may devour, or rather whom they may inveigle into paying for their devouring. (p. 214)

The combination of gambling and women is particularly unpalatable to Steinmetz. When, in William Makepeace Thackeray's *Vanity Fair* (1847–8), Becky Sharp re-emerges in continental Europe, she too attempts to dress extravagantly, and she similarly employs her sexual allure to gain a material advantage. At one point it is even implied that she has prostituted herself: 'when she got her money, she gambled; when she had gambled it, she was put to shifts to live; who knows how or by what means she succeeded?'[97]

Following on from his evident disdain for women gamblers, Steinmetz devotes an entire chapter to 'Lady Gamestresses', the inclusion of which he justifies somewhat spuriously by stating that it is 'only with the view of avenging good and honourable women, that I now proceed to speak of those who have disgraced their sex' (p. 258). He is concerned with the consequences of women gambling, noting that losers 'were often reduced to beggary, or to what is far viler, to sacrifice, not only their honour, but that of their daughters' (p. 260). He does not furnish us with any examples of this particular practice, but he remains keen to remind us of the moral risks inherent in women gambling:

> The consequences of such gaming were often still more lamentable than those which usually attend such practices. It would happen that a lady lost more than she could venture to confess to her husband or father. Her creditor was probably a fine gentleman, or she became indebted to some rich admirer for the means of discharging her liabilities. In either event, the result may be guessed. (p. 262)

The cautionary tale in *The Gaming Table* comes at the end of the book under the heading, 'A Reclaimed Gambler's Account of his Career'. The victim describes his downfall:

> A young nobleman of very distinguished family undertook to be my conductor. Alas! to what scenes did he introduce me! To places of debauchery and dens of destruction. I need not detail particulars. From the lures of the courtesans we went to an adjoining gaming room. (p. 387)

Steinmetz repeatedly associates gambling with prostitution. To partake of one vice is to be lured into all. In the story, the gambler's downfall is very swiftly secured and he is led to the brink of suicide:

> I rang for my servant to bring me some gunpowder, and was debating with myself whether to direct its force to my brain or my heart, when he entered with a letter. It was from Harriet ————. She had heard of my misfortunes, and urged me with the soul and pen of a heroine, to fly the destructive habits of the town, and to wait for nine months, when her minority would expire, and she would come into the uncontrolled possession of £1700. With that small sum she hoped my expenses, talents, and domestic comfort, under her housewifery, would create a state of happiness and independence which millions could not procure in the mad career which I had pursued. (p. 388)

Salvation is attained when the hero leaves the city for a domestic idyll. The characteristically Victorian values of selflessness and duty are reaffirmed in this finally happy parable. Similarly, forty years earlier, in Disraeli's *The Young Duke* (1831) the hero was saved from a life of debauchery by the intercession of May Dacre, the morally upright heroine.

As the century entered its last decade, hostility to gambling increased further. 'Gambling', a lengthy article in *Quarterly Review* (1889) endeavours to justify its anti-gambling polemic by undertaking a broad historical overview, but this transparently functions to feed the overall argument.[98] It locates 'the earliest statute to restrict the power of enforcing gambling debts' in Charles II's reign (p. 143), and goes on to identify further examples of anti-gambling legislation, noting that the relevant laws were 'aimed more at the lower than the privileged classes' (p. 144). By listing the parliamentary measures imposed to combat gambling and by simultaneously displaying its persistence, the article shows the unstoppable, tenacious and therefore threatening nature of gambling. The article also gains some credibility as a historical survey.

'Gambling' is keen to highlight historical examples of excessive play and its injurious effects. Gambling was, apparently, particularly prevalent amongst the aristocracy in pre-revolutionary France. Furthermore, it damages the state because: 'at the death of the great King, gambling had deprived the French nobility of all interest in their country's welfare' (p. 141). The lesson here is that gambling is a threat to a nation's stability. The article is equally scathing about the French Republic:

> The Republic, revelling in excitement, did not deny herself the excitement of play. Citizens gambled with all the frenzy, if not with all the meanness, of the *ancienne noblesse*, whom they flattered by the imitation of one at least of their vices. Play produced all its attendant evils, but passion being less controlled, those evils took a more than usually malignant form, and murder and robberies abounded. The first Napoleon gambled with kingdoms, but not with cards. He despised men who were gamblers in the ordinary sense. (p. 142)

Here we find a grudging admiration for the nation's former adversary because, within the context of the article, Napoleon represents control and authority in opposition to the irresponsibility of the general population.

Gambling is also highlighted in England in the late eighteenth century. The article quotes the following sentiment from Lord Kenyon, expressed in 1796:

> It is extremely to be lamented (. . .) that the vice of gambling has descended to the very lowest orders of the people. It is prevalent among the highest ranks of society, who have set an example to their inferiors and seem to think themselves too great for the law. I wish they could be punished. If any prosecutions are fairly brought before me, and the parties are justly convicted, whatever may be their rank or station in the country – though they should be the first ladies in the land – they shall certainly exhibit themselves in the pillory. (p. 147)

The text records the excesses of the aristocracy and the ignorance of the masses, leaving a self-congratulatory middle class to claim moral authority. The misdeeds of the late eighteenth century continued in the early years of the nineteenth:

> in 1818 nearly every month of the year was distinguished by a duel or duels resulting from gambling quarrels. In a word, the law seemed utterly unable to cope with a habit, which produced disasters of terrible frequency, but of the advantages of which it is impossible to discover a trace. (p. 148)

This period is seen to be the high-water mark of excessive gambling, prior to the introduction of the Victorian era and a more orderly social and moral climate: 'soon after the commencement of the present reign there occurred a considerable lull in the fever of high play' (p. 151). Similarly, as the article turns its attention to the contemporary situation of gambling in England, it notes that 'there is no such card play as characterized the last quarter of the eighteenth century and the first three decades of this' (p. 155). The credit for this does not lie with the new legislation concerning gambling, commencing with the1845 Act. Instead, it is chiefly the product of a different attitude amongst the ruling class.

> But the Act, though it did much by making wagers incapable of legal enforcement, did less to discourage gambling than a change in the attitude of those who had influence on the habit of English society. (p. 152)

It appears that a moral transformation was primarily responsible for a social change. A newly dominant philosophy rejected gambling. 'Gambling' is troubled by a perceived increase in betting on horse racing:

> Every class of society, from the highest to the lowest, is more or less affected with a mania for betting, for the development of which there are unhappily ample opportunities. (p. 137)

The anxiety of the *Quarterly Review* regarding gambling in general, and betting on horse races in particular, rises into the hysterical:

> That vice and misery are eating into the heart of the nation. They are sapping, surely and not slowly, the honest instincts which, maintained through many generations and in spite of many difficulties, made our commerce the most successful in the world. Not only is racing, as at present pursued, the direct cause of ruin to many a home and the destruction to many a career, but it tends to foster habits and methods absolutely antagonistic to national progress. (p. 162)

The article concludes with a clarion cry for action:

> The present state of things is a scandal to our cities, a grave danger to our position as a nation. It loudly calls for the anxious thought of all who care for the welfare of the people. (p. 166)

There may be some justice in the *Quarterly Review*'s position. It is likely that gambling, particularly within the working classes and especially on horse races, increased during the 1880s. However, the simple explanation for the growth in gambling is that, until the 1880s, working people did not have sufficient disposable income to afford a modest gambling expenditure.[99] Furthermore, the absence of alternative facilities for gambling, the high profile of the sporting press and technological advances which allowed results to be spread at speed across country, created the conditions in which gambling on horse racing increased in popularity.

The anti-gambling movement reached its full height in the form of the National Anti-Gambling League. The League emerged around 1889–90. Its President was the Earl of Aberdeen and amongst its numerous Vice-Presidents were the Bishop of Wakefield, the Dean of Rochester and Dr W. T. Moore, editor of the *Christian Commonwealth*. The League adopted the fiercest anti-gambling rhetoric: 'there is humiliation in the thought that the chosen Anglo-saxon race, foremost in the civilisation and government of the world, is first also in the great sin of Gambling'.[100] It later ran a hymn-writing competition, one of the prize-winning entries being 'A Leprosy is o'er the Land'. The League published a fairly regular newspaper, *The Bulletin*, together with occasional tracts, for example, 'A Blot on the Queen's Reign', written by John Hawke, Organising Secretary of the League, in 1893, and alluding in its title to the Prince of Wales's attendance at horse racing meetings.[101] This was not the Prince of Wales's only involvement with gambling. In 1891 he featured in the Tranby Croft case, in which it emerged that he had instigated and participated in a game of baccarat for money. Furthermore, it was commonly believed that he contracted large gambling debts, from which he was discharged by financiers.[102]

Every issue of the NAGL's bulletin featured accounts of crimes and suicides brought about through gambling. *The Bulletin* also boasted regular features, such as 'Pithy Paragraphs from the World's Press', which, in the May 1894 edition (vol 1, no 8) reprinted an article from *Christian Pictorial*, which, attacking the Prince of Wales's patronage of The Two Thousand Guineas horse race, stated: 'the vice of gambling is eating its way like a canker into the vitals of every class of the community, and for this the royal and aristocratic families of the land are chiefly responsible' (p. 85). The League was thus, in its early years, quite prepared to challenge the gambling of the ruling class. However, despite this willingness to confront gambling across the social spectrum, upper-class gamblers showed themselves to be impervious to attack, ignoring the League's proclamations and finally defeating it in court (see below). The League, therefore, increasingly turned its anger on working-class gamblers; what had started as an attempt to halt all gambling resulted in another assault solely on gambling within the working class.[103]

The League had a sense of being on a crusade against gambling. It was religious in the fervour of its utterances. It regularly printed an extended series of slogans, entitled 'Shall I Bet?'

'Yes!' – shout 20,000 Bookmakers:- ('for we live on the losses').
'No!' – cry half a million of fathers, mothers, sisters, wives:- 'that's how the misery of our home began.'

'Yes!' – whispers Covetousness:- 'you may win money more quickly than by working.'

'No!' – answers Prudence:-'very few win in the long run.'

'Yes!' – urges Selfishness:- 'you will have easy times if you're lucky.'

'No!' – replies Conscience:- 'others would suffer for your ease: you may drug me for a while, but there will be remorse afterwards.'

'Yes!' – say the Sporting Newspapers:- 'you will buy us more eagerly.'

'No!' – rejoins Duty:- 'you will neglect me, and employ your thoughts elsewhere.'

'Yes!' – laughs the Publican:- 'betting men are my best customers.'

'No!' – murmurs the Savings Bank:- 'they seldom patronize me for long.'

'Yes!' – votes the Tipster:- ('what shall I do without you?')

'No!' – sighs the Prison Governor:- 'my jail is getting full.'

'Yes!' – mutters the Devil:- 'it's the shortest road in my direction.'

'NO!' – commands your Maker:- Do as you would be done by. Work in faith and hope. Strive to be honest and pure. The reward shall come some day. 'Fear not, I will be with thee.'

Members of the League were encouraged to cut out 'Shall I Bet?' from *The Bulletin*, or buy it at five shillings for a thousand copies, and to hand them to people whom they felt might be tempted to gamble.[104] This manifesto of anti-gambling associates it with the neglectful and indeed the diabolical, thereby demonstrating the extent to which gambling was perceived as a threat to society at a time when the economic health of Victorian England was deteriorating.

In 1897, the League endeavoured to use the 1853 Gaming Act to ban betting at race courses. The Act had stated that it was illegal to resort to a place for the purposes of gambling, and the League argued that a race course was a 'place' within the definition of the Act. The League won the case, against the Kempton Park Racecourse Company, but the decision was overturned at the Court of Appeal. The Appeal Court's decision is neatly summed-up by David C. Itzkowitz (1988): 'everyone recognized that the strained decision in the Kempton Park case had been made simply to allow the sport of horse racing to continue as before while not disturbing the legal prohibition against gambling in other areas.'[105] Once again, the favoured mode of gambling of the upper class was protected by the state. Despite the ferocity of the National Anti-Gambling League's opposition, the commercialization of gambling did not cease. When an ideological and an economic interest collided, the latter triumphed.

One of the characteristic features of gambling in the nineteenth century was that it was attacked from all points of the political spectrum. Much of the above material has addressed gambling from an orthodox, middle-class perspective. However, as a formal labour movement emerged some of its spokespersons considered gambling and its impact on the working classes from a socialist position. On 4 January 1902, John Burns, MP, delivered a speech entitled *Brains Better than Bets or Beer*.[106] Burns implies a connection between gambling and poor living conditions, generated by personal irresponsibility: 'one home is clean, bright, attractive, and in the same street, with more money, and often more room, others are dirty, untidy, noisome in their conditions. Why? Because too many workmen work hard five days, but on the sixth are generally found at the "Corner Pin" spotting winners and catching losers. (Cheers.)' (p. 5). Burns's proposed solution is a form of autonomous, working-class self-help and thus self-improvement. He encourages the working class to 'spend on the improvement of their lot, even on rent for better homes, what is now devoted to drink, betting and worse' (p. 7). The advice he gives is specific:

> To each married man I make this appeal – when you have a spare hour take the missus out. (Loud cheers.) Take the missus and children to theatre, music halls, parks, libraries, museum, and the number of places of healthy diversion and recreation that the London County Council and the State, by collective effort, have secured for the musical, artistic, and recreative enjoyment of all. Spend on books what is often given to beer; to mental improvement what is given to gambling. (pp. 9–10)

For Burns, alcohol and gambling are both impediments to working-class development. They are not accredited with any status as legitimate forms of recreation. However, although Burns criticizes aspects of working-class behaviour he blames the aristocracy for the popularity of gambling: 'their vicious prodigal example is spreading to every class less fortunate than themselves' (p. 11). There is some socialism in Burns's analysis as he sees upper-class ignorance and profligacy as part of the problem, but there is also a sense of paternalism, with working people being told how they should entertain themselves.

Another left-wing critique of gambling may be found in J. Ramsay Macdonald's essay, 'Gambling and Citizenship', published in *Betting and Gambling: A National Evil* (1905).[107] Ramsay Macdonald was himself a member of the National Anti-Gambling League and, at the time of the publication of 'Gambling and Citizenship', he was also Secretary of the Labour Representation Committee. Like Burns, he identifies gambling specifically as 'a class disease' (p. 118), which 'spreads downwards to the industrious poor from the idle rich' (p. 120). Macdonald thus highlights explicitly one of the concerns raised, though not legislated upon specifically, by the Select Committee on Gaming more than fifty years previously. The idea of the upper class setting a bad example to the working class clearly persisted through the second half of the century although, in practice, the working class were much more likely to be at the receiving end of the state's hostility than their upper-class counterparts. Ramsay Macdonald likens the time at which he was writing to the late eighteenth century, when gambling and politics were closely linked:

> The gamblers were in power. There was plenty of party but little politics, and what politics there was was largely an art of recouping gaming losses from the public purse. (p. 125)

Ramsay Macdonald points to corruption in high places, associating gambling with a dereliction of social duty, a technique also used by Disraeli, most explicitly in *Sybil*, although Disraeli came from the opposite end of the political spectrum. Both commentators, however, were able to employ gambling as a signifier for aristocratic irresponsibility, but while Macdonald employed the device to condemn the aristocracy, Disraeli was interested in redeeming it.

Ramsay Macdonald, like Disraeli in *Sybil*, is interested in the political consequences of an obsession with gambling although, unlike Disraeli, he is most interested in its impact on working-class politics:

> Men who are too weary to think, too overworked to attend political meetings or take positions of responsibility in their trade unions, can nevertheless speak authoritatively about the pedigree of an obscure horse and the record of a second-rate footballer. (p. 126)

He is explicit about the implications of a preoccupation with gambling for the development of the labour movement: 'to hope, for instance, that a labour party can be built up in a population quivering from an indulgence in games of hazard is folly' (p. 127). 'Gambling and Citizenship' shows how gambling is antithetical to citizenship, as gambling imbues working people with a false perspective. The most interesting point to note, however, is the extent to which both Burns and Macdonald were out of sympathy and indeed out of touch with their own constituency. There are good grounds for suggesting that the majority of gambling in the nineteenth century was controlled and pleasurable, given its persistence through increasingly aggressive prohibitive measures and the fact that society did not implode as a result of gambling, despite the NAGL's warnings. For socialist commentators to attack working-class gambling with such vitriol was to make assumptions about working people having no self-discipline and no right to enjoy themselves as they best saw fit.

Discussion of the novels featured in the chapters that follow will draw upon the historical aspects of gambling detailed in this chapter. Benjamin Disraeli records the profligacy of upper-class gamblers in their clubs and at the races. Charles Dickens is similarly aware of the gambling of aristocrats, but also of excessive gambling lower down the social scale. William Makepeace Thackeray features the gaming-house and the card-table: his representations derive from his own experiences of gambling hells and card games. For George Eliot, gambling is especially (though not exclusively) a signifier for irresponsibility, and both the continental gaming-house and the pub feature as arenas for gambling in her novels. Thomas Hardy's accounts of gambling are largely removed from their wider social context, focusing rather on the physical process of the gamble, whereas, for Anthony Trollope, gambling is located firmly in its social context, being a legitimate upper-class pastime compromised by personal irresponsibility. For George Moore, horse racing and bookmaking is crucial to the progress of *Esther Waters*, which leans heavily on the actual world of gambling in Victorian England and exposes the hypocrisy pervading the state's treatment of gamblers. The connections between the individual novels and the historical context in which they were written will become more apparent in the individual chapters and more explicit in the conclusion.

chapter two

'A Dissipated Career'

Benjamin Disraeli and a Failing Aristocracy

In 1824 and 1825 Benjamin Disraeli undertook a series of disastrous speculations on the stock exchange. He did not discharge the debts arising out of this misadventure until 1849, and in the intervening period Disraeli wrestled constantly with financial worries. It was Disraeli's first serious encounter with the world of speculation and gambling (although he had visited a casino in Frankfurt in August 1824) and it was to be the most significant gambling experience of his life. However, Disraeli's political ambitions brought him into contact with the gambling culture of the time, including the gaming-houses of St James's. This chapter focuses on gambling in Disraeli's fiction and in his life, from 1831 (the year in which *The Young Duke* was published) to the period surrounding the end of the Young England trilogy.[1] Within this period gambling became a matter of concern to parliament, resulting in both a Select Committee and legislation.

The Young Duke (1831, 1853)

Disraeli wrote *The Young Duke* to raise money, following his stock exchange misfortunes.[2] In a letter of 8 December 1829, he referred to the dangers of becoming 'a literary prostitute' with his publisher, Henry Colburn, as 'the bawd'.[3] The novel centres on George Augustus Frederick, Duke of St James, and his personal development from youthful hedonism to maturity. The title is significant, as the parish of St James was, until the mid-nineteenth century, notorious for its gaming-houses. The Duke's name thus associates him with wealth and self-indulgence.

The Young Duke is not particularly realistic, nor was it intended to be. In the preface Disraeli notes that, 'to draw caricatures of our contemporaries is not a very difficult task: it requires only a small portion of talent, and a great want of courtesy'. Matthew Whiting Rosa, in *The Silver-Fork School* (1964), a study of the early-nineteenth century literary genre otherwise known as 'the fashionable novel', describes *The Young Duke* as 'a fashionable novel to end fashionable novels'.[4] He compares the novel with the Silver-Fork criteria: 'the characters must be of high station – therefore, this one is about a duke. (. . .) The sins must be glamorous – this novel's sins include the latest dancer from the opera; the money gambled away is enough to impair fifty thousand a year'.[5] In fact, Rosa's view is that the high-life in *The Young Duke* is represented so hyperbolically that it exceeds the conditions of the Silver-Fork, a notable achievement in relation to a genre which was not renowned for its restraint. However, by noting the genre within which Disraeli loosely operated in *The Young Duke*, we can see some of the conditioning influences on his representations of glamorous lifestyles and gambling.

The Duke gives notice of his hedonistic disposition from a young age, as he is forced to leave Oxford in the aftermath of an undergraduate prank. He thereafter travels in Europe, and 'gamed a little at Paris' (I, 18). The social world he inhabits is indolent and carefree; this state of affairs exists at the highest tier of society in *The Young Duke* and is in evidence in Parliament during a debate in the House of Lords. The speeches are unedifying, the motion is withdrawn, but the narrator is equally interested in the non-participating members.

> While all this was going on, some made a note, some made a bet, some consulted a book, some their ease, some yawned, a few slept; yet, on the whole, there was an air about the assembly which can be witnessed in no other in Europe. Even the most indifferent looked as if he would come forward if the occasion should demand him, and the most imbecile as if he could serve his country if it required him. (I, 45)

The narrator makes an attempt to salvage national pride by indicating the heroic potential of the parliamentarians but the prevailing image is of lethargy and disinterest. True leadership in the country is slumbering and feckless and, at best, waiting to be catalyzed. Disraeli's representation of the ruling class in the first half of the nineteenth century shows them failing to live up to their responsibilities. He later repeated this technique at the beginning of *Sybil*, where gambling is a more prominent element.

The Duke fits nicely into his social and political context. He has enormous wealth and therefore enormous potential to improve society but he squanders his riches. We soon form an idea of how he passes the time: 'think of Crockford, think of White's, think of Brooks', and you may form a faint idea how the young Duke had to talk, and eat, and flirt, and cut, and pet, and patronize!' (I, 74–5). He is a member of all the most exclusive gaming clubs in London. He is, by virtue of his wealth and status, a leader of fashion with tremendous social influence. He also has easy access to women of similar social standing. In the midst of his flirtation with Lady Aphrodite: 'the women began to stare, the men to bet' (I, 54). Any emotional response of which these incidental characters may be capable is omitted. All they engage in is gossip and gambling.

The Duke's prestige leads to him being appointed as a steward at a horse racing meeting in Doncaster. The races are an occasion of general festivity, available to the whole community in the pre-enclosure era. The meeting is referred to as 'the Carnival of the North' (I, 120). The Duke's own horse, Sanspareil, is defeated in the St Leger by May Dacre, a horse named after the woman whom the Duke is pursuing. Unaccustomed to loss, he is defeated both in the race and, albeit temporarily, in his romantic aspirations. Prior to the race, the Duke and May Dacre have a conversation in which she comments on the number of requests she has received from men eager to dance with her: 'we damsels shall soon be obliged to carry a book to enrol our engagements as well as our bets' (I, 144). Social and romantic intercourse is here associated with gambling, as both are competitive and both involve the pursuit of a sought-after prize. In the same conversation, May tells the Duke, in reference to his horse, that 'favourites always win' (I, 145). This turns out to be ironic, as the horse May Dacre defeats Sanspareil. Furthermore, the Duke, a social favourite, has to reorganize his own life fundamentally in order to gain the approval of May herself. The presumption that favourites always win is challenged in *The Young Duke* when a character of moral substance refuses to fall in with the expectations of fashion.

The unexpected outcome of the St Leger is costly to many.

> The Dukes of Burlington and Shropshire exchanged a few hundreds; the Duchess and Charles Annesley a few gloves. The consummate Lord Bloomerly, though a backer of the favourite, in compliment to his host, contrived to receive from all parties, and particularly from St Maurice. The sweet little Wrekins were absolutely ruined. Sir Lucius looked blue, but he had hedged; and Lord Squib looked yellow, but some doubted. Lord Hounslow was done, and Lord Bagshot was diddled.
>
> The Duke of St James was perhaps the heaviest sufferer on the field, and certainly bore his losses the best. Had he seen the five-and-twenty thousand he was minus counted before him, he probably would have been staggered; but as it was, another crumb of his half-million was gone. The loss existed only in idea. (I, 164–5)

The Duke is stoic in defeat, but his sanguine response is more an expression of his ignorant profligacy than his aristocratic training. A later race meeting at Newmarket is more serious and socially exclusive, 'a sacred ceremony', free from crowds, the 'thoughtless thousands', who attend race meetings merely 'to sport their splendid liveries and to disport their showy selves' (II, 24). The Duke is an élitist: his involvement with horse racing is consistent with his social and economic position, as the maintenance of horses requires wealth and influence. On a personal level his involvement is a strategy to offset romantic disappointment in the aftermath of May Dacre's refusal of his proposal: 'if the form of May Dacre ever flitted before his vision for an instant, he clouded it over directly by the apparition of a bet' (II, 31–2). Gambling here is compensatory, relevant on a personal as well as a social level.

Gambling in *The Young Duke* begins as a pastime for the wealthy, but it becomes more sinister when the Duke becomes acquainted with a set of debauched aristocrats, including the aptly-named Lord Dice. His gambling intensifies rapidly. The entire episode is prefaced by Disraeli's own perspective on gambling (III, ch. 6).

> I know that I am broaching a doctrine which many will start at, and which some will protest against, when I declare my belief that no person, whatever his apparent wealth, ever yet gamed except from the prospect of immediate gain. We hear much of want of excitement, of ennui, of satiety; and then the gaming-house is announced as a sort of substitute for opium, wine, or any other mode of obtaining a more intense vitality at the cost of reason.

Thereafter the narrator demystifies gambling: 'gambling is too active, too anxious, too complicated, too troublesome; in a word, "too sensible" an affair for such spirits, who fly only to a sort of dreamy and indefinite distraction. The fact is, gaming is a matter of business. (...) It pre-supposes in its votary a mind essentially mercantile. (...) No man flies to the gaming-table in a paroxysm.'

Gambling, according to the narrator, is unglamorous labour which depends, paradoxically, upon a commercial spirit.

> The first stake will make the lightest heart anxious, the firmest hand tremble, and the stoutest heart falter. After the first stake, it is all a matter of calculation and management, even in games of chance. Night after night will men play at 'rouge et noir', upon what they call a system, and for hours their attention never ceases, any more than it would if they were in the shop or on the wharf. No manual labour is more fatiguing, and more degrading to the labourer, than gaming. Every gamester (I speak not of the irreclaimable) feels ashamed.

Hereafter, controversially, the narrator challenges the popular conception that gambling is an inescapable vice.

> And this vice, this worst vice, from whose embrace, moralists daily inform us, man can never escape, is just the one from which the majority of men most completely, and most often, emancipate themselves. Infinite are the men who have lost thousands in their youth, and never dream of chance again. It is this pursuit which, oftener than any other, leads man to self-knowledge. Appalled by the absolute destruction on the verge of which he finds his early youth just stepping; aghast at the shadowy crimes which, under the influence of this life, seem, as it were, to rise upon his soul; often he hurries to emancipate himself from this fatal thraldom, and with a ruined fortune, and marred prospects, yet thanks his Creator that his soul is still white, his conscience clear, and that, once more, he breathes the sweet air of heaven. (III, 52–4)

Disraeli's description is a broadly rational, if unconventional, critique of gambling. It is very unlike the position adopted in the contemporaneous 'Hells in London' article (see chapter one), and presents an alternative analysis of gambling in the 1830s. Its pragmatism foreshadows the 1844 Select Committee on Gaming. Furthermore, Disraeli argues that gambling performs some good as it facilitates self-knowledge. Disraeli's assessment excludes the absolute hostility to gambling by which the latter part of the century came to be characterized.

The Duke's gambling reaches its height when he loses £100,000 at écarté during a virtually continuous forty-eight hour game. The seriousness of the contest is made apparent early in the chapter (III, ch. 8): 'there seemed a general understanding among all the parties, that tonight was to be a pitched battle, and they began at once, very briskly' (III, 67). The game is open combat, emphasizing the adversarial nature of this form of gambling, as the contestants compete directly against each other. During the first break the Duke relinquishes social niceties: 'he passed over the delicacies, and went to the side-table, and began cutting himself some cold roast beef. (. . .) He devoured the roast beef, and rejecting the hermitage with disgust, asked for porter' (III, 68). Gambling has fractured the Duke's sophisticated veneer: his manner of eating becomes bestial, the drink he requests is associated with the working class, from whom he normally cultivates distance. The card game is stewarded by Tom Cogit. He is illegitimate, an implicit comment on the proceedings, which occur without society's sanction.

> They played till dinner-time without intermission; and though the Duke made some desperate efforts, and some successful ones, his losses were, nevertheless, trebled. Yet he ate an excellent dinner, and was not at all

depressed; because the more he lost, the more his courage and his resources seemed to expand. At first, he had limited himself to ten thousand; after breakfast, it was to have been twenty thousand; then, thirty thousand was the ultimatum; and now he dismissed all thoughts of limits from his mind, and was determined to risk or gain every thing. (III, 70)

The Duke is losing all self-control and all his money. His conduct, irrational rather than rooted in a desire for profit, contradicts Disraeli's view of gambling, but the earlier section was an intrusion by Disraeli into the narrative, manipulating the text to accommodate his own analysis. The Duke, Disraeli's invention, does not share Disraeli's perspective. The Duke's fellow card-players also alter within this closed environment. Aristocrats prey upon each other and any pretence at decorum is abandoned: 'the atmosphere was hot, to be sure, but well it became such a hell' (III, 71). The effect of gambling on the players manifests itself in their physical appearance.

> There they sat, almost breathless, watching every turn with the fell look in their cannibal eyes, which showed their total inability to sympathize with their fellow-beings. All forms of society had been long forgotten. (. . .) Lord Castlefort rested with his arms on the table: -a false tooth had got unhinged. His Lordship, who, at any other time, would have been most annoyed, coolly put it in his pocket. His cheeks had fallen, and he looked twenty years older. Lord Dice had torn off his cravat, and his hair hung down over his callous, bloodless cheeks, straight as silk. Temple Grace looked as if he were blighted by lightning; and his deep blue eyes gleamed like a hyena. (III, 72)

As the Duke decides to end the game, he catches a glimpse of himself in the mirror: 'a blight seemed to have fallen over his beauty, and his presence seemed accursed. He had pursued a dissipated, even more than a dissipated career' (III, 73). This is the point of self-realization for the Duke. Gambling has performed a useful act in accordance with Disraeli's earlier description as it has forced the Duke to view his own profligacy and its consequences. His awareness of his own degradation is then considered alongside an alternative image: 'in the darkness of his meditations, a light burst from his lurid mind, – a celestial light appeared to dissipate this thickening gloom, and his soul felt as it were bathed with the softening radiancy. He thought of May Dacre' (III, 74–5). Like the parliamentarians in the early part of the novel, the Duke's personal irresponsibility is compounded by his act of class betrayal: he has ignored the duties of leadership which have been placed upon him since birth. May Dacre now appears as the antithesis of gambling and the personification of a life free from corruption and parasites, leading the Duke to end the game.

Despite the implausible aspects of *The Young Duke* there are grounds for suggesting that this particular form of gambling for extraordinarily high stakes did have some foundation in reality. Captain Gronow, in his *Reminiscences and Recollections*, details a private card game at the Roxburgh Club in St James's Square.

> Upon one occasion at the Roxburgh, the following gentlemen, Hervey Combe, Tippo Smith, Ward (the Member for London,) and Sir John Malcolm, played at high stakes at whist; they sat during that night, viz., Monday, the following day and night, and only separated on Wednesday morning at eleven o'clock; indeed, the party only broke up then owing to Hervey Combe being obliged to attend the funeral of one of his partners who was buried on that day. Hervey Combe, on looking over his card, found that he was a winner of thirty thousand pounds from Sir John Malcolm.[6]

Spectacular gambling at cards was clearly not unknown among the well-off, and one of the effects of the commercialization of gambling in the second half of the nineteenth century was to lessen the adversarial features of the practice. It became less common for individuals to gamble between themselves and more regular for gambling to be accommodated by some commercial agency, even though bookmaking had to operate in circumstances in which it was illegal. In *The Young Duke*, in the absence of a commercial framework, the contest between individual gamblers is more pronounced.

The Duke of St James's redemption occurs through the intercession of the Dacre family. Mr Dacre is initially the Duke's guardian, but the Duke shuns him in favour of more glamorous company. He puts off a visit to the Dacres' home for as long as possible and, when he finally arrives, he finds 'no manoeuvring mothers, no flirting daughters, no gambling sons, for your entertainment. (. . .) The Jockey Club may be quoted, but Crockford will be a dead letter' (I, 214). The Jockey Club is tolerated, as it is the governing body of horse racing, consisting of titled people of considerable reputation. Crockford, a dissolute former fishmonger, does not figure.

Castle Dacre is also the home of May Dacre, to whom the Duke proposes marriage. His proposal adopts a gambler's vocabulary: 'I have staked my happiness upon this venture' (I, 289). In the wake of her rejection, the narrator dwells on the Duke's bitterness: 'bitter are a losing card, a losing horse' (I, 293). Romance is viewed as a gamble: the Duke is unable, at this stage, to engage with serious emotions, and instead expresses various modes of human conduct as forms of gambling. His language also reflects the extent to which marriage was a gamble, an irreversible and financially significant act with far-reaching consequences. Eventually he faces absolute financial ruin. He allows Mr Dacre to administer his affairs, stays at Castle Dacre and falls in with its routine. His proximity to May and a general moderation in his lifestyle bring happiness. The Duke becomes a fit suitor and May finally accepts his proposal. *The Young Duke*, therefore, ends happily. This is a predictable outcome in a novel in which a moral instruction co-exists with a light tone and levity of style, a novel in which the narrator apparently feels the need to step into the foreground when describing the unexpected outcome of the St Leger, announcing 'pardon me! The fatal remembrance overpowers my pen. An effort and some *Eau de Portingale*, and I shall recover' (I, 164). Despite its portrayal of upper-class excesses, however, *The Young Duke* maintains that the aristocracy is essentially honourable. The Duke feels like a criminal after he has gambled because he has broken a long-standing social contract which perpetuates the notion of upper-class decency.

A revised version of *The Young Duke* was published in 1853, the same year in which a major piece of anti-gambling legislation was passed.[7] The main difference between the 1831 text and the 1853 text is the role adopted by the narrator. In the later version the speaker is more detached and removed from the central protagonist. In the two decades separating the two editions, attitudes towards aristocratic excess had hardened. Furthermore, Disraeli himself was, by the 1850s, more of an establishment figure, having been elected to Parliament in 1837. It is possible that Disraeli was eager to establish a sense of distance from a hero whose conduct is, for a large part of the novel, antithetical to the Victorian ideal. The gap between the two versions is acknowledged in Disraeli's advertisement for the 1853 edition.

> The reader will be kind enough to recollect that *'THE YOUNG DUKE'* was written 'when George the Fourth was King' (1829), nearly a quarter of a century ago, and that, therefore, it is entitled to the indulgence which is the privilege of juvenile productions. Though its pages attempt to portray the fleeting manners of a somewhat frivolous age, it is hoped that they convey a moral of a deeper and a more permanent character.

This apologetic introduction stresses the morally instructive nature of the text. With specific regard to gambling, its representation in the 1853 version is virtually the same as in the 1831 version. The very few changes that do occur, however, are noteworthy. In the lengthy passage on gambling in volume three (as discussed earlier) Disraeli writes, in the

1831 text, 'Every gamester (I speak not of the irreclaimable) feels ashamed'. In the 1853 text, the section in parentheses is omitted. The effect of the omission is to make the statement even more categorical. In the main gambling episode (III, ch. 8), the differences between the two texts are very slight indeed, with only the occasional personal pronoun being altered. For example, 'I use the word advisedly' (p. 68), in 1831, is changed to 'we use the word advisedly' (p. 243), in 1853, and 'let me say' (p. 73), in 1831, is changed to 'let us say' (p. 245) in 1853, which has the effect of withdrawing the narrator from the incident. He no longer exists as a character in his own right and, instead, voices a group perspective, reflecting mainstream society's less tolerant attitude to gambling in the 1850s.

Although gambling is a prominent theme in *The Young Duke*, it was less important to Disraeli himself in the 1830s and 1840s. There were, however, several occasions when it affected his life. In November 1831 Disraeli brought a friend, Henry Stanley, to London. Stanley thereafter disappeared, until he was tracked down at a gaming-house in St James's, owned by Effie Bond, a moneylender with whom Disraeli had had dealings.[8] It was suspected that Disraeli had introduced Stanley to the gaming-house, and Disraeli's reputation suffered in consequence. On balance, however, it seems unlikely that Disraeli was involved in this incident, and, in a letter to his sister, dated 14 November 1831, he expressed concern about Stanley's plight.[9]

Disraeli himself was a member of numerous clubs, including the Cocoa Tree, but he found it difficult to gain membership of Crockford's. In July 1834 Baron Ossulton offered to nominate Disraeli for membership, but Disraeli felt sure that the application would be rejected.[10] However, he was aware of what was going on in Crockford's, referring in a letter to the fact that he was praised there (20 January 1835), and, in a letter dated 7 February 1835, knowing the odds being given at Crockford's on the identity of the new Speaker of the House of Commons.[11] Disraeli eventually became a member of Crockford's on 6 February 1841, by which time Crockford himself had retired from the club. Crockford announced his resignation on 1 July 1840, concerning which Disraeli wrote, ''tis a thunderbolt and nothing else is talked of'.[12] Following his own election to membership Disraeli was most impressed, writing that it 'is like a French palace and very different to any club'.[13] Within a short period of time he became an established figure at Crockford's and was confident enough to nominate someone for membership himself in March 1843.[14] Crockford's, as a point of congregation for society's élite, was useful to Disraeli, and in March 1842 he twice referred, in letters to his wife, to being congratulated at Crockford's by prominent society figures, for a speech he had made in Parliament concerning consular service.[15] Because of his success at the club, its imminent closure, arising out of the 1845 Act, came as a disappointment to him, as evidenced in a letter to his sister, dated 23 August 1845.

> I am afraid that the new gaming Act, smuggled thro' the House, during one of the damned morning sittings without a gentleman present, will absolutely knock up Crockford's. They say it will positively be dissolved. What folly! It was the only place in London where there was no cheating![16]

Disraeli laments the fate of Crockford's but he did not use the club for its gaming facilities. Instead, Crockford's served his larger ambition of increasing his social reputation and political influence. Disraeli recognized the importance of Crockford's as an arena where the powerful congregated.

The Young England Trilogy

The Young England movement was a faction within the Tories in the 1840s. It was a reaction against the utilitarian spirit of the times, hearkening back to a mythical past characterized by benign feudalism. In Parliament there were four 'Young Englanders' working together in the House of Commons. They were Disraeli, George Smythe, Lord John Manners and Alexander Baillie-Cochrane. In Disraeli's fiction, Smythe is the inspiration for the eponymous hero of *Coningsby* and he also appears as Waldershare in Disraeli's final novel, *Endymion* (1880). Manners and Baillie-Cochrane are also featured in *Coningsby*, as Lord Henry Sydney and Buckhurst respectively. The Young England movement was essentially romantic: Smythe was heavily influenced by Byron's poetry and Scott's novels, and in 1852 he fought the last known duel on English soil. The Movement's actual political influence was negligible, though it did reflect a pervading disquiet in Tory circles pertaining to the decline in the influence of the aristocracy, a process signified by the Reform Act of 1832 which extended the electoral franchise and, in the 1840s, by the repeal of the Corn Laws which had, it was believed, done much to safeguard the landed interest. Despite the movement's minimal influence politically, it provided Disraeli with the basis for his trilogy of the 1840s which addressed explicitly the problems of his own era.

Coningsby (1844)

Disraeli's literary reputation is centred on the Young England trilogy, the first volume of which is *Coningsby*, published in May 1844.[17] The plot concerns Harry Coningsby and his rejection of the limitations of his aristocratic heritage personified by his grandfather, Lord Monmouth (based on the Third Marquess of Hertford). Disraeli had been introduced to the Third Marquess of Hertford in 1834, on whom the character of Lord Steyne in William Makepeace Thackeray's *Vanity Fair* is also based.[18] Instead of following Lord Monmouth's guidance, Coningsby symbolically unifies aristocracy and industry through his marriage to Edith Millbank, daughter of a successful and philanthropic manufacturer. *Coningsby* covers the period from the passing of the Reform Bill in 1832 to the Tory election victory in 1841.[19] Gambling in *Coningsby* is an aristocratic pastime and it also figures in the political realm. Lord Monmouth's disposition towards the rest of humankind is evident from the outset: 'Lord Monmouth always looked upon human nature with the callous eye of a jockey' (p. 10). One of the very few people towards whom he is not exploitative is Mr Ormsby, who is also rich and 'won money with him (Lord Monmouth) at play'. Lord Monmouth 'liked his companions to be very rich or very poor; to be his equals, able to play with him at high stakes, or join him in a great speculation; or to be his tools, and to amuse and serve him' (p. 26). Mr Ormsby reciprocates Lord Monmouth's friendship to a large extent but, along with Lord Eskdale, he expresses a wish to bet on the future of Lord Monmouth's marriage (Bk. 8, ch. 7). Friendship is expendable when set against the prospect of a profitable wager. Lord Monmouth's enthusiasm for gambling spills over into both his political conduct and his personal relationships. He bets a thousand pounds with a Whig minister on the outcome of an election, and, on the day of his wedding, he feels 'calm as if he were winning the St Leger' (p. 295). Again in Disraeli we find romantic and gambling discourses intertwined, indicating both the ubiquity of gambling and the gamble inscribed in marriage.

Other aristocrats in *Coningsby* are gamblers. Lord Eskdale, a friend of Lord Monmouth, is 'the best judge in the world of a horse or a man; he was the universal referee; a quarrel about a bet or a mistress was solved by him in a moment, and in a manner which satisfied both parties' (p. 25). Women are not prioritized over gambling stakes: both are male possessions. Another aristocrat in *Coningsby*, Lord Beaumanoir, owns racehorses, an orthodox signifier of wealth and status. In addition, an Italian nobleman, Prince Paul Colonna, 'was a man dissolute and devoted to play' (p. 22). His gambling is not commendable, arguably because he is a foreigner. Furthermore, gambling remains a feature of life when the highest level of all in society is discussed. Rigby, an associate of Lord Monmouth, tells Coningsby that, 'as for Loyalty, if the present King went regularly to Ascot races, he had no doubt all would go right' (p. 125). Rigby's view, that William IV would increase his popularity if he patronized Ascot races, highlights the extent to which horse racing was regarded as an occasion for large-scale, highly visible social assembly. Ascot was also one of the most glamorous meetings in the racing calendar and it was therefore an opportunity for the monarch to be seen by important and influential people. Greville's record of the indifferent reception of the crowd to the arrival of the monarch at the races shows that this was a significant ritual.

The language of gambling in *Coningsby* is also employed in the political arena. The narrator, in book two, draws attention to the link between gambling and politics: 'it was a lively season, that winter of 1834! What hopes, what fears, and what bets! From the day on which Mr Hudson was to arrive in Rome to the election of the Speaker, not a contingency that was not the subject of a wager!' (p. 92).[20] Elsewhere in *Coningsby*, a forthcoming election in Darlford is the subject of 'bravado bets and secret hedging' (p. 280). Lord Monmouth, anticipating a general election, tells Coningsby, 'we can beat them; but the race requires the finest jockeying' (p. 404). His outlook is shared by Rigby, who is a contestant in the Darlford election. The narrator informs us that 'all his hopes were now staked on the successful result of this contest' (p. 469) but, on two occasions before the vote, we are informed that he is 'a beaten horse' (pp. 404, 468). The gambling metaphor degrades politics, which becomes a contest to be won rather than an opportunity to serve.

Coningsby's own quest is to steer politics away from blind competition and to pursue a more substantial agenda. One of the few other characters in *Coningsby* to possess moral substance is Sidonia, a highly successful and influential financier who also voices words of wisdom which (notwithstanding the fact that they are sometimes enigmatic) have a considerable impact on Coningsby. Lord Monmouth is fully aware of Sidonia's qualities, thinking that he 'was the best man in the world to bet on' (p. 306). In book four, chapter fourteen, Sidonia and Coningsby compete in a steeplechase, on the outcome of which bets are made. Coningsby rides his grandfather's horse, named Sir Robert. Sidonia looks over the course 'with the eyes of a workman' (p. 242), thus distinguishing him from the rest of the competitors, many of whom are aristocrats or their sycophantic companions. Once the race has started Prince Colonna takes the lead with Sidonia in the rear. The prince, however, is dismounted at the first serious obstacle, showing himself to be extravagant but insubstantial, and Coningsby takes the lead. It looks as though Coningsby is going to win but he falls at the last fence and, although he remounts and finishes second, Sidonia comes through and wins the race. In the final words of the chapter, Sidonia delivers a moral to Coningsby: "'You rode well,' said Sidonia to Coningsby; "But your horse was more strong than swift. After all, this thing is a race; and, notwithstanding Solomon, in a race speed must win"' (p. 246). It is significant that Coningsby is defeated when he rides his grandfather's horse because, within the novel, his personal progress depends upon him freeing himself from Lord Hertford's influence. Both in the race and in his life, he cannot experience substantial and enduring prosperity with his grandfather; he must separate from him and find his own way. The race expresses the relative worth of the characters and it also signposts the way ahead for Coningsby. Coningsby is not a gambler, and the characters who do gamble belong to the old generation who have failed both politically and morally. The fact that politics becomes the subject of gambling in *Coningsby* highlights the extent to which the contemporary body politic is corroded. However, whilst Coningsby is not a gambler in the most obvious sense, in his pursuit of Edith Millbank he is not averse to using gambling terms. When he suspects that her affections are directed elsewhere, he experiences difficult emotions: 'these were the first pangs of jealousy that Coningsby had ever experienced, and they revealed to him the immensity of the stake which he was hazarding on a most uncertain die' (p. 332). Here, the use of a gambling image emphasizes the risk that Coningsby feels he has taken. It also shows the pervasiveness of gambling in British society in the 1830s and '40s, as it is used to articulate a variety of experiences, not all of which are connected with gambling organically. At a time when anxiety over gambling was increasing, its presence in other discourses can be read as a reflection of that anxiety, as it was never far removed from mainstream consciousness. Furthermore, the pervasive quality of the language of gambling serves to highlight contradictions within society in the first half of the century, as a practice that was subject to growing condemnation was yet being undertaken in different guises on a variety of economic and social levels.

Sybil (1845)

Sybil (1845) is Disraeli's most widely praised literary achievement.[21] Within the novel the aristocratic hero, Charles Egremont, witnesses both the splendour and the squalor of England during the period 1837–44.[22] He is thus exposed to what Disraeli describes as 'Two Nations', or, more explicitly, 'the Rich and the Poor' (p. 77). *Sybil* reflects the perspective of the Young England movement, a loosely organized faction within the Conservative party with which Disraeli was associated. The movement was, according to Louis Cazamian (1903) rooted in three main principles: 'the landed gentry were outraged by the encroachments of industrial radicalism; romantic young men were filled with imaginative enthusiasm for the majestic monarchy and beautiful religion of the past; and there was a feeling of simple, humane sympathy for the poor in town and country'.[23] The novel opens in an exclusive club on the eve of the Epsom Derby.

> 'I'll take odds against Caravan.'
> 'In poneys?'
> 'Done.'
> And Lord Milford, a young noble, entered in his book the bet which he had just made with Mr Latour, a grey-headed member of the Jockey Club.
> It was the eve of the Derby of 1837. (p. 1)

Henry Blyth (1969) and Robert Blake both state that this chapter is set in Crockford's; Paul Bloomfield (1961) and Barbara Dennis (2000) are equally certain that it is set at the Jockey Club in London.[24] The actual location, however, is not important. The main point is that the setting is upper-class and socially exclusive. Following this initial round of betting the narrator moves into a dining room.

> The seats on each side of the table were occupied by persons consuming, with a heedless air, delicacies for which they had no appetite; while the conversation in general consisted of flying phrases referring to the impending event of the great day that had already dawned.
> 'Come from Lady St Julian's, Fitz?' said a youth of very tender years, and whose fair visage was as downy and as blooming as the peach from which with a languid air he withdrew his lips to make this inquiry of the gentleman with the cane.
> 'Yes; why were you not there?'
> 'I never go anywhere,' replied the melancholy Cupid, 'everything bores me so'. (p. 2)

The young character (Alfred Mountchesney) is joined shortly by his companion, Lord Eugene De Vere. Both of them, 'had exhausted life in their teens' (p. 3). Again in Disraeli, the aristocracy is static and jaded. We are presented with one of the two nations, wherein there is nothing to admire. At the end of the chapter a sudden storm draws the members away from their conversations and focuses their minds on what is to come, as any rainfall could significantly affect the outcome of the race. Later in *Sybil*, a political storm, in the form of Chartism, similarly confronts the aristocrats.

In chapter two, at the race itself, bookmakers, including Hump Chippendale, 'keeper of a second-rate gaming-house' (p. 7), mingle with the aristocrats. Each person is seeking an advantage over those around him; this is a competitive and duplicitous environment, in which entrepreneurs vie with aristocrats, reflecting wider economic and social tensions in the first half of the century. In the event, an un-fancied horse, Phosphorus, wins the race. The horse is, in its appearance, relatively unimpressive, with 'both his forelegs bandaged' (p. 9). Furthermore, Egremont declines the invitation to bet on him. However, appearances are shown to be deceptive and Egremont's judg-ment is, at this stage, imperfect. The notion of an unlikely competitor winning the contest re-emerges in *Sybil*, with the modest, eponymous heroine eventually regaining her aristocratic status. The opening two chapters contain the only detailed descriptions of gambling in the novel, but they establish themes which reverberate throughout *Sybil*. First, we have an irresponsible aristocracy, living in idle luxury and gambling away its wealth. Secondly, we have the theme of competition. As the action unfolds it focuses upon adversarial contests between the polit-ical parties. In these political intrigues, individuals and factions jockey for position. The prize of a seat in Parliament requires a large financial stake with which to buy up the electorate. One Whig politician relies upon the language of horse racing when describing a forthcoming polit-ical contest: 'the stake is worth playing for, and don't suppose we are such flats as to lose the race for want of jockeying' (p. 45). The fact that the Derby is won by an outsider suggests that the manoeuvrings of the governing classes are not infallible. At times the narrator draws atten-tion explicitly to the links between gambling and the state of contemporary politics, speaking of 'a gambling foreign commerce' (p. 24) and thereby highlighting what he sees as reckless and debt-laden systems of international trade. Elsewhere he draws attention to apathy and shows how the public tolerates a lack of access to Westminster Abbey. His analysis is scathing: 'but the British public will bear anything; they are so busy in speculating in railroad shares' (p. 266). Here, a form of gambling is seen to be distracting people away from matters of greater importance to do with civil and religious liberties. This may be a pertinent moment at which to remind ourselves of Disraeli's own market speculations and the consequences that they brought about. Moreover, in 1845 Disraeli held shares in the Duffryn,

Llynvi and Porth Cawl Railway. As most of *Sybil* was written in the early part of 1845 it is therefore very likely that Disraeli himself was practising the speculations of which, in *Sybil*, the narrator strongly disapproves.[25]

The last chapters of *Sybil* recall the Chartist strikes and riots of 1842. The most militant section of the workers is led by the 'Liberator of the People', a drunken, thuggish figure who ignites an orgy of destruction and, finally, self-destruction. The narrator thereby condemns autonomous, working-class militancy. Social salvation eventually occurs through the marriage of Egremont and Sybil (a symbolic unification of the past with the present) and through Sybil's restoration to her proper, aristocratic status. At the novel's conclusion the narrator identifies the root of the nation's problems.

> In the selfish strife of factions two great existences have been blotted out of the history of England – the Monarch and the Multitude; as the power of the Crown has diminished, the privileges of the People have disappeared; till at length the sceptre has become a pageant, and its subject has degenerated again into a serf. (p. 489)

Disraeli's political views were based on a highly subjective view of the past, although there was considerable popular enthusiasm for Medievalism in the mid-nineteenth-century, as it was seen as a time of stability in opposition to a present characterised by uncertainty in the context of the world's first industrial economy. Disraeli's romantic response to industrialism was not pragmatic but, as an imaginative possibility, his blueprint for social restoration caught the mood of at least part of his own political party.

Tancred (1847)

In the final part of the trilogy, *Tancred* (1847), gambling again features.[26] It sets the scene in the opening chapter, in which the narrator focuses on the neighbourhood of aristocrats' servants.

> They bet upon the Derby in these parts a little, are interested in Goodwood, which they frequent, have perhaps, in general, a weakness for play, live highly, and indulge those passions which luxury and refinement encourage; but that is all. (. . .) Here may be found his grace's coachman, and here his lordship's groom, who keeps a book and bleeds periodically too speculative footmen, by betting odds on his master's horses. (p. 2)

The novel then focuses on Tancred's ancestors. Gambling is used to signify his grandfather's degeneracy. The former Duke of Bellamont was 'a man of pleasure, the chosen companion of the Regent in his age of riot' (p. 11). Tancred's father (a mid-century rather than early-century member of the upper class, with a more elevated sense of duty and conduct) uses gambling to help define his personality as he considers his own father's deplorable excesses in the context of his aristocratic lineage: 'death was preferable, in his view, to having such a name soiled in the haunts of jockeys and courtezans and usurers' (p. 13). An incidental character, Lord Milford, when speaking of the Duke, considers him in relation to gambling: 'I mean to say he never played, was never seen at Newmarket' (p. 19). Tancred follows in his father's footsteps to the extent that he does not gamble, but he differs from him in that he expresses a dissatisfaction with all aspects of contemporary society by wanting to go on a journey to the Holy Land, a cause of distress within his immediate circle, although his father is relatively sanguine: '"as long as he does not take to play," said the duke, "I do not much care what he does"' (p. 81). Gambling is still the ultimate pitfall, against which the hazards of a journey to Palestine seem manageable.

In the second half of the novel when the action moves to Palestine, references to gambling virtually disappear from *Tancred*. On the one occasion when it is mentioned it is associated with the less favourable aspects of Western life. When a character, Besso, tries to tell his daughter about the personalities of English men, he includes gambling: 'they pass their days in the chase, gaming, and all violent courses' (p. 242). The lack of references to gambling in the second half of *Tancred* is explained by the fact that the Holy Land is the environment within which the hero finds spiritual wisdom and guidance, although there is still conflict and intrigue in the region. Gambling does not belong in Palestine, where many of the characters are motivated by spiritual concerns. Eva, the character to whom Tancred proposes at the end of the novel, seeks consistently, from her very first conversation with Tancred in book three chapter four, a theological understanding of the world and her place therein. It is the absence of this firm moral framework in contemporary English society that Disraeli laments in the Young England trilogy, offering the prospect of a new moral direction through Coningsby, Egremont and Tancred.

Away from his writing, Disraeli's involvement with gambling continued to be modest. His letters show that he played cards in April and September 1843, losing one pound five shillings on one occasion and winning five pounds ten shillings on another.[27] In May 1848 he referred, in a letter to his wife, to Lord George Bentinck winning eleven thousand pounds on the Derby, but he does not mention whether he himself also gambled on the event.[28] In another letter, dated 11 August 1848, he makes reference to an acquaintance losing large sums on the Derby and at lansquenet.[29] A few years later, in March 1851, he wrote of a dispute over a game of whist, with which he himself was not involved.[30] These are the only references to gambling in Disraeli's letters following the conclusion of the Young England trilogy. It thus appears that the closure of the gaming-houses in 1845 had not caused him any great distress and that, notwithstanding his poor speculations in business in his earlier years, he was in no sense an inveterate gambler. He was, however, extremely ambitious and his desire to court the leading figures of his day invariably brought him into the gambling environment of Crockford's and other exclusive clubs.

Disraeli often uses horse racing to express the qualities and future directions of characters. In *The Young Duke* the Duke's horse is defeated by one called May Dacre. The woman May Dacre triumphs over the Duke in life (albeit to the Duke's benefit). In *Coningsby* the horse race encapsulates Prince Colonna's vacuity and Sidonia's wisdom. In *Sybil* the race is won by the unfancied outsider, as the political and moral contest is won by the unassuming heroine. Horse racing in Disraeli's fiction plays out contests between opposing individuals and opposing ideologies.[31]

The connections Disraeli drew between contests, gambling and politics were not limited solely to the literary realm. In a speech in Parliament on 15 May 1846 he attacked Peel's administration and referred to 'a people debauched by public gambling'.[32] In a letter of 23 May 1846 he made this assessment of the prospects of forming a protectionist government: 'the game is over for the moment, but it is a great game, and I think, that, "yet a little time", and the people of England will rally round it'.[33] Disraeli viewed politics in competitive terms. In his novels, his critical use of gambling terms in relation to politics is therefore disingenuous, as his own political strategy appeared to feed off his competitive instinct as much as his moral fibre. Based on his comments cited here, it appears that Disraeli's own outlook on politics did not differ radically from that of the characters in his novels. In the Young England trilogy gambling is used to expose character flaws in individuals, but it is also a representation of the malaise in the contemporary political world, in which competition and speculation replace true leadership. Moreover, Disraeli presented a gambling and indolent upper class awaiting galvanization from a dynamic individual, a situation not far removed from his perception of his own career in the Conservative party.

—————— *chapter three* ——————

'Tumult and Frenzy Reigned Supreme'

Charles Dickens's Gambling Characters

Gambling cannot be described as a major theme in the novels of Charles Dickens. However, given Dickens's status as the central English novelist of the early and mid-Victorian period, his use of gambling in his fiction is worthy of attention in a canonical study of this kind. This chapter investigates the one Dickens novel in which gambling is an important theme, *The Old Curiosity Shop*, and three others in which gambling contributes significantly towards the development of the plot and the representation of characters.

Nicholas Nickleby (1838–9)

Gambling is featured incidentally in Dickens's first published collection, *Sketches by Boz* (1836–7).[1] In one episode, 'The Tuggses at Ramsgate', gambling is part of an evening's entertainment: 'there were marriageable daughters, and marriage-making mammas, gaming and promenading, and turning over music, and flirting' (p. 349). Gambling, which, in 'The Tuggses at Ramsgate' takes the form of a dice game, is secondary to the mating game, in which the risk of a flirtation can lead to rejection or acceptance, or the innocent can be exploited by the wily and this is what happens when Captain Waters and his wife successfully dupe Cymon Tuggs. Clearly, gambling is little more than part of the detail of *Sketches by Boz*, but it emerges as a more significant element in *Nicholas Nickleby*.[2] Gambling is mentioned in the first paragraph: 'two people who cannot afford to play cards for money, sometimes sit down to a quiet game for love' (p. 1). Furthermore, the first chapter also details how Nicholas Nickleby's father lost his fortune through business speculations and thereby reduced his family to penury. The narrator describes entrepreneurial capitalism explicitly as a gamble.

> Speculation is a round game; the players may see little or nothing of their cards at first starting; gains *may* be great – and so may losses. The run of luck went against Mr Nickleby. A mania prevailed, a bubble burst, four stockbrokers took villa residences at Florence, four hundred nobodies were ruined, and among them Mr Nickleby. (p. 5)

Speculation is a card game, but here it also clearly refers to the general practice of speculation, and to the uneven nature of the practice as the wily profit and the innocent suffer. In a third reference to gambling in the early part of *Nicholas Nickleby*, a member of Parliament is referred to as having spent all of the previous night at Crockford's (ch. 2). Gambling is thus present in the political, commercial and emotional realms as *Nicholas Nickleby* opens, signifying its ubiquity within society.

In the sub-plot of *Nicholas Nickleby*, Kate Nickleby is plagued by unwanted attention from an aristocrat, Lord Frederick Verisopht, and his friend, Sir Mulberry Hawk, who attempts to seduce Kate through a form of bullying intrusiveness masquerading as chivalry. She is first introduced to them at a dinner party given by Ralph Nickleby, at which she is struck by 'the easy insolence of their manner towards herself' (p. 235). Kate is the sole female at the party, and her presence there is designed to draw Lord Verisopht further into Ralph Nickleby's power. Ralph Nickleby has few qualms about exploiting his niece, and even at his most conscience-stricken point, when he internally debates whether or not it was wise to have introduced Kate to Verisopht and Hawk, he merely states, 'she must take her chance' (p. 341). His analysis evades his own responsibility for her predicament as he effected the introduction, risking her welfare for his own benefit. At the party Verisopht and Hawk make Kate the subject of a bet and thereby degrade her, with Hawk wagering fifty pounds against Lord Frederick that Kate cannot look Hawk directly in the face. On a later occasion, following further victimization of Kate, Hawk and Lord Frederick go off to gamble (ch. 27). She is adopted involuntarily as one of their leisure pursuits.

The main gambling incident in *Nicholas Nickleby* occurs in chapter fifty, when Hawk and Verisopht clash in a gambling booth at a race course. As the novel progresses the two characters grow apart, with the young aristocrat emerging as feckless but not villainous. He is unhappy with Hawk's treatment of Kate Nickleby and his threats of violence against Nicholas. Conversely, Hawk's personality is consistent throughout the novel. In a card game during his convalescence, following an altercation with Nicholas, Hawk 'caught up the stakes with a boastful oath' (p. 489). Later, Ralph Nickleby anticipates Hawk's revenge on Nicholas: 'his wrath will have lost nothing of its violence in the meanwhile. Obliged to live in retirement – the monotony of a sick-room to a man of his habits – no life – no drink – no play – nothing that he likes and lives by' (p. 569). Ralph influences Hawk's anger by telling him how the news of the attack on him by Nicholas has spread: 'every club and gaming-room has rung with it' (p. 491). Hawk is thus repeatedly connected with gambling; in his actions, in analyses of his personality and in reports concerning him.

Remarks about Kate Nickleby are the immediate cause of the disagreement between Verisopht and Hawk (culminating in a duel) but the hostility builds up during the chapter, through gambling and its context. The opening words of the chapter direct the reader's attention towards 'the little race-course at Hampton' (p. 653), before detailing a crooked gambling enterprise, where the operators try 'to entrap some unwary customer', and 'a motley assemblage of feasting, laughing, talking, begging, gambling and mummery' (p. 654). It is 'into one of these booths that our story takes its way' (p. 654), where one of the most striking features of the game is the commentary of the croupier.

> 'Rooge-a-nore from Paris! Gentlemen, make your game and back your own opinions – any time while the ball rolls – rooge-a-nore from Paris, gentlemen, it's a French game, gentlemen, I brought it over myself, I did indeed! – Rooge-a-nore from Paris – black wins – black- stop a minute, sir, and I'll pay you directly – two there, half a pound there, three there – and one there – gentlemen, the ball's a rolling – any time, sir, while the ball rolls!' (p. 656)

The croupier's speech patterns mimic the circular motion of the ball around the wheel. As the pace of the chapter accelerates, images of delirious spinning recur creating the overall impression of an environment which is reeling out of control.

As Lord Frederick and his party approach the gaming table, they are 'wild, burning with wine, their blood boiling, and their brains on fire (. . .). In that giddy whirl of noise and confusion, the men were delirious'. In this feast of debauchery all pretence of decorum has been abandoned. It is a place in which 'tumult and frenzy reigned supreme', and Hawk and Verisopht are found to be 'seizing each other by the throat' (p. 662). The illustration for this episode underlines the riotous nature of the proceedings: cards, bottles and chairs are strewn around

*The Last Brawl between Sir Mulberry and his Pupil
(Hablot Browne, alias 'Phizz'), from Charles Dickens,* Nicholas Nickleby

the room as Verisopht and Hawk, in the height of their argument, are held apart. Others in the picture are shown to be helpless with drink or wholly immersed in gambling (plate I). In the aftermath of the confrontation, as Lord Frederick prepares for the duel, he contemplates the street, its 'free, fresh, wholesome air' contrasting with the 'hot, close atmosphere' of the gaming booth. Lord Frederick, however, 'shrank involuntarily from the day as if he were some foul and hideous thing' (p. 664). He has been separated from nature, fatally compromised by corruption and gambling and he is killed in the duel. At the end of the novel Sir Mulberry Hawk dies in jail, 'as such high spirits generally do' (p. 830). There is thus a cautionary tale element to the presentation of gambling in *Nicholas Nickleby*, with the focus on upper-class gamblers in an era in which the exclusive gaming clubs of St James's were highly visible although, paradoxically, the confrontation occurs in a context in which all the social classes are mixing. Perhaps Dickens could not have staged the argument in an exclusive club such as Crockford's, where Captain Gronow had noted: 'a most gentlemen-like feeling prevailed'.[3] Assumptions about the different social classes dictated the context for the confrontation.

Gambling also features in *Nicholas Nickleby* in the character of the irresponsible Mr Mantalini, whose wife refers 'to certain agreeable weaknesses on that gentleman's part, such as gaming, wasting, idling, and a tendency to horse-flesh' (p. 259). In addition, gambling in *Nicholas Nickleby* establishes atmosphere. Ralph Nickleby and Wackford Squeers, in their pursuit of Mrs Skilderskew, go to 'low lodging-houses, and taverns kept by broken gamblers' (p. 776), thereby establishing the socio-economic and moral complexion of the neighbourhood and the activities therein. However, despite the use of gambling in *Nicholas Nickleby* to signify exploitative conduct, card playing is sometimes shown to have a more benign function. Mrs Nickleby harks back to card parties formerly held in her household as a way of highlighting former glories (ch. 45) and a game of cards on Tim Linkinwater's birthday is harmonious and socially inclusive (ch. 37). Games themselves are enjoyable entertainment, although a card game in chapter nine does become a point of disagreement when Fanny Squeer's romantic aspirations are thwarted. At the beginning of the novel we are presented with an image of the exploitation of the innocent. Gambling is closely associated with the former, but the novel is concerned with the triumph of the benign and thus the gamblers are crushed.

The Old Curiosity Shop (1840–1)

Gambling is still more prominent in Dickens's next novel *The Old Curiosity Shop*.[4] Nell's grandfather's mania for gambling is central to the novel, culminating in his theft from Nell. His gambling addiction is fully revealed by Daniel Quilp in chapter nine, but his own perception of his situation is more complicated: '"I am no gambler," cried the old man fiercely. "I call heaven to witness that I never played for gain of mine, or love of play; that at every piece I staked, I whispered to myself that orphan's name and called on heaven to bless the venture, which it never did."' The grandfather claims that his gambling is motivated by a desire to provide for Nell. He thus seeks to pass the responsibility for his conduct onto her, yet, when he does gamble, his immersion in the game is total. Throughout the novel his fate is often catalyzed by a gambling situation. Gambling in *The Old Curiosity Shop* is therefore significant on a narrative level: it accelerates a character's progress and, in the case of Nell and her grandfather, their deterioration.

Evicted from their shop by Quilp, Nell and her grandfather experience a life of vagrancy. They first come into contact with a group of itinerant entertainers heading for the horse races, seeing 'carts laden with gambling booths' (p. 136), and a space where 'some small gambler drove his noisy trade' (p. 147). The races are a point of large-scale social congregation and are surrounded by a general air of holiday and festivity. The race course is situated on an open heath in the pre-enclosure era and includes people right across the social spectrum.[5] However, within this context gambling is shown to be a contaminating presence, through the eyes of the morally flawless Nell who thinks 'how strange it was that horses who were such fine honest creatures should seem to make vagabonds of all the men that drew about them' (p. 151). Her mixture of despair and disdain for gambling exposes a common perception of the early 1840s when concern over the effects of gambling was rising.

At the Valiant Soldier Inn Nell's grandfather overhears card players in action.

'Nell, they're – they're playing cards,' whispered the old man, suddenly interested. 'Don't you hear them?'
'Look sharp with the candle,' said the voice; 'its as much as I can do to see the pips on the cards as it is; and get this shutter closed as quick as you can, will you? Your beer will be the worse for tonight's thunder I expect. – Game! Seven-and-sixpence to me, old Isaac. Hand over.'

'Do you hear, Nell, do you hear them?' whispered the old man again, with increased earnestness, as the money chinked upon the table.
'I haven't seen such a storm as this,' said a sharp cracked voice of most disagreeable quality, when a tremendous peal of thunder had died away, 'since the night when old Luke Withers won thirteen times running upon the red. We all said he had the devil's luck and his own, and as it was the kind of night for the Devil to be out and busy, I suppose he was looking over his shoulder, if anybody could have seen him.' (p. 220)

The storm reflects the grandfather's inner turmoil. The mention of the Devil generates, in conjunction with the weather, a diabolic undertone to the situation. The gamblers, List and Jowl, are, at this stage, only identifiable by their voices, at least one of which is unpleasant to the ear. Moreover, the language they use is aggressive. The childlike grandfather will be no match for the bullying men. Nell and her grandfather have exchanged one set of villains (Codlin and Short Trotters, ch. 19) for a worse pair. The drama of the scene is amplified when Nell sees the reaction that the game provokes in her grandfather: 'the child saw with astonishment and alarm that his whole appearance had undergone a complete change. His face was flushed and eager, his eyes were strained, his teeth set, his breath came short and thick, and the hand he laid upon her arm trembled so violently that she shook beneath its grasp' (p. 221).[6] The grandfather tells Nell that 'the means of happiness are on the cards and in the dice'. He deifies 'fortune', stating 'we must not reproach her, or she shuns us; I have found that out' (p. 223). However, Nell's grandfather loses their money. The illustration accompanying the game juxtaposes Nell's grandfather against the other three players. The player closest to him is the largest of all and he looks down upon the old man. All three of the players against whom the old man is competing have drinks in front of them. One of them is smoking a pipe. Conversely, Nell's grandfather has no such luxuries, merely Nell's open purse. He is smaller than the other characters, hunched and feeble (plate II).[7] Nell retires to bed and shortly thereafter becomes aware of a shadowy figure in her room. She follows the figure to her grandfather's chamber, fearing for his safety.

The door was partly open. Not knowing what she meant to do, but meaning to preserve him or be killed herself, she staggered forward and looked in. What sight was that which met her view!
The bed had not been lain on, but was smooth and empty. And at the table sat the old man himself, the only living creature there, his white face pinched and sharpened by the greediness which made his eyes unnaturally bright, counting the money of which his hands had robbed her. (p. 229)

[89]

A Game of Cards (George Catermole), from Charles Dickens, The Old Curiosity Shop

Dickens ends the chapter by focusing on the grandfather's hands, thereby emphasising the bare, physical act of theft. He also foregrounds his face, which is harsh and angular, and his eyes, which have become inhuman. Essentially, the grandfather becomes 'Quilpine' and is associated with words such as 'savage', 'wild', and 'ravenous' (pp. 223–4).[8] The effects of the crime are not only economic. Nell is damaged by the theft, as noted by Paul Schlike (1985): 'from this moment Nell's strength fails until she collapses and dies'.[9] The crime is essentially murderous.

Nell's grandfather continues to gamble and steal from her. She encounters him in the company of List and Jowl in a gypsy encampment, with her grandfather 'leaning forward upon a stick on which he rested both hands' (p. 312). He is physically and, through his gambling mania, morally weak. He is now openly exploited by List and Jowl.

> 'Well, are you going?' said the stout man, looking up from the ground where he was lying at his ease, into her grandfather's face. 'You were in a mighty hurry a minute ago. Go, if you like. You're your own master, I hope?'
> 'Don't vex him,' returned Isaac List, who was squatting like a frog on the other side of the fire, and who had so screwed himself up that he seemed to be squinting all over; 'he didn't mean any offence.'
> 'You keep me poor, and plunder me, and make a sport and jest of me besides,' said the old man, turning from one to the other. 'Ye'll drive me mad among ye.' (p. 313)

The old man is infantilized by the gamblers, to such an extent that he is called 'the grey-haired child' by the narrator (p. 313). His mania for gambling has effected a total regression of his personality. Furthermore, he is coerced by List and Jowl into attempting to commit a robbery, which Nell prevents. The old man drinks a toast to his proposed crime, which Nell overhears: 'the gypsy produced three tin cups, and filled them to the brim with brandy. The old man turned aside and muttered to himself before he drank. Her own name struck upon the listener's ear, coupled with some wish so fervent, that he seemed to breathe it in an agony of supplication' (p. 316). One unsettling possibility here is that Nell's grandfather is invoking her name as a talisman of fortune to bring him luck. He cites Nell's welfare as his prime motivating factor, but as the means by which he seeks to achieve it are morally unacceptable they are therefore of no use to her. Towards the end of the novel, however, we are presented with a substantial explanation of the grandfather's fear of poverty, which has led him into gambling (ch. 69). There is no space remaining in the novel for this theme to be developed, but it is clear that the grandfather's wrongdoing is connected substantially with his social situation, if not necessarily determined entirely by it. An alternative understanding of this late attempt at analysis by Dickens might suggest that he is seeking to bail out Nell's grandfather. The explanation offered for his gambling mania restores him to goodness by making him a victim rather than a villain.[10]

Daniel Quilp is not a gambler in the strictest sense. However, like Nell's grandfather, he is a card player. A game for Quilp is intensely combative. It is, furthermore, an opportunity for him to display his cunning, his lack of scruple and his fondness for exercising complete control. In chapter twenty-three, during a game of cribbage, he cheats and, in addition, he keeps a close watch on the other players, including his wife, whom he suspects of being attracted to Fred Trent. The game is also an opportunity for Quilp to torment his mother-in-law, whom he excludes deliberately from the proceedings. Quilp's behaviour in the game functions as a synopsis of his conduct as a whole. He uses the language of the card table when he introduces Dick Swiveller to Sampson and Sally Brass, describing him as 'an ace of trumps' (p. 248). Quilp habitually views others as impersonal devices to be utilized and exploited for his own ends. As Quilp exposes Nell's grandfather's gambling mania, he describes the process as if it were a card game: 'let me be plain with you, and play a fairer game than when you held all the cards, and I saw but the backs and nothing more' (p. 73). Quilp's entire existence is predicated on prosperity achieved through a particularly vicious brand of parasitism and conflict. As with Ralph Nickleby, a career of speculation and exploitation leads to Quilp finally being destroyed. At a time when an increasingly powerful capitalist class held enormous sway over those whose workplaces they governed, *The Old Curiosity Shop* flushes out the evil businessmen. Dickens thus draws a clear line between good and bad capitalism, with the latter being characterized in part by its association with gambling. An equally ignominious end befalls Fred Trent, though his death by drowning is only mentioned in passing (p. 670). Significantly, he too becomes involved with gambling, at one point securing a position in a gaming-house (p. 468). Appropriately, therefore, he meets with an unpleasant end. In addition, List and Jowl are apprehended by the forces of law and order.

Gambling in *The Old Curiosity Shop* generally takes the form of card playing, in which the participants compete against each other. This can be contrasted with roulette, in which the player is essentially passive as he awaits the result produced by the wheel and the ball (the distinction is dealt with in greater detail in the Conclusion). Gambling in *The Old*

Curiosity Shop is thus essentially combative, reflecting the fact that it was written before the full-scale commercialization of gambling had taken place. However, card playing is not always condemned in *The Old Curiosity Shop*. Dick Swiveller uses cards unashamedly for pleasure. Part of Dick's fantasy world involves playing cribbage with himself, 'for twenty, thirty or sometimes even fifty thousand pounds a side, besides many hazardous bets to a considerable amount' (p. 526). He begins to include in his game the Brass's servant, whom he calls Marchioness. Their actual stakes consist of two sixpences. Dick immerses himself wholly in this role playing, 'assuming the gay and fashionable air which such society required' (p. 528). Here, gambling, or (more accurately) mock gambling, becomes socially cohesive. It is also an important stage in the development of the character of Dick Swiveller. Initially, through his acquiescence to Fred Trent's plot to marry him to Nell, and his subsequent, albeit unwitting, dealings with Quilp, Dick's moral status in the novel is unclear. The manner in which he plays cards, however, suggests that his nature is fundamentally playful. His character is transformed by the fever into which he falls at the end of chapter sixty-three, from which he emerges with a sense of moral purpose. The fever expunges his hedonism without damaging his comic persona.[11] Card playing also forms a significant element in the development of the character of the Marchioness. She changes from a timid servant to a swift and adept cribbage player. She then further develops into Dick's saviour. Card playing imbues her with personality. At the end of *The Old Curiosity Shop*, Dick marries the Marchioness. Their union is most content, 'and they played many hundred thousand games of cribbage together' (p. 669). Recreational card playing is harmonious and unifying, freed from the taint of gambling which is appended harmlessly in Dick's fantasy world.

After *The Old Curiosity Shop*, gambling does not feature as a prominent theme in any of Dickens's novels. However, in *Martin Chuzzlewit* (1843–4) gambling is part of the persona acquired by Bailey when he enters the service of Montague Tigg, as he becomes 'a highly-condensed embodiment of all the sporting grooms in London; an abstract of all the stable-knowledge of the time' (p. 422).[12] Furthermore, the company founded by his employer, the Anglo-Bengalee Disinterested Loan and Life Assurance Company, attracts a number of reckless speculators, an idea which later becomes more important in relation to gambling in *Little Dorrit*. Gambling in *Martin Chuzzlewit* is also a signifier with regard to the personality of Jonas Chuzzlewit. We learn, at quite an early stage, that he is a card sharp (ch. 11), and it emerges much later that he exerts power over others by winning money from them at cards (ch. 48). In addition, in chapter seven Mark Tapley makes an allusion to the charging of 'race-week prices' (p. 104) at the Blue Dragon, showing how horse racing could be an economic stimulus to a local economy. *Martin Chuzzlewit* is thus conscious of gambling on both a micro and macro-economic level, implying its pervasiveness in mid-century culture.

Hard Times (1854)

In *Hard Times*, Thomas Gradgrind Junior gambles, leading him to accumulate debts and commit the crime for which Stephen Blackpool is blamed.[13] The issue is first raised by James Harthouse, who asks Thomas's sister, 'do you think he games at all?', adding, 'everybody does lose who bets' (p. 171). Harthouse's main ambition is to curry favour with Louisa, with whom he is in love, but he has sufficient experience of life, and therefore sufficient worldly wisdom, to suspect that Tom is a gambler. Harthouse's introduction of the idea of gambling helps to create the conditions in which the reader can deduce that Tom is responsible for the theft.

Harthouse himself is associated with gambling. Following his first appearance, he is discussed by Bitzer and Mrs Sparsit.

> 'What do you think of the gentleman, Bitzer?' she asked the light porter, when he came to take away.'Spends a deal of money on his dress, ma'am.
> 'It must be admitted,' said Mrs Sparsit, 'that it's very tasteful.'
> 'Yes, ma'am,' returned Bitzer, 'if that's worth the money.'
> 'Besides which, ma'am,' resumed Bitzer, while he was polishing the table, 'he looks to me as if he gamed.'
> 'It's immoral to game,' said Mrs Sparsit.
> 'It's ridiculous, ma'am,' said Bitzer, 'because the chances are against the players.' (p. 122)

Mrs Sparsit objects to gambling on moral grounds, thus reflecting the orthodox view of gambling around the time of the 1853 Act. Bitzer, however, opposes gambling on economic grounds. He is a product of Thomas Gradgrind Senior's utilitarian educational methods. He is not interested in the ethical status of gambling, merely its arithmetical certainties. Mrs Sparsit later refers to Harthouse as 'the kind of gentleman (. . .) whom one might wager to be a good shot' (p. 208), an opinion in which Bitzer concurs. No actual bet is intended and the two characters are referring implicitly to Harthouse's romantic pursuit of Louisa, yet it is noteworthy that the language of gambling is employed by two characters who have already declared their opposition to the practice: a hostile disposition towards Harthouse is thus implied. Harthouse makes his feelings known to Louisa, and he is heard by Mrs Sparsit to tell Louisa 'how she was the stake for which he ardently desired to play away all that he had in life' (p. 212). The gambling metaphor is appropriate because, as Louisa is a married woman, Harthouse's romantic declaration is hazardous. However, Harthouse departs without Louisa and thus his use of a gambling metaphor in his declaration of love exposes his shallow affections.

There are other incidental references to gambling in *Hard Times*. Mr Childers, a horse-riding entertainer, is first seen 'dressed in a Newmarket coat' (p. 29), an extravagant garment favoured by the patrons of Newmarket race course. Mrs Sparsit comes from an ancient and socially superior family 'who could trace themselves so exceedingly far back that it was not surprising if they sometimes lost themselves – which they had rather frequently done, as respected horse-flesh, blind hookey, Hebrew monetary transactions, and the Insolvent Debtors' Court' (p. 42). Thomas Gradgrind Junior nurtures the suspicions against Stephen Blackpool, 'offering to wager that he had made off before the arrival of those who were sent in quest of him, and that he would not appear' (p. 254). Gradgrind's use of the gambling term exposes his own predilections, and while it does not alert the other characters in the novel to the possibility that he committed the crime, it reminds the reader of Gradgrind's gambling habit and financial worries. Gambling in *Hard Times* signifies villainy in Tom Gradgrind and shallowness in Harthouse. Neither character is rewarded in the resolution of the novel, which highlights the restorative nature of the imagination.

Little Dorrit (1855–7)

In *Little Dorrit* a large number of characters gamble following Mr Merdle, whose skill in speculation is far renowned.[14] His failure, leading to his suicide, precipitates a wider collapse in the fortunes of many characters. Twenty years later the character of Melmotte in Anthony Trollope's *The Way We Live Now* meets with a similar fate, in a novel in which gambling of all kinds is commonplace (see chapter seven). Gambling also features in *Little Dorrit* in the language used by characters and, in addition, it is employed to help define characters, principally Rigaud. References to gambling occur from the first chapter. A jailer recommends John Baptist Cavaletto not to gamble, and

Rigaud describes his own fortunes thus: 'shaken out of destiny's dice-box into the company of a mere smuggler' (p. 9). Rigaud repeats the phrase, 'shaken out of destiny's dice-box', when he is reunited with Cavaletto in chapter eleven (p. 133). Rigaud is a rootless (and ruthless) character who shifts from one situation to another with alacrity. His use, therefore, of a gambling image to express his mode of living is appropriate because his life is not methodical, rather he seeks to exploit the opportunities of whatever situation he finds himself in. He sees himself essentially as the dice, thrown randomly by destiny. His one detailed plan in the novel, the pursuit of blackmail payments from Mrs Clennam, is, in itself, the product of chance as it relies upon the fortuitous discovery of the particulars of Arthur Clennam's lineage. Gowan, considering Rigaud, 'supposed him to live by his wits at play-tables' (p. 490). Rigaud is the untrustworthy outsider, travelling under various pseudonyms, with a criminal past, a gambler's vocabulary and (it is thought) a gambling history. Furthermore, Dickens's association of Rigaud with dice ten years after the dice game of hazard had effectively been banned underlines the character's nefarious nature as he is connected with a discredited practice.

As Rigaud's plan nears completion, he espouses a philosophy of sorts to Clennam: 'words, sir, never influence the course of the cards, or the course of the dice. Do you know that? You do? I also play a game, and words are without power over it' (p. 745). Rigaud sees impartial fate as pre-eminent, a position which diminishes morality as there is no correlation between conduct and reward. The narrator rejects this standpoint through the violent death of Rigaud when Mrs Clennam's house collapses. Rigaud, believing himself to be negotiating from a position of strength, dismisses the arguments and accusations levelled against him, suggesting that he is supremely confident. However, it is noticeable that 'he had charged himself with drink for the playing out of his game' (p. 763). While this may be simply a characteristic exhibition of arrogance, it is perhaps more likely (bearing in mind the use of the word 'charged') that the alcohol is generating the courage necessary to undertake his plan and, therefore, that he is generally less relaxed about being shaken out of destiny's dice-box than he would like his listener to believe. Rigaud professes himself to be sanguine about life's gambles but, underlying this, he is finally conscious of risk.

Chapter thirteen of book two of *Little Dorrit* is entitled 'The Progress of an Epidemic'. It deals with what Clennam calls, 'these Merdle enterprises' (p. 580). Clennam is initially cautious about backing Merdle's judgment, stating, 'very strange how these runs on an infatuation prevail' (p. 581). He sees that the rampant speculation going on in *Little Dorrit* has more to do with rumour and fashion than with economic analysis. However, his companion, Pancks, is entirely confident: 'they're the best schemes afloat. They're safe. They're certain' (p. 582). The characters in *Little Dorrit* have such blind faith in Merdle's judgment that they are not even conscious of the fact that they are actually gambling by risking their capital on the uncertainty of what is to come. Pancks describes the monies ventured following Merdle's lead as 'investments' rather than 'speculations' (p. 582). He urges Clennam to follow Merdle's advice, saying 'go in and win', and when Clennam replies, 'but what of Go in and lose?' Pancks is dismissive (p. 585). Everyone is seeking to get rich quick through gambling rather than through hard work. One of the few exceptions to this rule is Doyce, who tells Clennam, 'if I have a prejudice connected with money and money figures (. . .) it is against speculating' (p. 673). Doyce is industrious and he earns his wealth. Most of the other characters in *Little Dorrit* attempt to by-pass this process, but they are brought down after Merdle commits suicide. The character of Merdle owes something to John Sadleir (1814–56), a corrupt financier who also committed suicide. Dickens acknowledged the influence in a letter written in March 1856.[15] Thus, although the gambling in *Little Dorrit* is fictional, it is rooted in a contemporary reality.[16] Furthermore, there was a commercial crisis in 1857 after a good harvest had brought down the cost of wheat, thereby damaging financial organizations with commitments in this market.[17]

There are further references to gambling in *Little Dorrit*. When Mr Dorrit is first admitted to the Marshalsea debtors' prison he asks a turnkey (a warder) whether his children will be allowed in.

> 'Children? Why, we swarm with 'em. How many a you got?'
> 'Two,' said the debtor, lifting his irresolute hand to his lip again, and turning into the prison.
> The turnkey followed him with his eyes, 'and you another', he observed to himself, 'which makes three on you. And your wife another, I'll lay a crown. Which makes four on you. And another coming, I'll lay half-a-crown. Which'll make five on you. And I'll go another seven and sixpence to name which is the helplessest, the unborn baby or you!' (p. 59)

There is no actual bet, as the turnkey is talking to himself. However, his use of the language of gambling is significant because, first, it emphasizes his certainty with regard to Mr Dorrit's character and circumstances, a certainty that is borne out in reality. Secondly, it illustrates the lack of sympathy which is prevalent within the prison. Mr Dorrit's situation is merely a matter for comment and speculation. When a doctor in the Marshalsea is summoned to attend Mrs Dorrit in childbirth, he and his companion are found to be 'playing at all-fours, smoking pipes, and drinking brandy' (p. 60), showing him to be uncouth. When Mr Dorrit is suddenly made rich and released from the Marshalsea, some of his fellow inmates think 'that the thing might in the lottery of chances have happened to themselves, or that something of the sort might yet happen to themselves, some day or other' (p. 425). Crushed by society, they have relinquished control over their own lives, and hope for elevation by chance as no other option is available to them. Following the sudden change in the Dorrit family's fortunes, their lifestyles change profoundly. Edward Dorrit is generally to be found 'in diceing circles' (p. 481). He is a reprobate before he becomes rich, and his wealth nurtures corruption. *Little Dorrit* challenges the get rich quick mentality, but it also shows some of the less wholesome effects of sudden wealth and thus implicitly advocates sober, accumulative industry.

Mr Sparkler, Mrs Merdle's son, is 'in the habit of frequenting all the races' (p. 248). He is a typical wealthy young man of the 1820s, the period in which the novel is set.[18] When he pursues Fanny Dorrit to Venice, and constantly drifts past the house in which she is staying, 'he might have been supposed to have made a wager for a large stake to be paddled a thousand miles in a thousand hours' (p. 506). Again, the bet is wholly fictitious and illustrates a state of mind rather than an actual gamble. When Fanny Dorrit describes Mrs General to Little Dorrit, she states, 'if she had the ace of trumps in her hand, at whist, she wouldn' say anything, child. It would come out when she played it' (p. 505), showing her to be a careful and strategic thinker. It further highlights the fact that Fanny believes Mrs General to be cunning in her reticence. A game of whist takes place at Mr Meagles's house in chapter sixteen of book one, but it is an occasion for harmonious family interaction, in which gambling has no place. Finally, in looking at references to gambling in *Little Dorrit*, at the Circumlocution Office, Clennam enters a room in which two characters are talking about a fixed dog fight, on which money had been staked. Their keen immersion in an inconsequential conversation is an aspect of How Not To do It, the governing principle of the office.

Charles Dickens makes little mention of gambling in his letters. In a letter to John Forster, probably dating from 16 September 1842, he describes briefly his impressions on visiting a race course: 'at the Isle of Thanet races yesterday I saw – oh! who shall say what an immense amount of character in the way of inconceivable villainy and blackguardism! I even got some new wrinkles in the way of showmen, conjurors, pea-and-thimblers, and trampers generally.'[19] Pea-and-thimble also receives an incidental mention in chapter fifty of *Nicholas Nickleby* and in the opening paragraph of chapter thirty-seven of *Martin Chuzzlewit*. In September 1857 Dickens visited Doncaster at the time of the St Leger race meeting, again giving his account to Forster: 'the impressions received from the race-week were far from favourable. It was noise and turmoil all day long, and a gathering of vagabonds from all parts of the racing earth. Every bad face that had ever caught wickedness from an innocent horse had its representative in the streets.' Dickens concludes his letter by stating, with regard to gambling, 'I vow to God that I can see nothing in it but cruelty, covetousness, calculation, insensibility, and low wickedness'.[20] Dickens's condemnation of gambling in this letter is more vehement than his general treatment of the subject in his fiction. Dickens consistently presents gamblers in his novels as irresponsible and dissolute, but he rarely if ever subjects them to the derogatory adjectives that he employs in his letter to Forster. Dickens remained in Doncaster for the St Leger. His fortune on race day is detailed in a further letter, which is here quoted in full (with Dickens referring to himself in the third person).

On the St Leger day a wonderful, paralysing coincidence befell him. He bought a race-card; facetiously wrote down three names for the winners of the three chief races (never in his life having heard or thought of any of the horses, except that the winner of the Derby, who proved to be nowhere, had been mentioned to him); and, if you can believe it without your hair standing on end, those three races were won, one after another, by those three horses!!! He also thought it noticeable that, though the losses were enormous, nobody had won, for there was nothing but grinding of teeth and blaspheming of ill-luck. On the night of the Cup Day a groaning phantom lay in the doorway of his bedroom and howled all night. The landlord came up in the morning to apologise, and said it was a gentleman who had lost £1500 or £2000; and he had drunk a deal afterwards; and then they put him to bed, and then he – took the 'orrors, and got up, and yelled till morning.[21]

Dickens also believed that the sight of Doncaster races would deter young men from gambling.[22] However, on balance, it is unlikely that the races at Doncaster were any more uproarious than the races in most other parts of the country, although a witness to the 1844 Select Committee on Gaming (Robert Baxter) had suggested, from an anti-gambling perspective, that Doncaster was particularly rife with gambling (as discussed in chapter one). Therefore, and given that horse racing generally became increasingly popular from the 1830s onwards in Victorian England, Dickens's belief that people would be dissuaded from gambling by witnessing the excesses of behaviour at Doncaster races is not borne out by the available evidence.

In the one phase of Dickens's career when he used gambling as a significant theme, Crockford's was still in full swing. The figure of the debauched aristocrat, therefore, was familiar to his readers and thus Lord Frederick Verisopht was an instantly recognizable character type. The relocation of the gambler lower down the social scale in *The Old Curiosity Shop* reflects a wider judgment that gambling was corrosive in its effects. This is underlined when we consider that games without gambling in Dickens are enjoyable social events. When gambling increased significantly as a matter of social concern, in the period between the Gaming Acts of 1845 and 1853, Dickens approached it through non-fiction, perhaps reflecting the seriousness and urgency of the problem as it was perceived at the time. Gambling was not at the center of Dickens's concerns, but we learn enough from his representation of it to support the view that it did increase as a source of anxiety as the nineteenth century moved into its fourth and fifth decades.

chapter four

'Gambler, Swindler, Murderer'

William Makepeace Thackeray's Losses and Gains

In the summer of 1829, Thackeray, then an undergraduate student at Cambridge, visited France. During this holiday he had his first significant encounter with gambling. In a letter to his mother, written in July, he describes the boarding-house in which he stayed and the habits of its clientele: 'they are most inordinate card players here, and I am told play rather high'.[1] Thackeray, at this stage, was simply a spectator. In a further letter to his mother, dated 6 August 1829, he stated, 'the boarding house was an idle, dissipated écarté-playing boarding house'.[2] At this stage he did not appear to be susceptible to the lure of gambling. However, the same letter also records Thackeray's first impressions on visiting Frascati's, a well-known casino on the Rue de Richelieu in Paris.

> The interest in the game Rouge et Noir is so powerful that I could not tear myself away until I lost my last piece – I dreamed of it all night – and thought of nothing else for several days, but thank God I did not *return*. The excitement has passed away now, but I hope I shall never be thrown in the way of the thing again, for I fear I could not resist.[3]

Frascati's was a luxurious gaming house with an aristocratic clientele. It was also, according to Captain Gronow, a place where 'some of the most celebrated women of the *demi-monde* usually congregated'.[4] However, at this point in his life, Thackeray's gambling was not yet problematic. In another letter to his mother in August 1829, he describes how a game of écarté amongst friends is 'delightful and rational amusement', with the proceeds being used to fund travel excursions.[5] Furthermore, Thackeray was in no sense entranced by this form of gambling, noting on a later occasion, 'écarté again this evening I am sick on't'.[6] Far from being a problem gambler, Thackeray just included some gambling in his normal recreation. His letters to his mother at this time evidently provoked a concerned response from her, as shown in a letter written by Thackeray on 21 August 1829, in which he assures her, 'I have learnt the full extent of the evil'.[7] At the end of the letter Thackeray tries to be reassuring: 'I said in my last letter I think, that I should go into one of the low gaming houses – this of course unless I receive permission from you – I shall not now do.'[8] Thackeray was sufficiently interested by what he had seen at Frascati's to seek out more gaming houses, but the less reputable establishments (located in and around the Palais Royal) would have been much more hazardous. In any event, Thackeray was greatly attracted to Paris and paid it another visit in the spring of 1830. On this second occasion, however, he appears to have avoided any significant contact with gambling.[9]

In the summer of 1830 Thackeray suffered a catastrophic gambling loss. He fell victim to two professional gamblers, who initially allowed him to win small sums at écarté, whereafter the stakes were raised and Thackeray lost fifteen hundred pounds. The experience caused profound financial damage to Thackeray, but creatively it was not without its rewards. Thackeray's sketch, 'Sharpers', shows two such gamblers in operation. The dealer, tight-lipped and slightly smiling, stares confidently at the viewer. He shows one card only and holds the remainder close to his body. His companion stands close behind him and looks down at the cards; they are both well dressed (plate III). Furthermore, one of the gamblers who exploited Thackeray later became his model for the character of Deuceace in *The Yellowplush Papers*.

In a letter to his mother of 31 December 1830, Thackeray talks of his reasons for leaving Cambridge without a degree. He does not cite gambling as a factor in his decision to leave, but it seems reasonable to suggest that it was an important element in his failure to graduate from Cambridge. Gordon Ray (1945) cited as reasons for Thackeray's departure from Cambridge, 'his heavy losses at play and his fear that the temptation to gamble might prove too strong for him if he remained at the University'.[11]

A year later, in December 1831, Thackeray wrote to his stepfather and spoke of having raised some money to pay a gambling debt. In 1832 Thackeray's gambling became even more intense. His diary entry for 3 April shows that he lost at 'No 60', which was a gambling house at 60 Regent's Quadrant.[12] The entry for the following day shows that Thackeray 'went to 60 *for the last time, so help me God* where I won back the exact sum I had lost the day before'.[13] From this it appears that Thackeray's visits to the gaming house were more compulsive than recreational. However, he continued to play écarté with his friends and, according to the diary entries, this was a much less torturous process.[14]

Sharpers (William Makepeace Thackeray), from The Letters and Private Papers of William Makepeace Thackeray

In May 1832 Thackeray again succumbed to the lure of the gaming-houses. On 2 May he wrote, 'broke my vow and won five pounds at play at 60 Quadrant'; on the 8th Thackeray, 'went to 64 and lost £10', this being another gaming-house in Regent's Quadrant.[15] Further successes and failures in gambling are recorded on 11 and 17 May: 19 May is described by Thackeray as 'one of the most disgraceful days I ever spent – playing from after breakfast till 4 o'clock at chicken hazard.'[16] Chicken hazard (otherwise known as English hazard) differs from normal hazard (or French hazard) in that, in the former, the competitors bet directly against each other, rather than staking their bets in opposition to the bank. It is therefore a more confrontational and adversarial game than ordinary hazard.

Thackeray's diary entries for June 1832 continue to detail his progress, or lack of it, in gambling, and in July 1832 he again went to Paris where he gambled frantically. The experience caused him severe anxiety, as evidenced in a diary entry from 17–18 August: 'may Almighty God give me strength of mind to resist the temptation of play, and to keep my vow that from this day I will never again enter a gaming house'. His resolution, however, was short-lived and on 19 August he wrote, 'I broke the vow I solemnly made yesterday – and thank God lost the last halfpenny I possessed by doing so.'[17] Thackeray was no longer in control of his gambling. His diary shows that he continued gambling into September and October. On 17 November 1832 he states how he had gone 'for a minute to Frascati's where I lost all I had'.[18] An earlier diary entry from the same trip to France offers an insight into Thackeray's gambling. On 22 August, having read a history of philosophy, he wrote, 'the excitement of metaphysics must equal almost that of gambling at least I found myself giving utterance to a great number of fine speeches and imagining many wild theories which I found it impossible to express on paper.'[19] From this entry it would appear that Thackeray was prone to exuberance and enthusiasm and was thus susceptible to the kind of intense excitement that gambling can produce. This aspect of his personality sat uneasily alongside his clear revulsion for his gambling practices.

Thackeray was by no means unique in experiencing great anxiety about his gambling habit. The same clash of feelings was experienced by Charles Greville and recorded in his diaries. In 1843 he wrote:

> if I chose to tell more stories of the turf, somebody would be found to read them in times remote; but I always feel so ashamed of the occupation, and a sort of consciousness of degradation and of deterioration from it, that my mind abhors the idea of writing about it; in fact, I often wonder at my own

sentiments or sensations, and my own conduct about the business and the diversion of racing. It gives me at least as much of pain as pleasure, and yet so strong is the habit, such a lingering, lurking pleasure do I find in it, such a frequent stimulus does it apply to my general indifference and apathy, that I cannot give it entirely up.[20]

Both Thackeray and Greville were from respectable families, and this may be one of the reasons for their contradictory emotions. Despite the long-standing association between horse racing and the aristocracy (a connection which undoubtedly lent greater respectability to horse racing than to other practices with which gambling was intertwined), the idea that gambling was intrinsically wrong on moral grounds was in circulation and effected both men's perception of their conduct. Thackeray's diary entries were written in the 1830s when gambling was going through a transitional phase, as the gaming houses were in their prime and concern was beginning to be raised about their effect on the working classes. Greville's diary entry is taken from a time when anxiety over gambling had increased and, whilst new legislation on horse racing was not one of the recommendations of the 1844 Select Committee on Gaming, it is significant to note that concerns about gambling were not limited to the gaming houses. Greville's sense of self-disgust does not exceed Thackeray's, but Greville experiences these feelings in relation to a practice which, legislatively at least, enjoyed a veneer of respectability.

In February 1835 Thackeray was involved in an incident which later gave rise to 'A Gambler's Death', in his first published book, *The Paris Sketch Book* (1840).[21] Thackeray narrates how he met a former school-fellow who had since become a ruined gambler, and how Thackeray lent him a small amount of money which the gambler then turned into a fortune at the gaming tables, later squandering the whole sum. He describes his initial encounter with his former companion thus: 'a dark-looking, thick-set man, in a greasy well-cut coat, with a shabby hat, cocked on one side of his dirty face, took the place opposite me, at the little marble table, and called for brandy' (p. 117). The narrator lends the man, Attwood, five pounds, which he thereafter turns into thirteen thousand francs. This turn of fortune provokes an uncharitable reaction in the narrator: 'the passion of envy entered my soul'. Elaborating on this feeling, the narrator states, 'I hated Attwood for *cheating* me out of all this wealth' (p. 119). There is very little in the way of genuine friendship in 'A Gambler's Death', merely opportunism. Thackeray presents a shallow environment, in which gambling is central. Attwood, when next encountered by the narrator, is 'pale and agitated' (p. 120).

The title of the piece has already signalled the final outcome and this sudden change in Attwood's demeanour signals that the end is not too far away. The news of Attwood's suicide is broken to the narrator by another acquaintance, who is eating as he breaks the news: 'the man's mouth was full of bleeding beef as he delivered this gentlemanly witticism' (p. 122). This image emphasizes the cruelty and callousness of the life led by Attwood and his companions. The characters seem incapable of civilized or compassionate behaviour.

Thackeray stressed the fact that 'A Gambler's Death' was rooted in an actual incident. The details of Attwood's death were explained in a footnote, including the items that were found in the vicinity of the corpse: 'in order to account for these trivial details, the reader must be told that the story is, for the chief part, a fact; and that the little sketch in this page was *taken from nature*. The letter was likewise a copy from one found in the manner described' (p. 123ff). At Attwood's burial, the narrator wonders, 'was he worse than any of us, his companions, who had shared his debauches, and marched with him up to the very brink of the grave?' (p. 124). The point of 'A Gambler's Death' is made explicit by the narrator in the final paragraph, which is prefaced by a sub-heading.

MORAL

'When we turned out in our great-coats,' said one of them afterwards, 'reeking of cigars and brandy-and-water, d——e, sir, we quite frightened the old buck of a parson; he did not much like our company.' After the ceremony was concluded, these gentlemen were very happy to get home to a warm and comfortable breakfast, and finished the day royally at Frascati's. (p. 125)

The characters are unrepentant and pursue the same course of action as they had done prior to Attwood's death. Thackeray presents a bunch of indecorous pleasure-seekers who choose to gamble in the wake of a suicide. Thackeray's own periodic revulsion to gambling, as evidenced in his diary entries, feeds through into this part of 'A Gambler's Death'. His own susceptibility to gaming-houses, however, is not presented.

Two years earlier, in February 1838, Thackeray published (in *Fraser's Magazine*) 'The Amours of Mr Deuceace: Dimond Cut Dimond', part of *The Memoirs of Mr C.J. Yellowplush*.[22] It is written from a servant's perspective in a servant's vernacular, and is of interest here because it focuses on a gambling exploit to which Thackeray's personal gambling experiences are relevant. Yellowplush's employer, Deuceace, frequents Almack's and Crockford's, spelt 'Holmax' and 'Crockfud's' by the narrator (p. 190). Yellowplush further points out and comments upon the exact calibre of person by whom he is employed.

> For it's no use disgysing it – the Honrabble Halgernon was a GAMBLER. For a man of wulgar family, it's the wust trade that can be – for a man of common feelinx of honesty, this profession is quite imposibil; but for a real thoroughbread genlmn, it's the easiest and most prophetable line he can take. (p. 191)

Yellowplush highlights the different perceptions of gamblers by society as a whole, perceptions which depend on the social class to which the gambler belongs. The text highlights satirically the license granted to the aristocracy, who did not suffer the same constraints as people lower down the social order. Deuceace's partner in the gambling scheme is Blewitt, who is also 'a bettin man' who 'went reglar to Tattlesall's' (p. 192). Their victim is Dawkins, described by the narrator as 'a pidgin' (p. 192). A 'pigeon', in gambling parlance, is a willing gambler, with money but utterly without guile.

Deuceace's first plan is to recruit Blewitt as an accomplice. He does this by flattering him, exaggerating his acumen as a gambler. He claims that the Duke of Doncaster knows Blewitt, 'as every sporting man in England does, I should think. Why, man, your good things are in everybody's mouth at Newmarket' (p. 195). Together, they lure Dawkins into a game of cards. Their first game is described by Yellowplush: 'after dinner and praps 8 bottles of wine between the 3, the genlm sat down to *écarty*. It's a game where only 2 plays, and where, in coarse, when there's only 3, one looks on' (p. 203). The accompanying illustration, also by Thackeray, shows the three gamblers in action. Dawkins is clearly younger than the other two players. He is looking up deferentially towards Blewitt who, in turn, is leaning over Dawkins, invading his body space (plate IV). Gambling thus acquires a parasitical undertone at this point, which the narrative itself underlines. After initially allowing Dawkins to win (in much the same way that the young Thackeray was allowed to win small stakes at first when he was duped), Deuceace and Blewitt take £4,700 from the younger man. Thereafter, Deuceace dupes Blewitt, with whom he will not share the winnings, with the narrator thereby showing how there is no honour among thieves. The story is thus given a slight moral dimension, but this aspect of 'Dimond Cut Dimond' is muted, with the main emphasis being on the rakish behaviour of Deuceace and the informed observations of Yellowplush.

Barry Lyndon (1844)

In 1844 Thackeray published *The Memoirs of Barry Lyndon*.[23] The plot follows the rise and fall of an Irish adventurer in the second half of the eighteenth century and gambling forms a significant element in the narrative. With regard to the hero's lineage, we are told that his father was a member of White's who came to the notice of George II by riding a winning horse at Newmarket (ch. 1). Gambling is thus inscribed in Barry Lyndon's personal history from the outset. In common with Thackeray, Barry Lyndon is exploited by a wily pair of professional frauds and gamblers, the Fitzsimmons. Thereafter he becomes a soldier, in which role he states, 'drinking and gambling are, I am sorry to say, our principal pastimes' (p. 64). For conscripted soldiers, however, gambling holds additional significance: 'those who had anything to risk gambled' (p. 87). Later in the novel, Barry Lyndon is himself conscripted and thus rendered utterly powerless. Gambling becomes an expression of desperation within an oppressed community. With no means at their disposal for improving their situation, they strive for an unlikely elevation through fortune. Barry Lyndon meets up with his uncle, whereafter the two of them make a fortune through gambling. Thackeray's presentation of his upper-class gamblers makes them seem honourable: 'there is a sort of chivalry among the knights of the dice-box' (p. 108). With this image in place the contests between the gamblers become titanic struggles for supremacy. Upper-class gambling becomes imbued with merit: all the values of the jousting field are relocated to the gaming table. Barry Lyndon even presents a code of conduct for gamblers: 'play grandly, honourably. Be not, of course, cast down at losing; but above all, be not eager at winning, as mean souls are' (p. 109). The problem with this analysis is that it denies flatly the most obvious feature of gambling. It seeks to distance itself from money, as this is the preoccupation of a class lower down the social scale, but, in fact, the gambling of Barry Lyndon and his uncle is wholly focused on material gain.

However, Barry Lyndon's analysis becomes more adventurous and sophisticated. In chapter nine he considers gambling in relation to commerce.

> In later times, a vulgar national prejudice has chosen to cast a slur upon the character of men of honour engaged in the profession of play; but I speak of the good old days in Europe, before the cowardice of the French aristocracy (in the shameful revolution which served them right) brought discredit and ruin upon our order. They cry fie upon men engaged in play; but I should like to know how much more honourable *their* modes of liveli-

Mr Dawkins advises with Mr Blewett upon a Difficult Point at Écarté
(William Makepeace Thackeray), from The Yellowplush Correspondence

hood are than ours. The broker of the Exchange who bulls and bears, and buys and sells, and dabbles with lying loans, and trades on state-secrets, what is he but a gamester? (p. 119)

Later, he compares himself to a farmer, as 'a crop is a chance, as much as a game of cards' (p. 169). He sees the principles of gambling inhering in the wider society and, moreover, he refuses to accept the distinction between stock exchange speculation and gambling. Thackeray was writing in the mid-century, but the memoirs were supposedly written in the early-nineteenth century before speculation had distanced itself from other forms of gambling. The fact that traders on the exchange sold lottery tickets as well as shares until 1826 suggests that the close connection between gambling and financial speculation was widely recognized.

In a section of the narrative located in 1772, the narrator focuses on aristocratic gambling in London.

> We have no idea in this humdrum age what a gay and splendid place London was then: what a passion for play there was among young and old, male and female; what thousands were lost and won in a night; what beauties there were – how brilliant, gay and dashing! Everybody was delightfully wicked: the royal Dukes of Gloucester and Cumberland set the example; the nobles followed close behind. (p. 217)

In the same paragraph he mentions White's, Wattier's and Goosetree's. Shortly thereafter, we hear of a game of cards between Barry Lyndon, Lord Sandwich, Lord Carlisle and Charles Fox. The novel thus condenses the upper-class gambling culture of the late-eighteenth century. A card game, as in Disraeli's *The Young Duke*, becomes a test of endurance as much as skill. However, *Barry Lyndon* also looks at gambling at the opposite end of the social scale. On one occasion, the hero loses money to students and soldiers 'in a tavern room thick with tobacco smoke, across a deal table besmeared with beer and liquor'. He describes the loss as 'ignoble' and 'shameful' (p. 122). Later, Barry Lyndon's wife objects to him 'gambling and boozing with low Irish black-legs' (p. 174). Lower-class gambling in the novel is not glamorous: it is merely the sordid pursuit of profit. By removing, wholly artificially, the discourse of the pursuit of money from upper-class gambling Thackeray imbues it with glamour, but this strategy is profoundly self-delusional. By effectively ignoring economics Thackeray depoliticizes upper-class gamblers who become spectacular social celebrities instead of wasteful social parasites.

Towards the end of the novel Barry Lyndon's luck begins to fail. In this position he now sees upper-class gambling with greater insight. Having lost money to aristocrats at Newmarket race course he states, 'there was no set of men in Europe who knew how to rob more genteelly' (p. 233). He now sees the false veneer of upper-class respectability but he is powerless to do anything about it. The novel shows how the odds are ultimately stacked against the adventurer. Barry Lyndon seeks fame, fortune and upper-class respectability, but social mobility on this scale is not possible. The extent of class stratification is apparent in the different perceptions of gambling which are determined by the class position of the gambler.

Vanity Fair (1847–8)

Vanity Fair[24] covers the years 1812–30, and thus we have a Victorian narrator looking back on the conduct of the preceding generation. Gambling occurs repeatedly in *Vanity Fair*. Furthermore, it is strikingly apparent in the language used by the characters. When love is discussed, betting proposals are more common than marriage proposals. For example, a friend of Joseph Sedley's says to him: 'I bet you thirteen to ten that Sophy Cutler hooks either you or Mulligatawney before the rains' (p. 30). George Osborne attempts to talk Dobbin into marrying Jane Osborne by favourably assessing his prospects of success: 'I'll bet you five to two she will' (p. 272). The characters and the narrator are equally at home using gambling terms in relation to death and legacies. The Reverend Bute Crawley does not think much of the elderly Miss Crawley's chances of survival: 'I lay five to two, Matilda drops in a year' (p. 124). We are told that his wife mishandles her monopoly of Miss Crawley's attentions and that she 'had really played her cards too well' (p. 409). Rawdon Crawley was 'once first favourite for this race for money' (p. 432). An imminent death is merely a potential financial windfall. Miss Crawley finds that her relatives are speculating on the contents of her will and are not too bothered about her actual welfare. Any concern they show is conditional upon future reward. The narrator refers to this process as 'these speculations in life and death' (p. 114). The Reverend Bute Crawley, notwithstanding his religious title, is himself a gambler. We are told how he lost money through bookmaking on the Derby in his younger years. He talks of racing his dog for money and, later, he and his son 'fall to talking about odds on the St. Leger'. Becky Sharp, in a letter to Amelia, refers to him as 'the abominable horse-racing rector' (p. 121).

This enhances Becky's status as a young lady of decorum in the eyes of her friend, but it is in no way an accurate reflection of Becky's true feelings about gambling.

Gambling terms in *Vanity Fair* also feature in the political world. Set against the backdrop of the Napoleonic Wars, the narrator refers to the period as a time when 'empires were being staked' (p. 136). It is later suggested that Napoleon's resurgence might 'cause Russia to drop his cards' (p. 211), and we are told that 'Napoleon is flinging his last stake' (p. 212). The link constructed between war and gambling stresses the drama, recklessness and precariousness of conflict. Wellington, we are told, was 'enabled to win the last great trick' (p. 456) at Waterloo. Thackeray is not alone in establishing a connection between gambling and warfare. It features prominently in the opening paragraph of 'A Fashionable Gaming-House – Confessions of a Croupier', from *Bentley's Miscellany* (1844): 'the revolutions of empires from his day to that of Napoleon, a period of some forty centuries, have been nothing but mighty games of chance, in which the destinies of nations were staked by Kings and Emperors.'[25] At a time when war was a very recent memory it is not surprising that references to conflict, and particularly references to Napoleon, were commonplace. *Vanity Fair* compares warfare to a gamble, the outcome of which is by no means certain. Jos Sedley is characteristically panic-stricken in his reaction to the battle, although his response also illustrates the fact that the result is uncomfortably close. By contrast, Becky Sharp's cool closure of a business deal, selling her horses for an extraordinary price to Jos during the battle, indicates her composure and ability to gamble calculatedly. The description of the aftermath of Waterloo features the victorious soldiers engaging in boisterous celebrations.

> The city was a vast military hospital for months after the great battles; and as men and officers began to rally from their hurts, the gardens and places of public resort swarmed with maimed warriors, old and young, who, just rescued out of death, fell to gambling, and gaiety, and love-making, as people of Vanity Fair will do. (p. 442)

In a release of tension and within a general atmosphere of abandonment, gambling forms part of the merriment.

Numerous characters in *Vanity Fair* are gamblers and sportsmen. George Osborne is 'excellent in all games of skill' (p. 135), and has 'won the Garrison Cup at Quebec races' (p. 143). He goes to the gambling houses in St James's and he resents Amelia Sedley doting on him because 'there's no fun in winning a thing unless you play for it' (p. 145). George's shallowness, however, rebounds on him as he meets his match at games in Rawdon Crawley and encounters someone even more heartless than himself in Becky Sharp. Rawdon and Becky exploit him while he tells unconvincing lies to Amelia: 'he pretended regimental business to Amelia (by which falsehood she was not in the least deceived), and consigning his wife to solitude or her brother's society, passed his evenings in the Crawleys' company – losing money to the husband, and flattering himself that the wife was dying of love for him' (p. 354). Throughout Osborne's life his egotism is his undoing. He is also self-deceptive, hence his assertion, concerning his gambling with Crawley, that 'with fair play it comes to pretty much the same thing at the year's end' (p. 353).

Osborne gambles with particular energy following a liaison with Becky.

> Osborne meanwhile, wild with elation, went off to a play table, and began to bet frantically. He won repeatedly. 'Everything succeeds with me tonight,' he said. But his luck at play even did not cure him of his restlessness, and he started up after a while, pocketing his winnings, and went off to a buffet where he drank off many bumpers of wine. (p. 358)

He seeks to maintain the level of excitement he has just experienced with Becky by gambling. It does not, however, satisfy him. Becky shows herself to be a greater stimulant to George than betting and he thereafter drinks in a further effort to maintain his inner momentum. Becky has previously warned Amelia about George's gambling, but this is hardly sincere or compassionate advice, given that Rawdon is the main beneficiary of George's gambling losses. The fact that Becky immediately thereafter leaves Amelia to dance with George suggests that her real intent is to wound her friend rather than guide her.

Rawdon Crawley starts out in *Vanity Fair* in a similar vein to Osborne. According to a letter from Becky to Amelia, 'he drinks, bets, rides, and talks about hunting and shooting' (p. 122). The Reverend Bute Crawley holds a more forthright opinion of Rawdon: 'he's a gambler – he's a drunkard – he's a profligate in every way' (p. 124). He also calls him 'gambler, swindler, murderer' (p. 125), and accuses him of fixing a prize-fight. Rawdon is happy to gamble with and win money from Jos Sedley and George Osborne, and he uses the proceeds to pay his and Becky's bill at an inn. He is also said to have made Lord Dovedale (a young nobleman) drunk, and then 'fleeced (him) of four thousand pounds' at the Cocoa-Tree. In this incident he is described as an 'abominable seducer and perverter of youth' (p. 228). Amongst men he is a champion: 'with the men at the club or the mess-room he was well enough; and could ride, bet, smoke, or play at billiards with the boldest of them' (p. 616). However, he has no other talents: 'the only book he studied was the Racing Calendar' (p. 658). Within the novel, however, Rawdon Crawley is transformed by marriage and father-hood.

> In all his life he had never been so happy as, during the past few months, his wife had made him. All former delights of turf, mess, hunting-field, and gambling-table; all previous loves and courtships of milliners, opera-dancers, and the like easy triumphs of the clumsy military Adonis, were quite insipid when compared with the lawful matrimonial pleasures which of late he had enjoyed. (p. 365)

Unfortunately, Rawdon's image of domestic bliss is an illusion. His wife is unfaithful. Nevertheless, his extremes are tamed when he steps into the mainstream of society, foregoing selfish pleasures, including gambling, and engaging in family life. Following his arrest he passes the time in detention cutting cards for low stakes, but this is more of an effort to alleviate despair and loneliness than a return to his profligate ways.

The debauched upper class is most vividly exemplified in *Vanity Fair* by Sir Pitt Crawley. Early in the novel we are told that 'he speculated in every possible way' (p. 101). Following Sir Pitt's death, the Marquis of Steyne refers to him as 'that old scoundrel' (p. 621) and later adds, 'he might have been a peer if he had played his cards better' (p. 633), although Steyne's own conduct is very far from being above reproach. Aside from Steyne's seduction of Becky, his gambling exploits are also well known and a minor character relates how the Marquis and Egalité Orleans 'won a hundred thousand pounds from a great personage at Hombre' (p. 589). Conversely, the new man of the nineteenth century is pre-figured in the character of Mr Osborne senior. He is a successful businessman. He is, however, conscious of being inferior to the titled and landed gentry, and is eager to ensure that his son is on a par with the aristocracy.

> 'Mix with the young nobility. There's many of 'em, who can't spend a dollar to your guinea, my boy. And as for the pink bonnets' (here from under the heavy eyebrows there came a knowing and not very pleasing leer) – 'why, boys will be boys. Only there's one thing I order you to avoid, which, if you do not, I'll cut you off with a shilling, by Jove, and that's gambling, sir.'
> 'Oh, of course, sir,' said George. (p. 155)

Osborne senior, from an emerging rather than established class, reflects the anti-gambling feeling which gathered momentum as the century progressed. However, the advice he gives to his son goes unheeded.

One of society's alternatives to the debauched aristocrat in *Vanity Fair* is seen in Dobbin. As his name suggests, he is a workhorse: steadfast and uncomplaining. He is predictably opposed to gambling, asking the young George Osborne (the son of George and Amelia) to pledge that he will never play at gaming-tables. He is the antithesis of Becky Sharp and, unsurprisingly, there is little love lost between them. Upon hearing of Becky's re-emergence abroad, he states, 'an honest woman always has friends, and never is separated from her family' (p. 836). He later describes Becky as 'a lady who is separated from her husband, who travels not under her own name, who frequents public gaming-tables' (p. 851). Dobbin's opposition to gambling is rooted in his fortitude, a quality which is moral as well as physical in him, and his heroic status is underlined in his successful union with Amelia Sedley at the end of the novel.

Becky Sharp's feminine charm is used to great effect. Her social ascent, from governess of questionable background to society belle, seems unstoppable until she is embroiled in scandal with Steyne, whereafter she disappears. She is next encountered at a gaming-table.

> A woman with light hair, in a low dress, by no means so fresh as it had been, and with a black mask on, through the eyelets of which her eyes twinkled strangely, was seated at one of the roulette-tables with a card and a pin, and a couple of florins before her. As the croupier called out the colour and number, she pricked on the card with great care and regularity, and only ventured her money on the colours after the red or black had come up a certain number of times. It was strange to look at her.
>
> But in spite of her care and assiduity she guessed wrong, and the last two florins followed each other under the croupier's rake as he cried out with his inexorable voice the winning colour and number. She gave a sigh, a shrug with her shoulders, which were already too much out of her gown, and dashing the pin through the card on to the table, sat thrumming it for a while. (pp. 808–9)

Metaphorically, Becky wears masks all the time, presenting different images to different characters. Appropriately placed at a gaming-table, she is still prepared to flout convention although her appearance shows that her fortunes have declined:

> When Becky left Brussels, the sad truth is that she owed three month's *pension* to Madame de Borodino, of which fact, and of the gambling, and of the drinking, and of the going down on her knees to the Reverend Mr Muff, Ministre Anglican, and borrowing money of him, and of her coaxing

and flirting with Milor Noodle, son of Sir Noodle, pupil of the Rev. Mr
Muff, whom she used to take into her private room, and of whom she won
large sums at écarté – of which fact, I say, and of a hundred of her other
knaveries, the Countess de Borodino informs every English person who
stops at her establishment, and announces that Madame Rawdon was no
better than a vipere. (pp. 821–2)

Becky is drinking, gambling and cheating her way around Europe: 'the
lucky Mrs Rawdon was known at every play-table in Germany' (p.
823). She tries to retain some sense of glamour in her life by gambling
at European resorts. The narrator's view is that she is essentially the
same person: 'she was not worse now that she had been in her days of
prosperity – only a little down on her luck' (p. 835).

At the height of Becky's triumph she consorts with royalty and she
is fully conscious of the scale of her achievement. One of her social
rivals, Mrs Winkworth, is described as being 'nowhere in the race' (p.
653). Following Becky's demise, however, she is less in control. In
Brussels she enjoys the social whirl but thirsts for gambling: 'she never
refused the champagne, or the bouquets, or the drives into the country,
or the private boxes; but what she preferred was the écarté at night, and
she played audaciously' (p. 821). She no longer fraternizes with the élite
and instead leads a Bohemian existence.

> It is said she was ordered out of Munich; and my friend Mr Frederick
> Pigeon avers that it was at her house at Lausanne that he was hocussed at
> supper and lost eight thousand pounds to Major Loder and the Honourable
> Mr Deuceace. We are bound, you see, to give some account of Becky's
> biography; but of this part the less, perhaps, that is said the better. (p. 823)

The introduction of Deuceace into *Vanity Fair* emphasizes the decadence of Becky's social milieu. Her appetite for the intrinsic qualities
of gambling, rather than the possibilities it holds for social and material
advancement, signifies that it answers her need for adventure and accelerated living. When conventional, social routes are closed off to her the
gaming table provides an arena for the expression of her vivacity and
ambition.

Becky's shrewd planning is shown when she urges Rawdon to quit
gambling, in the hope that it will induce Miss Crawley to leave him all
her money. She acknowledges, prior to her re-emergence in Europe,
that gambling 'is good to help your income, but not as an income itself'
(p. 457). She rapidly curries favour with Sir Pitt Crawley when she is
placed as a governess in his household, playing backgammon with him
to keep him amused. Becky finally trips up because cleverness un-

tempered by decency leads her to acquire many enemies. Moreover, her later significant immersion in gambling suggests a slump in her hitherto high standards of cleverness. Hope replaces planning; Becky is not adequately prepared for her fall.

For a brief period, Amelia Sedley shares Becky's life on the continent. Becky's acquaintances are eager to take advantage of Amelia in any way they can. The main danger to her welfare is Major Loder, who 'was caned by Sir John Buckskin for carrying four kings in his hat besides those which he used in playing at écarté' (p. 824), and Captain Rook, 'with his horse-jockey jokes and prize-ring slang' (p. 826). Their gambling credentials establish that they are untrustworthy. The environment is hazardous and, while Becky is prepared for the most challenging contest, Amelia is way out of her depth. Both Loder and Rook wish to seduce her and compete against each other: 'a couple of ruffians were fighting for this innocent creature, gambling for her at her own table' (p. 865). At this point Becky performs some good by seeking to reunite Amelia with Dobbin, although Amelia herself also acts independently towards the same end. However, this act of kindness by Becky is motivated by exasperation as much as charity. Becky Sharp, the cleverest character and most audacious gambler in *Vanity Fair*, is, unlike Amelia, well-equipped to survive in any climate. *Vanity Fair* presents a society in which gambling is endemic. Almost everybody is now an adventurer and consequently society is unstable. Dobbin's moral constancy eventually triumphs, but as Becky prospers too the social order can no longer be relied upon to reward virtue and punish vice with unfailing efficiency.

In the summer of 1848, following the publication of the last instalment of *Vanity Fair*, Thackeray again went to mainland Europe and once again became involved with gambling, although not to the extent that he had been in the 1830s. Following an initial, unspectacular loss at Spa, Thackeray was temporarily reduced to being merely a spectator. In a letter to his mother, dated 4 August 1848, he described some of the gambling he had witnessed.

> I go to the gambling shop and watch the people at play with a good deal of interest. The eagerness & feverishness of the women is very curious. There is one old fellow a scoundrel making his daughter play for him she is growing quite hot and feverish at it: so much so that I would like to pull his ears – Sometimes I have a shy myself but without any passion, and I don't lose or win 20 francs. There is a poor devil in the hotel here who has a favourite scheme about which he was bragging to me three nights ago, and with which he was enabled to win two hundred francs a day – A few years ago I should have believed him & I daresay try to join in the specu-

lation but I don't any more, and told him very kindly that he could not fail to blow up before long. Yesterday I saw him leaning against a pillar in the gambling room with the saddest hang dog look. The blow up had taken place. He could afford to lose 24 times running – but he lost 25 times. It was all over. He wont be able to pay his Inn-bill.[26]

Thackeray no longer exhibited the same degree of susceptibility to gambling schemes. His own gambling was no longer characterized by the excitement and recklessness which was apparent in his letters and diary entries in the early 1830s. At this point in his life, following the success of *Vanity Fair*, Thackeray's thirst for gambling may have diminished a little (although he was still able to write, 'O for shame! I lost *l*5 at the horrid rouge et noir & roulette' in a letter of 20 August 1848), but he was definitely not finished with it in his fiction.[27]

Pendennis (1848–50)

Thackeray's next novel was *Pendennis*, first published in instalments between November 1848 and December 1850.[28] It is an acknowledged self-portrait.[29] Thackeray, like Arthur Pendennis, the hero of the novel, attended public school, became involved with gambling and made a living writing for magazines. The novel is closely tied to the real world, featuring actual people and locations. In the opening paragraph the narrator introduces Major Pendennis.

> At a quarter-past ten the Major invariably made his appearance in the best blacked boots in all London, with a checked morning cravat that never was rumpled until dinner-time, a buff waistcoat which bore the crown of his sovereign on the buttons, and linen so spotless that Mr Brummell himself asked the name of his laundress, and would probably have employed her had not misfortunes compelled that great man to fly the country. (p. 1)

The appearance of Beau Brummell at the beginning of the novel has more than one function. First, it serves to locate the novel in time. Secondly, by implying an acquaintanceship between Brummell and Major Pendennis, it associates the Major with fashionable London life. Thirdly, the narrator is concerned with verisimilitude. It is established immediately that *Pendennis* is set in a real place and at a not too distant time. The novel also features a Captain Shandon, an Irish journalist, based on the real-life figure of William Maginn, one-time editor of *Fraser's Magazine*, and Mr Wagg, a celebrated wit, based upon Theodore Hook.[30] Actual locations in *Pendennis* are also plentiful.

News of the whereabouts of Sir Francis Clavering following his spectacular losses on the Derby reaches 'the neighbouring Tattersall's' (p. 769). St James's Street is mentioned on several occasions. The narrator repeatedly draws our attention to the actual world that forms the backdrop for fictional events. The wider social issues brought forward by the narrator are therefore both contemporary and pertinent.

The young Arthur Pendennis goes to university, where his career is short and inglorious. He lives beyond his means, neglects his studies and becomes involved in gambling. One game of hazard suggested by Bloundell-Bloundell, a fellow reprobate, is sufficient to ignite his enthusiasm and 'from that night Pen plunged into the delights of the game of hazard as eagerly as it was his custom to pursue any new pleasure' (p. 231). The experience does not offer any obvious benefits: 'Mr Arthur Pendennis did not win much money in these transactions with Mr Bloundell, or indeed gain good of any kind except a knowledge of the odds at hazard, which he might have learned out of books' (p. 232). Pendennis, like his creator at a similar point in his own life, has no discipline or restraint. He mimics the behaviour of the élite even though he lacks their financial resources as, compared to them, his origins are modest.

Gambling, particularly on sporting events, is prevalent in all ranks of society in *Pendennis*. Blanche Amory declares that horse racing is 'a national amusement, you know' (p. 757). For her it is fascinating because it is fashionable. She is not interested in gambling but she is very interested in social ostentation. Her involvement in gambling is limited to 'sportive bets' (p. 752) with young men as a form of flirtation at the Derby. Within the upper classes gambling is perceived as an embedded tradition. Lady Agnes Foker, the mother of Harry Foker, likens her son's lifestyle to that of the preceding generation: 'all the young men go to Spratt's after their balls. It is *de rigeur*, my dear; and they play billiards as they used to play macao and hazard in Mr Fox's time' (p. 495). Gambling is also a means of expressing social superiority. The upper classes remove themselves from the rest of the population to socialise and parade among themselves. Sir Francis Clavering is seen, along with his wife, at 'the baths and gambling-places of the Rhine and Belgium' (p. 259). Foreign places suggest something exotic in their own right, out of reach for the vast bulk of the population. Major Pendennis is said by his landlady to be visiting 'Badnbadn, with the Marcus of Steyne' (p. 355). Later, at Rosenbad, the Major resides 'at one of the great hotels, at the "Roman Emperor" or the "Four Seasons", where two or three hundred gamblers, pleasure-seekers, or invalids, sat down and over-ate themselves daily at the enormous table-d'hote' (p. 723). Gambling on the continent is also associated with the Bohemian community which Thackeray himself had experienced in the 1830s. For the morally upright character, however, the casino is a threatening place. Helen Pendennis is conscious of the 'croaking croupiers' (p. 723), making the environment sinister rather than glamorous.

Club-life in *Pendennis* is introduced immediately: 'one fine morning in the full London season, Major Arthur Pendennis came over from his lodgings, according to his custom, to breakfast at a certain Club in Pall Mall, of which he was a chief ornament' (p. 1). There is no evidence here to suggest that the Major's club is a centre for gambling. However, whether or not they were intended for gambling, clubs on this tier of society shared a policy of exclusivity. Their clientele was, more often than not, likely to gamble. An account of Crockford's club from *Bell's Life in London* (February 1828) emphasized the opulence of the surroundings and the high social rank of those by whom it was patronized.

> The St James's Club, alias Crockford's, is managed by a Committee of Noblemen and Gentlemen, under whose direction, and not under Mr Crockford's, the admission of members is regulated. The reputed splendour and magnificence of this edifice, and its gorgeous furniture, which exceeds anything of the sort, either in the palace of princes or the residences of subjects in any part of Europe, has induced many persons to solicit a private view; but this has recently been refused, and even the order of Mr Crockford himself, to admit a party, has been rejected. The most distinguished noblemen in the country are members of the club.[31]

The titled rich were a privileged and self-consciously superior breed. It was also widely assumed that the club-man was essentially honourable. In *Pendennis*, the Major attempts to elevate Pendennis socially and economically through marriage to Blanche Amory. This was too much for a reviewer of the novel in *The Scotsman* (18 December 1850).

> The Major Pendennis described to us would not have stooped to an intrigue so sullying as the one by which he tries to secure the Clavering seat and the Begum's fortune for his nephew. To suppress all knowledge of the existence of a felon father with the purpose of grasping a fortune and extorting a settlement – is a villainous meanness, too near kennel-practice for the average club man, be he ever so selfish, to stoop to.[32]

A gentleman, so *The Scotsman* would have us believe, conducted himself with propriety and decency. Interestingly, class snobbery in *Pendennis* is replicated, not challenged, by the servants of the wealthy, implying that the lower classes were more inclined to be aspirational than revolutionary. Morgan, Major Pendennis's footman, and Light-foot, the valet of Sir Francis Clavering, both frequent a gentleman's club 'held in the parlour of the "Wheel of Fortune" public-house'. Here the entertainment consists of 'fashionable town-talk; politics, cribbage, and other amusements', and the club practises its own form of exclusivity: 'the powdered heads of the largest metropolitan footman might bow down in vain entreating admission into the Gentleman's Club' (p. 783). The social descent of Sir Francis Clavering himself is signified by the fact that he frequents the Wheel of Fortune, a tavern whose very name brings forth images of gambling and chance. Alcohol and the drinking place were at the centre of working-class culture in the nineteenth century, and the publicans ensured that the pub remained the centre for gambling.[33] The Victorian middle class increasingly disapproved of pubs, and frequented them less and less. This did not necessarily denote total abstinence from alcohol. Instead, it signified a more general shift from public to private space; a withdrawal from public arenas to the family home.[34]

Lady Clavering, Sir Francis's long-suffering wife, speaks of her husband's 'incorrigible weakness and waste' (p. 768). In his library he 'smoked cigars and read *Bell's Life in London*, and went to sleep after dinner, when he was not smoking over the billiard-table at his clubs, or punting at the gambling-houses in Saint James's' (p. 472). Clavering is reputed to have a share in a gambling-house and 'is in a hell every night almost' (p. 503). He frequents 'the society of black-legs and profligates' (p. 762). His behaviour is an appalling transgression of class boundaries, and he leaves a family ball to go gambling. He is also a very unlucky gambler. Of his early life we hear that 'transactions at the gambling-table had speedily effected his ruin' (p. 259). Later, he gets his wife to pay his gambling debts. His biggest loss is on the Derby, when he takes a large number of bets, loses seven thousand pounds and faces ruin. The gamblers at the Derby are 'shabby bucks and dusky dandies', although the narrator is still conscious of the excitement of the event, drawing attention to 'that delicious and thrilling moment before the contest was decided' (p. 745). Sir Francis Clavering's vows to reform are as unconvincing as they are hyperbolic ('I'll go abroad out of the reach of the confounded hells, and I'll bury myself in a forest, by Gad!', p. 772) and, unsurprisingly, he continues to gamble. One of Clavering's hangers-on, Colonel Altamont, is the personification of vice. By his own admission he cannot resist 'a bottle of brandy, a box of dice, and a beautiful woman' (p. 547). Unlike Clavering, however, Altamont is sometimes a lucky gambler. He wins at the Derby, and at the end of

Pendennis his luck remains good at Baden. However, he is surrounded by parasites: 'a society of all sorts of sharpers, male and female, Russians, Germans, French, English' (p. 958). Earlier in the novel, Altamont tells of a gambling failure: 'a confounded run on the red had finished him, he said, at Baden-Baden' (p. 470). There is no reason to think that this will not happen again.

In contrast to Clavering and Altamont stands Arthur Pendennis's friend, George Warrington. In a conversation with Pendennis, Warrington states, 'a generous fellow plays for the play, a sordid one for the stake' (p. 571), thus voicing the questionable belief that gambling can be separated from economics. A review of *Pendennis* in *The Spectator* (21 December 1850) has this to say about Warrington.

> George Warrington, we have no doubt, will be the favourite by universal assent both with men and women. His surface coating of roughness is but a pleasant humour, and is seen through at a glance, revealing beneath it the finest humanity. A 'healthy animalism' is still a prominent character-istic of our better class of young men; and in spite of much dissipation, much dandyism, and much pseudo-philosophy, it is no very rare thing among that class to find the best scholars and the truest gentlemen neither too fine to drink beer and smoke short pipes, nor too delicate to have both the will and the power to thrash bargemen when occasion demands.[35]

Warrington is an ideal Victorian. He is intellectual yet robust; he is also fundamentally and consistently rational. He is to *Pendennis* what Dobbin is to *Vanity Fair*, a focus of moral strength resisting the dissipation by which he is surrounded.

Within the novel, Arthur Pendennis needs to compromise with the status quo. He manages to accomplish this, albeit with a measure of cynicism, as he tells Warrington in chapter sixty-one.

> An hereditary legislator, who passes his time with jockeys and blacklegs and ballet-girls, and who is called to rule over me and his other betters because his grandfather made a lucky speculation in the funds, or found a coal or tin mine on his property, or because his stupid ancestor happened to be in command of ten thousand men as brave as himself, who overcame twelve thousand Frenchmen, or fifty thousand Indians – such a man, I say, inspires me with no more respect than the bitterest democrat can feel towards him. But, such as he is, he is a part of the old society to which we belong; and I submit to his lordship with acquiescence; and he takes his place above the best of us all at dinner parties, and there bides his time. I don't want to chop his head off with a guillotine, or to fling mud at him in the streets. (pp. 796–7)

This may be read as an argument for political restraint. In the period in which Thackeray was writing there was an awareness that society was divided and, consequently, anxiety over the possibility of serious social unrest.[36] Events on mainland Europe, most notably the revolutions of 1848, gave substance to this fear and inflamed a general hostility towards all things foreign. *Pendennis* suggests that society is sound and only compromised by individual failings. Pendennis's personal journey accommodates him within Victorian society. In order to find contentment he has to renounce selfishness and embrace duty.

It is estimated that, in total, Thackeray lost around three thousand pounds through various forms of gambling.[37] The bulk of his gambling losses occurred in the early 1830s. In the latter half of his life, he scarcely gambled at all. It may be argued that this was because the gaming-houses had been abolished in the 1845 Gaming Act and thus the facilities for the sort of gambling by which Thackeray had been entranced were no longer available. However, the young Thackeray had gambled extensively at gaming-houses on the continent and these were still open and doing good business for most of the second half of the century. It therefore seems more likely that Thackeray simply moved away from gambling. In the aftermath of the success of *Vanity Fair*, Thackeray became a celebrity who enjoyed the trappings of fame. He may thereafter not have required the excitement of gambling, given how his own life became enhanced by his literary successes. This view is given additional credence if we recall that Thackeray, during the height of his immersion in gambling, became equally excited by metaphysics.[38] He sought and responded to excitement. Gambling fulfilled this need for a while (though it also inflicted considerable financial harm on him) but, eventually, he achieved more substantial fulfilment through his writing. With regard to representations of gambling in Thackeray's work, his own experiences fed into 'A Gambler's Death', 'Dimond Cut Dimond' and the adventures of Arthur Pendennis, although we should be wary of reading *Pendennis* as straightforward autobiography, as Gordon N. Ray has noted: '(Pendennis) is a much more spectacular figure than Thackeray had been, and his luxuries, dissipations, and eventual downfall are altogether more spectacular'.[39] *Barry Lyndon* shows us how the gambler rises and falls. When fortune fails the hero he has no deeply rooted social status (having misappropriated a title through a loveless marriage) with which to withstand the onslaught. In *Vanity Fair*, Becky Sharp's gambling is not simply an expression of irresponsibility or callousness. Instead, it is a metaphor for her existence as a survivor in an amoral universe. She gambles with her marriage and, when Rawdon unexpectedly returns to find her in her apartment in a compromising situation with Steyne, she loses the throw of the dice. But, unlike Amelia, paralyzed by her grief for George Osborne, Becky never gives up the game. Banished for a while by polite society to a Bohemian existence in mainland Europe, she regains a stake through Jos Sedley's insurance money and returns to *Vanity Fair* as a figure of respectability. In the novels in which Thackeray features gambling it is practically ubiquitous, pervading marriage, commerce and even language itself. Gambling thus expresses the spirit of the age, in which the adventurer could prosper, at least until they came upon the formidable barrier of class which exerted its own peculiar discrimination when it came to gambling.

chapter five

'Lose Strikingly'

Gambling with Life in George Eliot

George Eliot hated gambling with a passion. In the autumn of 1872 Eliot and her partner, George Lewes, took a trip to Homburg. The area was well known for its scenery, but the town itself was equally renowned for its gambling halls. In a letter written on 25 September to a friend, Mrs William Cross, Eliot voiced her feelings.

> We arrived at Homburg on Saturday night and settled in these comfortable lodgings the next morning. The air, the waters, the plantations are all perfect – 'only man is vile.' I am not fond of denouncing my fellow-sinners, but gambling being a vice I have no mind to, it stirs my disgust even more than my pity. The sight of the dull faces bending round the gaming tables, the raking-up of the money, and the flinging of the coins towards the winners by the hard-faced croupiers, the hateful, hideous women staring at the board like stupid monomaniacs – all this seems to me the most abject presentation of mortals grasping after something called a good that can be seen on the face of this little earth. Burglary is heroic compared with it. I get some satisfaction in looking on from the sense that the thing is going to be put down. Hell is the only right name for such places.[1]

In a further letter to Mrs Cross, dated 17 September 1873, she spoke of 'undesirable Homburg' and 'the joy of getting away again'.[2] To Eliot, the world of gambling was insensible and heartless.

Silas Marner (1861)

Eliot's novel *Silas Marner* (1861) affirms a set of values concerned with interconnection.[3] It is set at the time of the Napoleonic Wars and thus the society on which it concentrates is still predominantly agrarian. Silas Marner is a member of a religious community, Lantern Yard. He is betrayed by a fellow member of the community and is falsely accused of theft. He has no alibi because, at the moment when the crime takes place, he is stricken by a cataleptic seizure, with which he is also affected at a later point in the novel when an infant enters his cottage. At the time when the novel was written, catalepsy (a form of epilepsy characterized by sudden paralysis rather than fits) was not well understood by medical science. This fact is relevant because it alters the significance of Marner's cataleptic episodes by associating them with the mysterious and the unknown, as Sally Shuttleworth (1984) notes.

> Despite the increased interest in abnormal states of consciousness in the mid-nineteenth century, catalepsy still remained a mystery to psychologists. Inexplicable, and uncontrollable, catalepsy seemed to suggest the eruption of chance, rather than the operation of a uniform law.[4]

Marner's seizures are thus seen as chance events which trawl significant consequences in their wake, and chance emerges as a significant theme in the novel. The Lantern Yard community, believing in divine intervention, draws lots to establish Marner's guilt, believing that they are invoking providence when they are merely resorting to chance. The community thus paves the way for the introduction of the Cass family in *Silas Marner*, whose gambling habits denote irresponsibility and a reluctance to make mature, moral decisions.

The Cass family are landed and privileged. The narrator focuses on Squire Cass's sons, both of whom are corrupt. The conduct of Dunsey Cass is detailed in chapter three:

> people shook their heads at the courses of the second son, Dunstan, commonly called Dunsey Cass, whose taste for swopping and betting might turn out to be a sowing of something worse than wild oats. To be sure, the neighbours said, it was no matter what became of Dunsey – a spiteful jeering fellow, who seemed to enjoy his drink the more when other people went dry – always provided that his doings did not bring trouble on a family like Squire Cass's, with a monument in the church and tankards older than King George. (pp. 34–5)

The Cass family, belonging to the upper class in the early-nineteenth century, are held to have responsibilities as well as rights. Gambling is not necessarily an abrogation of those rights as it is a long-standing feature of aristocratic recreation but, when taken in conjunction with other modes of anti-social behaviour, it causes concern. Godfrey, Dunsey's elder brother, is also a morally weak individual. He is prone 'to that bitter rumination on his personal circumstances which was now unbroken from day to day save by the excitement of sporting, drinking, card-playing, or by the rarer and less oblivious pleasure of seeing Miss Nancy Lammeter' (p. 43). Alcohol and gambling function as a refuge from his problems, which remain unaddressed. He continues to court Nancy Lammeter despite his existing marriage.

Dunsey Cass sells his brother's horse and then causes the death of the animal before the deal is concluded. He steals Silas Marner's gold and disappears, leaving Godfrey to conclude that Dunsey 'had gambled away or otherwise squandered the price of the horse' (p. 97). Godfrey is quite prepared to believe that Dunsey is capable of gambling away something which is not his own. Furthermore, Godfrey continues to neglect his own duties and to trust in a dimly understood providence to liberate him from his dilemma.

> He fled to his usual refuge, that of hoping for some unforeseen turn of fortune, some favourable chance which would save him from unpleasant consequences – perhaps even justify his insincerity by manifesting its prudence.
>
> In this point of trusting to some throw of fortune's dice, Godfrey can hardly be called old-fashioned. Favourable Chance is the god of all men who follow their own devices instead of obeying a law they believe in. (pp. 112–13)

Trusting to the throw of fortune's dice involves the refusal to face up to one's position in the world. This idea is applicable not only in *Silas Marner* but, as we shall see, in *Middlemarch* and *Daniel Deronda*. Godfrey Cass's daughter by his secret marriage falls into Silas Marner's care and she imbues his life with new meaning as he is compelled to interact with her and with the community of Raveloe. As she gains adulthood, Godfrey Cass admits, both to Nancy and to Marner, that he is the girl's father. She, however, rejects biological continuity in favour of her immediate community by remaining with Marner. Heredity, itself a principle of chance, is shown to have little intrinsic merit. Gambling in *Silas Marner* is an individual vice, an abrogation of personal responsibility. In addition, it has social significance given the position of the Cass family within their community. The adherence of the two brothers to the principle of chance highlights their unreliability. The Lantern Yard community and Godfrey Cass place their trust entirely in chance and are disappointed; the former in the fact that the community has disappeared at the end of the novel, and the latter in that he is rejected by his daughter. Meanwhile, Marner melds into his community and prospers as a result.

Middlemarch (1871–2)

In *Felix Holt, The Radical* (1866) gambling features incidentally, with servants gambling in chapter seven. Furthermore, the character of Maurice Christian is wily and untrustworthy: it is no coincidence that he is an adept and successful card player. However, gambling next emerges as a significant theme in Eliot's work in *Middlemarch* (1871–2).[5] Set in the period leading up to the Reform Bill of 1832, a generation after *Silas Marner*, *Middlemarch* focuses on a period when industrialization was accelerating and intruding more into social life. It portrays life in a community which is increasingly being prevailed upon, and its continuity challenged, by economic and social changes. Gambling has the potential to threaten the community in *Middlemarch* by disrupting the lives of individuals and compromising their relationships with others. The first explicit reference to gambling in *Middlemarch* occurs towards the end of book one, 'Miss Brooke'. Peter Featherstone is being harangued by Mrs Waule, one of his numerous avaricious relatives. She seeks to discredit Fred Vincy, who is apparently favoured by Featherstone. Her strategy is to highlight rumours that Fred is a gambler: '"My brother Solomon tells me it's the talk up and down in Middlemarch how unsteady young Vincy is, and has been for ever gambling at billiards since home he came." "Nonsense! What's a game at billiards? It's a good gentlemanly game; and young Vincy is not a clodhopper. If your son John took to billiards, now, he'd make a fool of himself"' (1, 158). This exchange was probably one of the first parts of the novel to be written.[6] In establishing the character of Fred Vincy, Eliot used gambling to signify his unreliable and hedonistic streak. For Featherstone, gambling is a fit pastime for a gentleman. Conversely, Mrs Waule sees gambling as a symptom of irresponsible living: the contrasting views adopted by both characters act as a reminder of the shifting perception of gambling. As the narrative develops, Fred Vincy's gambling, in conjunction with his pleasure-seeking lifestyle as a whole, leads him into financial difficulty. Gambling, however, is clearly not the backbone of his existence.

> Fred was not a gambler: he had not that specific disease in which the suspension of the whole nervous energy on a chance or risk becomes as necessary as the dram to the drunkard; he had only the tendency to that diffusive form of gambling which has no alcoholic intensity, but is carried on with the healthiest chyle-fed blood, keeping up a joyous imaginative activity which fashions events according to desire and having no fears about its own weather, only sees the advantage there must be to others in going abroad with it. (1, 358)

Gambling is an aspect of Fred's personality but it is not its defining characteristic. It is further noteworthy that Eliot associates gambling with drunkenness, as both practices suggest personal weakness within a society increasingly concerned by the repercussions of behaviour likely to compromise economic and social stability.

Fred's profligacy is part of his personality. It is also predicated on his expectation of a large inheritance from Featherstone. Fred's speculative conduct in this respect, however, is shown to be unwise as Featherstone has made two wills. Fred is thwarted by Mary Garth who will not compromise herself by destroying Featherstone's alternative will. Fred is not alone in expecting great reward from Featherstone, whose relations gather around him as he draws closer to death. In chapter thirty-two his brother Solomon and Mrs Waule enter his bedroom and are distressed to note that 'the light-complexioned Fred, his short hair curling as might be expected in a gambler's, was lolling at ease in a large chair' (2, 52). Their dislike for Fred finds expression when they think of him as a gambler. Featherstone's prospective inheritees, particularly Fred, are in effect trading in expectations. The outcome, by disappointing all of them, judges their conduct, which is a form of gambling to the extent that it involves seeking a reward without being willing to work for it. The players stake their attention on the old man, but his caprice creates the conditions in which the outcome is uncertain. The fact of the second will emphasizes the precarious nature of his bequest: the resolution of the enigma is unclear up until the last moment. Gambling is disapproved of in this incident, even when the determining force is not blind chance but an irascible old man.

The most significant instance of gambling in *Middlemarch* occurs in book seven, 'Two Temptations', when Tertius Lydgate visits the Green Dragon inn (ch. 66). His childhood discovery of his scientific vocation highlights the impulsive streak in his personality which later emerges in his relationships with women and when he succumbs to gambling.

> The page he opened on was under the heading of Anatomy, and the first passage that drew his eyes was on the valves of the heart. He was not much acquainted with valves of any sort, but he knew that valvae were folding doors, and through this crevice came a sudden light startling him with his first vivid notion of finely adjusted mechanism in the human frame. A liberal education had of course left him free to read the indecent passages in the school classics, but beyond a general sense of secrecy and obscenity in connection with his internal structure, had left his imagination quite unbiassed, so that for anything he knew his brains lay in small bags at his temples, and he had no more thought of representing to himself how his blood circulated than how paper served instead of gold. But the moment

of vocation had come, and before he got down from his chair, the world was made new to him by a presentiment of endless processes filling the vast spaces planked out of his sight by that wordy ignorance which he had supposed to be knowledge. From that hour Lydgate felt the growth of an intellectual passion. (1, 217–18)

There is a paradox here: Lydgate's interest in science centres on investigation, method and rational analysis. The genesis of his passion, however, is much more spontaneous. This contradiction remains with Lydgate: his intellectual abilities rest uneasily alongside spontaneous effusions of feeling. His brief immersion in gambling exposes this internal tension.

Lydgate's biggest mistake, born of impulse, is his marriage to Rosamund Vincy. His general incompetence in money matters in the aftermath of his marriage is soon evident. During a conversation with the clergyman, Lydgate is disconcerted by Farebrother's fairly modest gambling, which he relies on to supplement his meagre income. Farebrother is more alert to the perils of debt, and he cautions Lydgate: "'take care not to get hampered about money matters. I know, by a word you let fall one day, that you don't like my playing at cards so much for money. You are right enough there. But try and keep clear of wanting small sums that you haven't got'" (2, 277). Farebrother and Lydgate are very different characters. The clergyman is neither idealistic nor a romantic and he is sanguine in his response to disappointments. Lydgate is shocked when he first learns of Farebrother's gambling and he believes that Farebrother's fondness for games is conditional upon the money that may be won from them. It is even rumoured that Farebrother has played billiards for money at the Green Dragon. This behaviour is shocking to Lydgate because he has never had to worry about money: 'he did not care for play, and winning money at it had always seemed a meanness to him; besides, he had an ideal of life which made this subservience of conduct to the gaining of small sums thoroughly hateful to him' (1, 272). Dorothea Brooke is similarly unable to comprehend Farebrother's gambling, asking, 'I wonder whether he suffers in his conscience because of that habit', and wanting 'to rescue him from his chance-gotten money' (2, 337–8). It is, for Dorothea, a morally compromised form of money obtained through an appeal to blind fortune rather than by work. However, Farebrother is clearly capable of morally serious and generous behaviour, as he agrees to represent Fred Vincy's case to Mary Garth and in so doing thwarts his own romantic aspirations. Farebrother gambles partly because he enjoys playing games and partly because he needs the money. Within the scope of George Eliot's representations of gambling (prior to *Daniel Deronda*) he occupies a curious position because his gambling is not an expression of irresponsibility. Gambling is what he is driven to do, by economics as much as inclination, although he is never gripped by a mania for gambling. Furthermore, Farebrother stops gambling when his material fortunes improve, as he informs Lydgate: 'I have no need to hang on the smiles of chance now' (3, 171).

Chapter sixty-six opens with Lydgate having to deal with severe financial pressures and a failing marriage: 'under the first galling pressure of forseen difficulties, and the first perception that his marriage, if it were not to be a yoked loneliness, must be a state of effort to go on loving without too much care about being loved, he had once or twice tried a dose of opium. But he had no hereditary constitutional craving after such transient escapes from the hauntings of misery'. He shortly thereafter finds himself considering an alternative source of consolation which connects more directly to his financial predicament.

> It was the same with gambling. He had looked on at a great deal of gambling in Paris, watching it as if it had been a disease. He was no more tempted by such winning than he was by drink. He had said to himself that the only winning he cared for must be attained by a conscious process of high, difficult combination tending towards a beneficent result. The power he longed for could not be represented by agitated fingers, clutching a heap of coin, or by the half-barbarous, half-idiotic triumph in the eyes of a man who sweeps within his arms the ventures of twenty chapfallen companions.
>
> But just as he had tried opium, so his thought now began to turn upon gambling – not with appetite for its excitement, but with a sort of wistful inward gaze after that easy way of getting money, which implied no asking and brought no responsibility. If he had been in London or Paris at that time, it is probable that such thoughts, seconded by opportunity, would have taken him into a gambling-house, no longer to watch the gamblers, but to watch them in kindred eagerness. Repugnance would have been surmounted by the immense need to win, if chance would be kind enough to let him. An incident which happened not very long after that airy notion of getting aid from his uncle had been excluded, was a strong sign of the effect that might have followed any extant opportunity of gambling. (3, 207–8)

Lydgate's general opinion of gambling, that it is a disease, closely shadows that of his creator. More interestingly, Lydgate's attraction to gambling emerges as his actual life prospects diminish. A flaw in his life strategy creates the conditions in which he throws himself on chance as it is the most immediate available option.

The Green Dragon is known for its gambling and general

dissipation. Lydgate goes there with the intention of consulting with a horse dealer. While he is waiting he starts playing billiards:

> the exceptional fact of his presence was much noticed in the room, where there was a good deal of Middlemarch company; and several lookers-on, as well as some of the players, were betting with animation. Lydgate was playing well, and felt confident: the bets were dropping round him, and with a swift glancing thought of the possible gain which might double the sum he was saving from his horse, he began to bet on his own play, and won again and again. (3, 209–10)

Fred Vincy enters the Green Dragon, and he, 'startled at seeing Lydgate, and astonished to see him betting with an excited air, stood aside, and kept out of the circle round the table' (3, 210). Within the gambling scene their normal roles become reversed, with Fred as the concerned, removed onlooker and Lydgate as the gambler.

Gambling temporarily restores a sense of optimism to Lydgate's prospects, but in the act of gambling he renounces his commitment to hard work and duty. His gambling is thus a process of moral descent. Furthermore, as observed by Fred, it has a transformative effect on his appearance. 'Lydgate, who had habitually an air of self-possessed strength, and a certain meditativeness that seemed to lie behind his most observant attention, was acting, watching, speaking with that excited narrow consciousness, which reminds one of an animal with fierce eyes and retractile claws' (3, 212–13). The animal imagery is significant, as his civilized veneer fades during the course of the game and his conduct becomes much more basic and unthinking.

Following the arrival of a new and skilled player Lydgate begins to lose but he continues to bet, 'for his mind was as utterly narrowed into that precipitous crevice of play as if he had been the most ignorant lounger there' (3, 213). Lydgate in a very short period of time (and in a Darwinian trope) has blended in with his environment. Fred stops Lydgate from losing too much by telling him that Mr Farebrother is also in the building. This interruption breaks the spell and brings Lydgate back to the real world. On the following day Lydgate has to face his conduct of the previous night. However, despite his misadventure, Lydgate still perceives a certain attraction in gambling, given the alternative with which he is faced.

> Nevertheless, though reason strangled the desire to gamble, there remained the feeling that, with an assurance of luck to the needful amount, he would have liked to gamble, rather than take the alternative which was beginning to urge itself as inevitable. That alternative was to apply to Mr Bulstrode. (3, 222)

[132]

Lydgate's approach to the corrupt financier arises out of necessity rather than choice and it is only seriously considered after gambling has failed. Lydgate, to his credit, is not a morally weak individual. This is most strikingly evident when he offers literal support to Bulstrode when the banker collapses, even though he knows that this will further besmirch him within the community. However, he is disabled in his personal affairs, as his constitutional flaws render him incapable of making informed judgments. His rational exterior rejects gambling, but his effusive nature generates a susceptibility to its promise of easy and abundant money.

Daniel Deronda (1876)

George Eliot began gathering material for her final novel, *Daniel Deronda* (1876), during the trip undertaken by George Lewes and herself to Homburg in the autumn of 1872.[7] There follows an extract from a letter written by Eliot in Homburg to John Blackwood, after Eliot had seen gambling at first hand.

> The saddest thing to be witnessed is the play of Miss Leigh, Byron's grand niece, who is only 26 years old, and is completely in the grasp of this mean, money-raking demon. It made me cry to see her young fresh face among the hags and brutally stupid men around her.[8]

The figure described by Eliot is not far removed from Gwendolen Harleth, the heroine. This is not to suggest that Gwendolen is based on Miss Leigh, but Eliot is clearly interested in, though simultaneously repelled by, the sight of the young woman at the gaming table. To Eliot, Miss Leigh is virtually possessed and thereby desensitized as a human being, languishing amongst dull and decrepit people.

Daniel Deronda is Eliot's only novel of contemporary life.[9] Lewes, in a letter to John Blackwood (22 November 1875), suggested that the advertisement for *Daniel Deronda* make mention of the fact that the novel is set in *'our own day'*.[10] Within the novel there is a mention of the Northern blockade of Southern ports in the American Civil War (which notes the significance of international events in opposition to Gwendolen's narcissism) and references to a slave uprising in Jamaica. The action may thus be dated in the mid-1860s, although a recent commentator has maintained that *Daniel Deronda* is set very deliberately in 1865.[11] The broad point, however, is that in *Daniel Deronda* George Eliot is writing of her own generation rather than an earlier one. The social and economic landscape that Eliot describes in *Daniel*

Deronda had undergone substantial change since the period in which either *Silas Marner* or *Middlemarch* was set. Marner's home of Raveloe is a generally stable agrarian community in which relationships exist within strata, the composition of which is determined by a hierarchical system in which the landed interest is pre-eminent. The community of Middlemarch maintains a form of integrated solidity which is disturbed unavoidably by encroaching industrialization, but which endures with a significant measure of continuity. There is a much more fundamental precariousness at the heart of *Daniel Deronda* (introduced, through gambling, in the very first chapter), with the narrator having to deal with the uncertainties of contemporary life, both socio-economic (in the form of industrialization) and intellectual (given the widespread impact of evolutionism from the mid-century onwards).

In a letter to Lewes of 3 November 1875, John Blackwood refers to 'the wonderful skill and power of the opening' of *Daniel Deronda*.[12] The narrator prepares us for the opening words in the epigraph to chapter one.

> Men can do nothing without the make-believe of a beginning. Even science, the strict measurer, is obliged to start with a make-believe unit, and must fix on a point in the stars' unceasing journey, when his sidereal clock shall pretend that time is at Nought.

The opening is not too dissimilar to saying 'once upon a time'. In effect the narrator is drawing attention to the arbitrary nature of beginnings.[13] The first words introduce us to a female character in the act of gambling. She is being observed by a male spectator.

> Was she beautiful or not beautiful? and what was the secret of form or expression which gave the dynamic quality to her glance? Was the good or the evil genius dominant in those beams? Probably the evil; else why was the effect that of unrest rather than of undisturbed charm? Why was the wish to look again felt as coercion and not as a longing in which the whole being consents?
>
> She who raised these questions in Daniel Deronda's mind was occupied in gambling: not in the open air under a southern sky, tossing coppers on a ruined wall, with rags about her limbs; but in one of those splendid resorts which the enlightenment of ages has prepared for the same species of pleasure at a heavy cost of gilt mouldings, dark-toned colour and chubby nudities, all correspondingly heavy – forming a suitable condenser for human breath belonging, in great part, to the highest fashion, and not easily procurable to be breathed in elsewhere in the like proportion, at least by persons of little fashion. (1, 3–4)

It is significant to note that R. H. Hutton, reviewing the novel in *Spectator* (1876), objected to the use of the word 'dynamic' in the novel's opening.[14] This is because, in the 1870s, the word still belonged largely to the discourse of science. In *Daniel Deronda*, it is apparent that Eliot is still very interested in science (in both *Silas Marner* and *Middlemarch* she very clearly delineates the whole process of cause and effect) but, as the epigraph suggests, she is also eager to blend scientific method with something more intuitive. The opening of *Daniel Deronda*, including the epigraph, introduces the reader to science but simultaneously undercuts this approach by placing us straight into the action, as the word 'dynamic' emphasizes activity. It is also pertinent to note Eliot's views on composition. In 'Leaves From A Note-Book', in the authorized edition of her essays first published in 1884, within a section entitled 'Story-Telling', she states, 'curiosity becomes the more eager from the incompleteness of the first information'.[15] This is what we have in the opening of *Daniel Deronda*: a character shown initially in action, without any build-up. The coming together of planning and intuition is also a common feature of gambling strategies. Furthermore, the presence of gambling at the beginning of *Daniel Deronda* stresses chance and hazard, themes which become significant as the text progresses.

The first paragraph contains five questions. Everything here is uncertain, yet to be determined. The questioner is Daniel Deronda, who is searching for a direction in his life. He is thus, in this receptive state, keenly alert to his surroundings. His attention is arrested by Gwendolen Harleth's vitality. The gambling community outlined in the first chapter of *Daniel Deronda*, like its eponymous hero, is not settled: it is uncertain and rootless. Gambling in the continental casino is associated immediately with corruption, as the narrator contrasts it with playing for coins in a less civilized and therefore comparatively innocent environment. A child in the casino is the only person not entranced by the roulette table. The arena where the actual gambling is taking place is referred to ironically as 'splendid'. A scientific image is reintroduced when the gaming salon is referred to as a condenser. The narrator repeatedly uses the vocabulary of science, partly in order to attain a sense of distance from the scene under consideration. The image of the condenser further suggests an enclosed, airless space, far removed from 'the open air under a southern sky' against which it is contrasted. In addition, the croupier's voice is described as 'an occasional monotone in French, such as might be expected to issue from an in-geniously constructed automaton' (1, 4). The casino is far removed from the world of authentic, human feelings. The ornamentation in the salon is coarse and unsubtle and an air of snobbery pervades the scene.

The narrator then turns to the other players. There is a cosmopolitan mixture, including 'English aristocratic and English plebian' (1, 5). Significantly, there is no mention of the English middle class. Gambling in the 1860s and '70s was still seen as a vice for indolent aristocrats and irresponsible sections of the lower classes, indulging in gambling in continental Europe after the abolition of gaming-houses at home in the 1845 Act. There is, however, a 'London tradesman' gambling, but in his manner and deportment he seeks to emulate the aristocracy, 'conscious of circulars addressed to the nobility and gentry, whose distinguished patronage enabled him to take his holidays fashionably, and to a certain extent in their distinguished company'. He apes the aristocracy who, despite his wealth, never fully admit him into their circle. He is also shown to be hypocritical, 'reflecting always that Providence had never manifested any disapprobation of his amusement'. However, he has no gambling mania: 'not his the gambler's passion that nullifies appetite' (1, 5–6). The narrator also notices 'a man with the air of an emaciated beau or worn-out libertine, who looked at life through one eyeglass, and held out his hand tremulously when he asked for change'. The last decrepit remnant of pre-Victorian society is characterized by 'fierce yet tottering impulsiveness' (1, 6). The cosmopolitan composition of this community does not make it daringly eclectic, merely unfounded, unconnected, and morally empty.

Gwendolen, as she gambles, becomes aware of Deronda's gaze, whereafter she begins to lose, although she has still made a considerable profit. This good fortune enables her to conjure up a fantasy scenario, whereby 'she had visions of being followed by a *cortege* who would worship her as a goddess of luck and watch her play as a directing augury' (1, 8). Gambling is a form of escapism for Gwendolen, enabling her to pretend that she has the potential to wield power whereas, in the actual society she inhabits, she is shown increasingly to be powerless. In this opening chapter, and for some time thereafter, Gwendolen's will is focused on the uncontrollable.[16] Her luck at the roulette table continues to decline under Deronda's gaze, but she continues to gamble. Her declared motive for so doing provides an insight into her character as a whole: 'since she was not winning strikingly, the next best thing was to lose strikingly' (1, 9). Gwendolen, more than anything, wants to live: fully and vitally. She wants to be noticed, to gain prestige and attention. Since, as a woman, she is not in a position to pursue a career, and since her talents are, in the final analysis, largely unexceptional (she is, for example, only a mediocre singer and musician) she gambles in order to make an impression in the world, and her recklessness in this respect expresses both ambition and frustration. As the novel progresses, Gwendolen is gradually compelled to realize that she is more passive than active. Gambling at roulette is itself fundamentally a passive process. Gwendolen trades on her beauty but finds that it is a limited commodity. She eventually gambles with it in marriage when the only alternative is genteel poverty.

As Deronda looks at Gwendolen, she feels that he 'was examining her as a specimen of a lower order', and that 'Deronda's gaze seemed to have acted as an evil eye' (1, 8). The intense attention of this male figure fractures the imaginary world that Gwendolen has created, a world which places Gwendolen herself in a supreme position. Later in the novel, another male figure, Mallinger Grandcourt, drags her into the harshest of realities in which she is maltreated. In both instances, Gwendolen's idea of supremacy involves her not being intruded upon. The maintenance of her idealized self-image forces her to be hermetic, and the inevitable arrival of significant others in her life breaks down her unrealistic self-definition. Gwendolen welcomes admiration from afar, but she is generally uncomfortable with anything more immediate. Deronda and Grandcourt affect Gwendolen in very different ways. However, it is significant that Gwendolen is disturbed by serious attention, particularly when it is from a male, which trespasses on the narrow psychological world that she inhabits.

Immediately following her loss at the roulette table, Gwendolen discovers that, in the aftermath of the business failure of Grapnell and Co., her family's fortunes have been decimated. She is clearly not the only person to have gambled unsuccessfully. The instability of her personal financial situation is replicated in her family as a whole and, through commercial speculation, in society. Gwendolen herself is now in a position whereby she has to stop playing at the roulette table and begin gambling in earnest.[17] Whereas, in both *Silas Marner* and *Middlemarch* a carefully articulated sequence of causes generally produces an event with a scientific, almost arithmetical, exactness, in the post-Darwinian world of *Daniel Deronda* chance is a much more important principle. In point of fact, as *Daniel Deronda* unravels it steps back in time to detail events leading up to Gwendolen's presence at the roulette table but, at the point of its occurrence in the opening chapter, Gwendolen's behaviour is given without a personal history or an explanation.

Following news of her family's loss, Gwendolen contemplates seeking to revive her financial prospects through roulette, and further considers pawning her jewellery in order to generate funds. Gwendolen imagines the scene 'with an agreeable sense that she was living with some intensity and escaping humdrum' (1, 18). It is clear that she rejects an ordinary, mundane life. Despite her ceaseless search for excitement, however, the narrator is eager to stress that she is not, constitutionally, a gambler: 'Gwendolen's imagination dwelt on this course and created agreeable consequences, but not with unbroken confidence and rising certainty as it would have done if she had been touched with the gambler's mania. She had gone to the roulette-table not because of passion, but in search of it' (1, 18). In common with Fred Vincy, Gwendolen Harleth (at this early stage in the novel) is a character who gambles rather than a gambler. However, Gwendolen can no longer play roulette as her wider financial situation has suddenly deteriorated. The risks undertaken by Gwendolen have been duplicated by more substantial speculators who have played with the security of her family. They are both financially irresponsible, although, of the two, Gwendolen is comparatively innocent. It is further significant that the Harleth family's fortune had been founded on Caribbean plantations, which keeps the wider social context in mind. Through the mentioning of contemporary uprisings of the oppressed, Gwendolen is aligned implicitly with wider groups of people, all struggling for self-determination.

Gwendolen's view of herself is rooted in the world's opinion of her. Her self-esteem resides in the attention she receives and thus, when Deronda retrieves the necklace that she has pawned in order to gamble, she experiences a sense of inferiority because he has witnessed her in a disadvantageous light. Given her youth and slightly more ambiguous beauty she is regarded as highly marriageable, but her own view of the institution is informed by cold reasoning.

> Her observation of matrimony had inclined her to think it rather a dreary state, in which a woman could not do what she liked, had more children than were desirable, was consequently dull, and became irrevocably immersed in humdrum. Of course marriage was social promotion: she could not look forward to a single life; but promotions have sometimes to be taken with bitter herbs – a peerage will not quite do instead of leadership to the man who meant to lead; and this delicate-limbed sylph of twenty meant to lead. (1, 52–3)

Gwendolen is ambitious but lacks worldly wisdom. Her potential (both physical and intellectual) is limited, but she misguidedly perceives the world around her as an index of possibilities to be accessed at will. She is clearly interested in the financial consequences of marriage, but she also wishes to maintain her personal autonomy. The emotional aspects of marriage are simply not considered. However, she cannot help becoming involved, whether with gambling or people. Hers is an ordinary, human trait of which, in the early stages of the novel, she is unaware.

Mallinger Grandcourt is an aristocrat. His eligibility as a husband is, however, damaged by the fact that he already has children by his mistress, Lydia Glasher. Grandcourt is not especially prone to gambling, describing it as 'a confounded strain' (1, 238–9). Flatness and existential fatigue characterizes his existence as a whole, and contrasts markedly with Gwendolen's vitality. Furthermore, during an early conversation with Gwendolen it emerges that he is uninterested in one of the more prevalent forms of gambling within aristocratic circles, horse racing.

> 'And do you care about the turf? – or is that among the things you have left off?' (Pause, during which Gwendolen thought that a man of extremely calm, cold manners might be less disagreeable as a husband than other men, and not likely to interfere with his wife's preferences.) 'I run a horse now and then; but I don't go in for the thing as some men do. Are you fond of horses?'
>
> 'Yes, indeed: I never like my life so well as when I am on horseback, having a great gallop. I think of nothing. I only feel myself strong and happy.' (1, 164)

Grandcourt is a tired and lifeless figure, almost as emotionally arid as Edward Casaubon in *Middlemarch*. Both of them impose harsh limits on their wives, and both of them seek to continue these limitations into the indefinite future through their respective wills. A last will and testimony is, of itself, a significant gesture because, as Gillian Beer (1983) has noted, wills are 'frail and often stultifying attempts to subdue the future to our purposes'.[18] Casaubon and Grandcourt seek to establish causes in order to generate or, perhaps more accurately, to prevent certain events, but reality shows itself to be recalcitrant in its willingness to be moulded to one individual's desire. The attempt to control chance is fundamentally flawed: a harsh lesson which many gamblers have to learn.

The conversation, detailed above, between Grandcourt and Gwendolen, in which she declares a love of horse riding is one instance in which Gwendolen Harleth is being completely honest. She is genuinely thrilled by horse riding. Her thirst for living, however, is thwarted by the restrictive nature of her society, particularly after her marriage. It is significant that, on more than one occasion, she is compared to a horse. She is, for example, referred to as 'a young race-horse in the paddock' (1, 32) and 'a high-mettled racer' (1, 148). During her engagement to Grandcourt, before the relationship sours, she sees horses as 'symbols of power and luxury' (2, 43) which, at this stage of the narrative, reflects her expectations of her own future. Later, when the extent of the error she has made in marrying Grandcourt becomes apparent to her, she is 'like an imprisoned dumb creature' (3, 68). By being compared to an animal she is reduced to being a possession: a creature of a lower order, devoid of the ability or opportunity to exercise control over her own life. Like a race horse she is the plaything of an upper-class man.

When Deronda is reintroduced to Gwendolen the two of them strike up a conversation about gambling.

> 'Mr Deronda, you must enlighten my ignorance. I want to know why you thought it wrong for me to gamble. Is it because I am a woman?'
>
> 'Not altogether; but I regretted it the more because you were a woman,' said Deronda, with an irrepressible smile. Apparently it must be understood between them now that it was he who sent the necklace. 'I think it would be better for men not to gamble. It is a besotting kind of taste, likely to turn into a disease. And, besides, there is something revolting to me in raking a heap of money together, and internally chuckling over it, when others are feeling the loss of it. I should even call it base, if it were more than an exceptional lapse. There are enough inevitable turns of fortune which force us to see that our gain is another's loss: – that is one of the ugly aspects of life. One would like to reduce it as much as one could, not get amusement out of exaggerating it.' Deronda's voice had gathered some indignation while he was speaking. (2, 89–90)

The tone of Gwendolen's question and its careful construction suggests that she is merely making polite and, on the surface, trivial conversation. Deronda commences by replying in kind, but his attitude rapidly hardens. Gwendolen is affected by his words, possibly because she feels that she is a practitioner of the avarice scorned by Deronda as, by accepting Grandcourt's proposal, she has disenfranchised his existing, albeit illegitimate, family. Deronda's heartfelt denunciation of gambling may reflect the author's own anti-gambling polemic, although Deronda's perspective on gambling is consistent with his generally humanitarian position. Deronda is opposed to exploitation, whether economic or emotional, and he has to turn away from contemporary society and seek salvation in an endeavour to construct a Jewish homeland, which was in reality a developing preoccupation in the 1870s. The Jewish race is admired within *Daniel Deronda* for its cultural continuity. Shuttleworth notes: 'Jewish culture represented for her [Eliot] the virtues of organic historical growth without the attendant disadvantages of the corruption of the English social organism'.[19] Eliot's utopia requires an unblemished history, characterized by uncorrupted development. Deronda has to leave Western society and Western history which, for the narrator, is morally irrecoverable, leaving behind Gwendolen in her barrenness. Western European civilization in *Daniel Deronda* has lost its way, first perceived in the novel as a loose congregation of gamblers, morally and culturally uprooted. By contrast, the Cohen family, with whom Deronda becomes involved, are steadfast. When Deronda leaves England at the end of the novel, he finally gives up on Victorian England.

Gwendolen's anxieties concerning her marriage are brushed aside on her actual wedding day, although it is the attendant crowd's attention that causes her most satisfaction.

> She had wrought herself up to much the same condition as that in which she stood at the gambling-table when Deronda was looking at her, and she began to lose. There was enjoyment in it: whatever uneasiness a growing conscience had created, was disregarded as an ailment might have been, amidst the gratification of that ambitious vanity and desire for luxury within her which it would take a great deal of slow poisoning to kill. (2, 116)

Gwendolen is on the cusp of her fortunes at this point. She is reminded on her wedding day of the moment at the roulette table when she began to lose. The reminiscence is unwittingly prophetic, for her wedding, too, marks a point after which she is set to lose, in this case spectacularly. Grandcourt is as impassive and as inaccessible as the forces of chance which dominate the roulette table; moreover he has the capacity to be wilfully cruel. Gwendolen's disposition at the altar further resembles her conduct at the roulette table, as she is conscious of attention and risk. Her marriage represents elevation for her but it is also an uncertain step. The moment, however, is clearly exhilarating for her: 'she felt herself standing at the game of life with many eyes upon her, daring everything to win much – or if to lose, still with *éclat* and a sense of importance' (2, 117). Gwendolen Harleth is the centre of the universe at this point in her experience. The material world appears to validate her own desires. Unfortunately this feeling, like the sense of herself as a talisman that she experienced at the roulette table, is illusory or, at best, short lived. She pays heavily for her moments of supremacy. Grandcourt confirms his cruelty by making Lydia Glasher and her children the principal beneficiaries of his will. Gwendolen's many and varied gambles, which she perceives as a potential means of liberation, are, without exception, disabling.

Gwendolen's marriage turns sour at a rapid pace. She increasingly looks towards Deronda as a source of spiritual rejuvenation. From the first chapter of the novel, when she believes that he exerts a malign influence over her play, Gwendolen gradually comes to perceive in Deronda an alternative perspective on life in which naked personal ambition is rejected in favour of a more generous, collectivist position. In a further conversation with him she sets aside social niceties and asks him a direct question: 'Suppose I had gambled again, and lost the necklace again, what should you have thought of me?' 'Worse than I do now' (2, 256). The question itself is the key point. Gwendolen is generally only interested in courting admiration, but with Deronda she seeks an honest appraisal. At one point in the conversation she reproaches him.

> 'You must tell me then what to think and what to do; else why did you not let me go on doing as I liked, and not minding? If I had gone on gambling I might have won again, and I might have got not to care for anything else. You would not let me do that. Why shouldn't I do as I like, and not mind? Other people do.' Poor Gwendolen's speech expressed nothing very clearly except her irritation. (2, 257)

The childlike and petulant nature of Gwendolen's speech indicates her sincerity. Her momentary resentful outburst against Deronda is also an expression of deep unhappiness in the context of much more fundamental growing pains. Gwendolen's desire to revert to the roulette table is also a wish for the restoration of control over her own life and her environment.

Gwendolen repeatedly uses images from gambling when assessing her life. As her fortunes continue to decline she considers the full consequences of her previous actions: 'it was all a part of that new gambling in which the losing was not simply a *minus*, but a terrible *plus* that had never entered into her reckoning' (3, 81). A loss is not an act in isolation: it percolates through into other areas of life. Gwendolen's reflection is oblique but it suggests that, in her life, the errors she has made in the chances she has taken have not simply resulted in the loss of the stake. Instead, one ill-advised risk has catalyzed a series of misfortunes. Gwendolen's knowledge of Grandcourt's illicit family, which comes to her before she marries him, creates the conditions in which he can humiliate her by openly visiting Lydia Glasher after the marriage. Later, in a conversation with Deronda, Gwendolen refers back to their earlier conversation and reinforces the idea of her life as a gamble: 'I wanted to make my gain out of another's loss – you remember? – it was like roulette' (3, 225). Gwendolen gambles when she marries Grandcourt and is aware of the scale of the risk because she is aware of Lydia Glasher. By gratifying her own narcissistic desires she does wrong and in due course she is punished. The scale of her suffering, however, outweighs her misdeeds because when she accepts Grandcourt she makes one of two available choices, the other being life as a governess. Fate presents Gwendolen with a 'Heads I win, Tails you lose' situation and she chooses the most dangerous option which at least offers the possibility of success although, in reality, it delivers abject failure. Her gamble in marriage also has a philanthropic dimension as it secures the financial well-being of her mother. Gwendolen's despair in marriage deepens to the extent that she eventually assists in her husband's death by not throwing him a rope as he drowns. Grandcourt's cruelty has desensitized his wife more effectively than gambling ever could.

Towards the end of *Daniel Deronda* George Eliot reintroduces her own view of gambling through the character of Lapidoth. Lapidoth has exploited his daughter, Mirah, and she has fled from him. From early on, when he is mentioned in passing by Mirah, she states that 'he was continually at a gambling-house' (1, 324). Mirah further relates an account given by her brother, Ezra: 'he says that my father had taken to gambling, which makes people easily distressed, and then again exalted' (3, 161). This signifies an unstable and unreliable personality. When Lapidoth appears he is shallow and duplicitous. Having begged some money from Mirah, he considers his next course of action.

> The father Lapidoth had quitted his daughter at the doorstep, ruled by that possibility of staking something in play or betting which presented itself with the handling of any sum beyond the price of starving actual hunger, and left no care for alternative prospects or resolutions. Until he had lost everything he never considered whether he would apply to Mirah again or whether he would brave his son's presence. In the first moment he had shrunk from encountering Ezra as he would have shrunk from any other situation of disagreeable constraint; and the possession of Mirah's purse was enough to banish the thought of future necessities. The gambling appetite is more absolutely dominant than bodily hunger, which can be neutralised by an emotional or intellectual excitation; but the passion for watching chances – the habitual suspensive poise of the mind in actual or imaginary play – nullifies the susceptibility to other excitation. In its final, imperious stage, it seems the unjoyous dissipation of demons, seeking diversion on the burning marl of perdition. (3, 350–1)

At a certain point in this paragraph, in the sentence beginning 'The gambling appetite', the narrator steps forward to present an aggressive, anti-gambling polemic. Lapidoth's thoughts are left behind and a more didactic procedure is adopted. Gambling in Lapidoth is, unambiguously, a sign of evil.

Lapidoth steals Deronda's ring and thereafter disappears, an act that paradoxically has benign consequences as it paves the way for Deronda's proposal of marriage to Mirah. Lapidoth's behaviour also demonstrates the strengths of family and community ties. His maltreated daughter is willing to welcome him back into the protection of the family. Jewish culture is shown to be solid and stable. Lapidoth's appearance in *Daniel Deronda* is brief and potentially destructive. His gambling addiction is central to the portrayal of his personality. Eliot is returning to familiar territory by using gambling as a signifier for personal irresponsibility. The ground, however, is never fully reclaimed because, in a sense, Eliot has already achieved too much with gambling in the character of Gwendolen Harleth. The contrast between Lapidoth's and Gwendolen's gambling could scarcely be greater: in him it is merely a sordid addiction, whereas for her it is the embodiment of her whole desire, frustration and hunger, connected by implication to wider struggles for independence in the 1860s and '70s.

George Eliot's robust hostility to gambling is documented occasionally in her letters and features repeatedly in her novels. Characters who rely on chance are condemned because, in so doing, they are neglecting their duty. However, Eliot was also keen to represent gambling with some degree of accuracy. She visited the horse races at Newmarket in September 1874 and she also gave serious thought to whether it was correct for Lush, Grandcourt's companion in *Daniel Deronda*, to say 'I will take odds' or 'I will lay odds' in chapter thirteen.[20] Each of the novels considered in this chapter offers a different perspective on gambling (from personal irresponsibility in *Silas Marner*, to impulsive weakness in *Middlemarch*, to frustrated ambition in *Daniel Deronda*), but there are also connections to be drawn between the works. Both Tertius Lydgate and Gwendolen Harleth begin by seeing the world as an index of possibilities. Both are finally compelled to accept defeat. Having had their idealistic aspirations thwarted in the harsh, actual world, they undertake a compensatory form of action. Lydgate and Gwendolen, both ambitious, are both broken by the nature of the society that they inhabit, which places insurmountable obstacles in their idealistic, romantic conceptions of the universe and their own place therein. Furthermore, Gwendolen and Lydgate both continue to gamble after they have started to lose, illustrating their vitality, their need to live with energy and momentum, but also their reluctance to face up to reality. In the aftermath of their respective defeats in life, they are, like the victims of conquering civilizations, confined to the pursuit of chance.[21] Gwendolen Harleth's fate is especially tragic. As the novel opens she is a gambler, but as it progresses she becomes both gambler and stake as she desperately hazards her future in a high-risk marriage. Gwendolen at the roulette table at the beginning of the novel signifies her own adventurous personality, and it further suggests precariousness, with the future being handed over to the forces of chance. In the aftermath of the publication of *Origin of Species* (1859), evolutionism had unsettled the intellectual and spiritual fabric of society. From this perspective the character of Gwendolen Harleth at the roulette table highlights the centrality of chance, but whereas nature is indifferent to human desires, Gwendolen Harleth's society is determined to maintain her in a lowly and ornamental position, and thus her ambition is denied any constructive outlet. Instead, she gambles and loses as the economics of the gaming-table insist that fortune is distributed upwards.

chapter six

'Doctrines of Chance'

Gambling as the Universal Trope in Thomas Hardy

Thomas Hardy knew practically nothing about gambling. On 26 May 1880, he went to Epsom on Derby Day. The incident is briefly recorded in *The Life of Thomas Hardy*.

> On his way he noticed that 'all the people going to the races have a twinkle in their eye, particularly the old men'. He lunched there with a friend, and together they proceeded, by permission, through Lord Roseberry's grounds to the Down. They saw and examined the favourite before he emerged – neither of the twain knowing anything of race-horses or betting – 'the jockeys in their greatcoats; little ghastly men looking half-putrid, standing silent and apathetic while their horses were rubbed down, and saddles adjusted'; till they passed on into the paddock, and the race was run, and the shouts arose, and they 'were greeted by a breeze of tobacco-smoke and orange-peels'.[1]

Hardy describes the participants and the atmosphere, but not the gambling, despite the fact that on-course betting was both legal and widespread. Similarly, in Hardy's fiction, references to gambling in its social context are few and far between. Hardy's gambling episodes tend to intensify an aspect of the narrative which has already been presented. In addition, his use of gambling connects with his wider idea of the centrality of chance.

An image from gambling appears in Hardy's first novel, *Desperate Remedies* (1871).[2] On the eve of Cytherea Graye's ill-advised marriage to Aeneas Manston, she hears a branch splintering from a tree and it sounds like a man 'shaking a dice' (p. 268). At this point in her life her destiny is the subject of a gamble. A different aspect of gambling is presented in *Far from the Madding Crowd* (1874).[3] Gambling appears in the novel in relation to the character of Sergeant Troy. In chapter thirty-nine he and Bathsheba return from the horse races. He has lost money belonging to her, an act signifying his lack of consideration for her. She, however, is clearly upset by his conduct: 'you have lost more than a hundred pounds in a month by this dreadful horse-racing' (p. 298). She is emotionally affected while he is indifferent; this brief incident is representative of their relationship and its fundamental flaws. In chapter forty-five Troy again visits Budmouth races but on this occasion he does not gamble, partly as a result of Bathsheba's entreaties, but mainly because he is saving his money for Fanny Robin. Troy's conduct illustrates where his affections really lie; Fanny Robin is more important to him than gambling, whereas his wife's wishes are always secondary to his own. Fanny's death, and the subsequent damage inflicted on her grave by nature, has a decisive impact on Troy: 'he simply threw up his cards and forswore his game for that time and always' (p. 365). At this point he disappears from the narrative until he returns at Greenhill Fair (ch. 50). The presence of the fair is one respect in which Hardy connects with his wider social context. As E.P. Thompson (1991) has noted: 'until late in the nineteenth century there was still a network of fairs held throughout the country (. . .) at which a fraternity of pedlars, card sharpers, real or pretended gypsies, ballad mongers and hawkers were in attendance'.[4] Hardy's presentation of the fair at Greenhill does not focus on gambling but his description of Troy's theft of an important piece of paper from Bathsheba is significant: 'the moment had come for saving his game, and Troy impulsively felt that he would play the card' (p. 400). Hardy's use of metaphor presents Troy as a reckless adventurer.

The Return of the Native (1878)

In *The Return of the Native*, Hardy's sixth published novel, a lengthy bout of gambling is placed at the centre of the action. *The Return of the Native* takes frantic and obsessed individuals and pits them against Egdon Heath, a virtually pre-historic terrain in which the entire action of the novel takes place.[5] The novel is set in the 1840s,[6] a significant phase in the history of nineteenth-century gambling, featuring the 1844 Select Committee on Gaming and the 1845 Gaming Act. In *The Return of the Native*, however, these events simply do not feature. Egdon Heath is a world apart, where the impact of wider social and political developments is muted. Paradoxically, this in itself is a reflection of the nature of life in rural, southern communities throughout the nineteenth century, as James Gindin (1969) has noted: 'although most of England became increasingly urban and industrial in the latter half of the nineteenth century, Dorset remained more agricultural and its populace more committed to the popular beliefs and superstitions surviving from earlier ages'.[7]

Within the novel, a network of relationships is altered by the desires of the characters and by the reverberations of chance incidents. The novel was originally rejected by Hardy's publisher, Leslie Stephen, editor of *The Cornhill*, who felt that there was a 'dangerous' potential in the relations between the characters.[8] Perhaps in response to this, Hardy changed the ending that he had originally planned for *The Return of the Native* and created the marriage between Diggory Venn and Thomasin Yeobright. The novel, therefore, ends happily, but the bulk of *The Return of the Native* is characterized by tense relationships and the consequences of random incidents, most notably (with regard to this discussion) the night-time gamble on the heath. In order to examine the full significance of the gamble it is necessary to first consider the characters whom it most affects and the environment in which it takes place, as both are significant with regard to the progress and resolution of the gamble.

Egdon Heath is the arena for the whole of the novel. It pervades and frequently participates in the action. The opening two paragraphs introduce us to its fundamental qualities.

> A Saturday afternoon in November was approaching the time of twilight, and the vast tract of unenclosed wild known as Egdon Heath embrowned itself moment by moment. Overhead the hollow stretch of whitish cloud shutting out the sky was as a tent which had the whole heath for its floor.
>
> The heaven being spread with this pallid screen and the earth with the darkest vegetation, their meeting-line at the horizon was clearly marked. In such contrast the heath wore the appearance of an instalment of night which had taken up its place before its astronomical hour was come: darkness had to a great extent arrived hereon, while day stood distinct in the sky. Looking upwards, a furze-cutter would have been inclined to continue work; looking down, he would have decided to finish his faggot and go home. The distant rims of the world and of the firmament seemed to be a division in time no less than a division in matter. The face of the heath by its mere complexion added half an hour to evening; it could in like manner retard the dawn, sadden noon, anticipate the frowning of storms scarcely generated, and intensify the opacity of a moonless midnight to a cause of shaking and dread. (p. 3)

The heath is dark, separate and out of time. Its darkness curtails the day. It is removed from the everyday world, populated only by a hypothetical furze-cutter, contrasting the brightness of the sky with the dimness of the earth. The heath has no immediate historical context. Its elemental simplicity renders it timeless: an enduring, pre-historic land-scape. At times it appears to be static: 'the sea changed, the fields changed, the rivers, the villages, and the people changed, yet Egdon remained' (p. 7). Change, however, is in evidence despite surface appearances to the contrary: 'this was not the repose of actual stagna-tion, but the apparent repose of incredible slowness' (p. 12). This quietly stated contrast sets in place an enduring opposition in the book, namely, fixity versus change. The sparse serenity of the heath contrasts with the feverish activity of the characters living on and around it.

The first stark contrast presented in the novel occurs when Diggory Venn is seen by Eustacia Vye's grandfather, walking across the heath.

> When he drew nearer he perceived it to be a spring van, ordinary in shape, but singular in colour, this being a lurid red. The driver walked beside it; and, like his van, he was completely red. One dye of that tincture covered his clothes, the cap upon his head, his boots, his face and his hands. He was not temporarily overlaid with the colour: it permeated him. (p. 9)

The contrast between Venn and the heath is most explicitly stated in terms of colour. The vivid red of Venn stands out against the darkness of his surroundings. Thus, from the outset, he is defined as the outsider. He does not fit in with the landscape although, like the heath, his outer passivity masks an active interior. His distinct appearance also separates him from every other character in the novel. Red is usually associated with passion, aggression, the demonic and the savage. As the novel progresses Venn exhibits each one of these qualities. He can be loving and devoted towards Thomasin Yeobright, his eventual wife, yet stand against Damon Wildeve, his rival suitor and the man against whom he gambles.

Damon Wildeve, Venn's rival, is, as his name suggests, undisciplined and impetuous. His switch in career from engineer to publican suggests a wayward disposition. His initial inability to supply the correct wedding certificate for Thomasin, and his clandestine meetings with Eustacia, show irresponsibility. He is capricious and inconstant in his affections, telling Eustacia that, 'the scales are balanced so nicely that a feather would turn them' (p. 97), when she enquires about his feelings. He is set on a collision course with Diggory Venn, whose unrecipro-cated love for Thomasin is stronger than Wildeve's own affections. Eustacia Vye, the tragic heroine of *The Return of the Native*, further complicates the situation. She has an affair with Wildeve but marries Thomasin's cousin, Clym. He is the returned native, coming back from Paris to his home on the heath. Eustacia associates him with the prospect of liberation. She wrongly thinks that he will take her to France. When she hears that he is coming to Egdon Heath, her thoughts become 'as animated as water under a microscope' (p. 127). Hardy's use of the idea of intense, microscopic focus on a character or incident is reintroduced and sustained throughout the gambling chapter. Eustacia feels stultified by the heath but it is an integral and inescapable aspect of her make-up. This is apparent when she is first sighted by Diggory Venn.

> There the form stood, motionless as the hill beneath. Above the plain rose the hill, above the hill rose the barrow, and above the barrow rose the figure. Above the figure was nothing that could be mapped elsewhere than on a celestial globe.
>
> Such a perfect, delicate, and necessary finish did the figure give to the dark pile of hills that it seemed to be the only obvious justification of their outline. Without it, there was the dome without the lantern; with it the architectural demands of the mass were satisfied. The scene was strangely homogenous, in that the vale, the upland, the barrow, and the figure above it amounted only to unity. Looking at this or that member of the group was not observing a complete thing, but a fraction of a thing. (p. 13)

Eustacia is associated with death, the heath and a sense of aspiration. She is standing on a barrow, a pre-historic burial mound. She is a part of the landscape, harmoniously, if involuntarily, blending in with her environment. She strives to be in the ascendant, climbing to the very peak of the hill. Like other characters in the novel she is defined in relation to the heath. Eustacia, Wildeve, Thomasin and Clym are linked in a state of virtually helpless attraction to one another, an attraction which is obsessive and largely unexplained. The reader can understand why Eustacia is attracted to Clym, but Diggory Venn's deep love for Thomasin is not fully explored. He, too, is affected by an irrational, gravitational pull. Collisions are inevitable. Clym cannot emotionally satisfy both his mother and his wife, as neither can comfortably tolerate the affection vouchsafed on the other. Thomasin cannot give herself to both Venn and Wildeve. The impassive heath bears witness to a series of feverish quests.

The gamble at the centre of *The Return of the Native* is a game of poker dice for one hundred guineas and it directs much of the rest of the action. An event featuring dramatic changes occurs on Egdon Heath, a landscape of conspicuous, if misleading, fixity. To separate the gamblers from their environment, however, is not a neat demarcation. The heath intrudes on the game as its life forms (insects, moths and horses) interrupt the gamblers. Egdon Heath is a strong and atmospheric presence, to such an extent that it is virtually a participant in the proceedings. It is the active context for the gamble. The gamble is an agent for change disrupting a previously fixed course, as the incorrect distribution of money in the aftermath of the gamble causes irrecoverable animosity between Eustacia Vye and Mrs Yeobright. The characters involved directly in the gamble, however, are not necessarily the most important figures in the novel as a whole. In a letter to Arthur Hopkins (the illustrator of *The Return of the Native*), dated 8 February 1878, Hardy set out the importance of the characters as he saw it.

> The order of importance of the characters is as follows.
> 1 Clym Yeobright
> 2 Eustacia
> 3 Thomasin & the reddleman
> 4 Wildeve
> 5 Mrs Yeobright.[9]

One of the characters who gambles in *The Return of the Native*, Christian Cantle, does not even figure in this chart. Furthermore, neither of the other two gamblers is classified as one of the two most important characters in the novel. However, the gamble in *The Return of the Native* is critically important because it affects everybody, creating discord between Clym, his wife and his mother. It also leads on quite quickly to the death of Mrs Yeobright. The subsequent emotional gap between Clym and Eustacia facilitates her reunion with Wildeve.

The Return of the Native consists of six parts. The gambling episode occurs at the end of part three, subtitled 'The Fascination'. This refers to the developing relationship between Eustacia Vye and Clym Yeobright, with Eustacia in particular being fascinated by the outsider with whom she associates the prospect of escaping Egdon Heath. 'The Fascination' also refers to the attraction of gambling for the three characters whom it affects directly: Diggory Venn, Damon Wildeve and Christian Cantle. When they gamble they become oblivious to external stimuli. The game of dice functions as the inevitable collision between Venn and Wildeve. It is a kind of shorthand, playing through in abbreviated form a struggle between two men in love with the same woman. Gambling provides the context for the resolution of their animosity. They are not simply gambling for money. They are also competing for psychological and moral supremacy. Venn gains a considerable advantage over his adversary in the former domain, and morally there is no contest between them. Venn's eventual prosperity may suggest that a moral message is being presented but this is countered by Wildeve's undeserved good fortune when he receives an inheritance. Their night-time meeting on the heath brings one thread of the plot to a close and, more significantly, it puts in place the chain of events which dominate the second half of the novel. Both Eustacia and Mrs Yeobright die as an indirect result of the gamble, and of Clym's subsequent inability to communicate with his loved ones. 'The Closed Door', the title of the fourth book of *The Return of the Native*, establishes an image of irrecoverability. The closed door presented by Eustacia to Mrs Yeobright leads directly to the latter's death. The emotional block between Clym and his wife and his mother is also a closed door. The gamble indirectly propels them into a position of mutual emotional inaccessibility.

The gambling episode begins in the chapter entitled 'The Morning and the Evening of a Day'. The opening move is another chance event, a raffle in The Quiet Woman inn decided by the casting of dice. The participants each contribute a shilling and the highest score takes the prize.[10] The specific theme of invoking chance with dice is introduced. The prize, material for a dress, is won by Christian Cantle. He feels empowered by his good fortune and by the means by which it has been brought about: 'what curious creatures these dice be – powerful rulers of us all, and yet at my command!' (p. 262). Christian is timid, simple and superstitious. His triumph in the raffle is useless to him as he has neither a wife nor a sweetheart. Hardy deflates the mystique of luck through this feckless character. Wildeve becomes aware of the fact that Christian is carrying money for Thomasin and Clym, as an indiscreet remark by Christian concerning the contents of his boots provokes his suspicion: 'Wildeve became lost in thought, and a look of inward illumination came into his eyes. It was money for his wife that Mrs. Yeobright could not trust him with' (p. 263). The two are followed at a distance by Diggory Venn who, unbeknownst to the other characters, has witnessed everything from a secluded corner of the inn.

In the original drafting of the novel, it is clearly implied that Wildeve, at this point in the narrative, deliberately seeks to take the money away from Cantle, as he says to himself, 'we will see if what belongs to the wife doesn't belong to the husband too'.[11] Furthermore, the original draft also excluded the passage in which Venn witnesses Cantle leaving the inn with Wildeve.[12] The final, published version of *The Return of the Native* is therefore more toned down than the original draft, to the extent that Wildeve's initial reasons for accompanying Cantle are not wholly mercenary, and Venn's subsequent appearance on the heath is explained in the text. The reader is slowly, rather than dramatically, prepared for the gambling scene, which is, in itself, intensely dramatic.

Later in the same chapter, Wildeve's intentions are again modified from the original draft to the final version. In the original, the narrator offers this analysis of Wildeve's reasons for pursuing the gamble with Cantle:

> as the minutes passed he had gradually formed an angry intention without knowing the precise moment of forming it.[13]

The published version of *The Return of the Native* contains a significant amendment:

> as the minutes passed he had gradually drifted into a revengeful intention without knowing the precise moment of forming it. (p. 268)

In the original draft Wildeve becomes frustrated, but in the final version his anger is more focused as he seeks revenge. Paradoxically, however, his arrival at this position in the final text is not a conscious process. Instead, he drifts towards seeking revenge. In the published version of *The Return of the Native*, Wildeve gradually arrives at a position in which he seeks to take Cantle's money in order to have his revenge on Mrs Yeobright and, once his thought process has unravelled, his position becomes unequivocal: 'it was extremely doubtful, by the time the twentieth guinea had been reached, whether Wildeve was conscious of any other intention than that of winning for his own personal benefit' (p. 269). The gamble in *The Return of the Native* finally evolves out of the narrative, with the characters responding both to external events and to inner feelings and frustrations.

The initial gamble between Christian and Wildeve is not, on Christian's part, wholly voluntary. He is induced to gamble by Wildeve, who entrances him with increasingly fabulous tales of gambling successes. This places Wildeve in a commanding position from the outset. It also establishes that he is unscrupulous. One of the stories he tells is of particular interest.

> 'Then there was a man of London, who was only a waiter at White's clubhouse. He began playing first half-crown stakes, and then higher and higher, till he became very rich, got an appointment in India, and rose to be Governor of Madras. His daughter married a member of parliament, and the Bishop of Carlisle stood godfather to one of the children.' (p. 266)

Allegedly, the essential details of this story are correct, with Sir Thomas Rumbold, an eighteenth-century Governor of Madras, having commenced his career as a waiter at White's. By re-telling it through Wildeve, however, Hardy attracted written complaints from two separate people claiming to be descendants of Rumbold.[14] In the original serial publication Rumbold was named, but when *The Return of the Native* appeared in book form his name, though not the anecdote itself, was deleted. There is therefore some limited connection between Hardy's gamblers and their wider context, although it is equally apparent that the gamble in *The Return of the Native* has a primarily narrative function.

Once the betting begins it arrests both characters. Wildeve directs the rays of a lantern upon a flat stone, the arena for the game. Everything else is excluded: 'both men became so absorbed in the game that they took no heed of anything but the pigmy objects immediately beneath their eyes; the flat stone, the open lantern, the dice, and the few illuminated fern-leaves which lay under the light, were the whole world to them' (p. 268). In this extract Hardy lists, like a simple formula, the temporary cosmos of Wildeve and Christian. The paraphernalia of the game is imbued with colossal significance. This is because the dice (small, material objects in themselves) have become, overtly, determinants: within a brief period of time their physical arrangement will alter the fortunes of Wildeve and Christian. The intensity of the situation, and of gambling as a whole, largely relies upon the speed with which it passes from enigma to resolution.[15] Wildeve and Christian decide to gamble, cast the dice and transfer the money with considerable haste.

In the first gambling scene in *The Return of the Native*, Wildeve wins all the money. Although his initial intention was simply to teach Thomasin's aunt a lesson, once he has won the money he resolves to keep it. He is, moreover, unsympathetic towards Christian whom he has clearly exploited, in so far as he induces him to gamble. Although the chances are theoretically equal on either side, Wildeve conducts the proceedings throughout. At this point Diggory Venn steps in, which introduces a new chapter, 'A New Force Disturbs the Current'. Venn's arrival, unexpected by Wildeve, is a sudden factor to be taken into account and events are set to be altered once again. His emergence on the heath in the immediate aftermath of Christian's defeat by Wildeve is ghost-like: 'a figure rose from behind a neighbouring bush and came forward into the lantern light. It was the reddleman approaching' (p. 270). The title of the chapter implies that Venn is active. He is a substantial opponent for Wildeve. The contest between Wildeve and Christian is merely a preliminary bout: this is the main event. Wildeve, theoretically, has the option of declining the contest but he does not do so. The narrator intervenes at this point, by way of explanation: 'now, gambling is a species of amusement which is much more easily begun with full pockets than left off with the same' (p. 271). The narrator is not generally opinionated in *The Return of the Native* and it is therefore a little surprising that the narrative voice interrupts the proceedings at this point. However, Wildeve's willingness to gamble with Venn when he has already won a substantial amount can hardly occur without some explanation, and to present it as a kind of aphorism deals with the issue neatly and conclusively. It is expressed as a homespun, inarguable wisdom.

At this point the landscape is practically mythical. Civilization is absent. The characters meet on a deserted part of a desolate heath at night-time. Venn has witnessed both the build-up to the gamble between Wildeve and Christian and the gamble itself. He has also seen Wildeve's callous celebration of his victory. Venn is here to set right this wrong. He has the status of an avenging angel. His words are calm and measured, his body language deliberate.

> Wildeve was a nervous and excitable man; and the game was beginning to tell upon his temper. He writhed, fumed, shifted his seat; and the beating of his heart was almost audible. Venn sat with his lips impassively closed and eyes reduced to a pair of unimportant twinkles; he scarcely appeared to breathe. He might have been an Arab, or an automaton; he would have been like a red-sandstone statue but for the motion of his arm with the dice-box. (p. 272)

Shortly afterwards, Venn is referred to as 'the red automaton' (p. 273). The absence of passions apparently enhances his abilities as a gambler, given the subsequent turn of events. Venn becomes the personification of chance as he is impassive and inaccessible, yet paradoxically he is also deeply invested in this struggle. The context of the gamble is small, Egdon Heath, but, through the mythic undertones, massive. In the ensuing contest Venn provokes Wildeve into a state of frustration and self-directed aggression. To an extent, Wildeve defeats himself. In the battle with dice, conversation is limited. Venn is at his most expansive when he repeats to Wildeve the fabulous stories of gambling success with which Wildeve had initially beguiled Christian.

> By this time a change had come over the game; the reddleman won continually. At length sixty guineas – Thomasin's fifty, and ten of Clym's – had passed into his hands. Wildeve was reckless, frantic, exasperated.
> '"Won back his coat,"' said Venn slily.
> Another throw, and the money went the same way.
> '"Won back his hat,"' continued Venn.
> 'Oh, oh!' said Wildeve.
> '"Won back his watch, won back his money, and went out of the door a

rich man,"' added Venn sentence by sentence, as stake after stake passed over to him. (pp. 272–3)

Here, Venn is, in effect, functioning as a mirror for Wildeve, forcing him to view his misdeeds. Wildeve does not like what he sees.

This second gamble is even more intense than the first. In a moment of extreme frustration Wildeve throws the dice away and they are only able to retrieve one. However, the game continues with the single die. This focuses the action still further as there is now only one object upon which so much depends. After a brief interval play is interrupted.

Ten minutes passed away. Then a large death's head moth advanced from the obscure outer air, wheeled twice round the lantern, flew straight at the candle and extinguished it by the force of the blow. Wildeve had just thrown, but had not lifted the box to see what he had cast; and now it was impossible. (p. 274)

Another sudden incident transforms the situation. The removal of the light is as instantaneous and dramatic as the revelation of the die. Wildeve and Venn gather thirteen glow-worms to illuminate the field of play, thus enabling them to keep on gambling. Wildeve in particular is desperate to continue with the game. The gamblers are also periodically interrupted by heath-croppers, wild horses grazing on Egdon Heath, 'dusky forms' gazing intently at the players (p. 274). The accumulative effect here is both ghostly and portentous. The death's head moth, the thirteen glow-worms, the scarcely visible silent observers, all serve to create a spectral and slightly sinister atmosphere. The worms throw 'a pale phosphoric shine' (p. 275) over the proceedings. There is also a significant contrast between the gamblers and their location: 'the incongruity between the men's deeds and their environment was great. Amid the soft juicy vegetation of the hollow in which they sat, the motionless and the uninhabited solitude, intruded the chink of guineas, the rattle of dice, the exclamations of the reckless players' (p. 275). The gamblers are a contaminating presence, disrupting the atmosphere of the heath.

The game concludes when Venn casts the die and it splits in two. Wildeve takes the view that this 'zero' score beats his own ace. There is no logic in this position and Venn is quite willing to concede the point. Wildeve, however, is adamant. In effect he surrenders his last five guineas. There is no obvious reason for this. Wildeve may be burdened psychologically by gaining the money unfairly in the first place and therefore by losing the money to Venn he releases his guilt. However, he is not, on the whole, unduly troubled by his conscience. Alternatively, he may simply be exhausted, a victim of battle fatigue. As he leaves the scene of the gamble he sees Eustacia passing in a carriage with Clym Yeobright: 'Wildeve forgot the loss of the money at the sight of his lost love' (p. 277). His gambling loss is echoed by his emotional loss and, like Troy in *Far from the Madding Crowd*, lost love hurts more than lost money.

The gambling scene in *The Return of the Native* becomes fateful as it dictates subsequent events, with the narrator noting the effects of the incorrect distribution of the money: 'it was an error which afterwards helped to cause more misfortune than treble the loss in money value could have done' (p. 279). The gamble and its aftermath causes havoc in the lives of the gamblers and those closest to them. The problem here (and this raises arguably the most paradoxical feature of gambling in general) is that, on the one hand, gambling suggests that everything is random and governed by the vagaries of chance whereas, on the other hand, the deterministic impact of gambling suggests that it is, in fact, shaping fate. The latter perspective is sustainable but it is important to remember that the gamblers are oblivious to the consequences of their actions. Fate is shaped by a blind and involuntary deity. Venn and Wildeve are not conscious of the effects of their conduct. These effects, however, are very considerable in determining the fate of others. In general terms, within an evolutionary order, an individual existence is not a sufficient register for change. Gambling creates the possibility of upsetting this process because it pushes fate. This is what the game of dice in *The Return of the Native* achieves as it phrases, in narrative incident, Hardy's view of the way the universe works.[16]

The Return of the Native highlights 'the near impossibility of return'.[17] Clym is unable to step back into and reclaim his former community. His quest to improve the education and therefore the welfare of the inhabitants of the heath involves the importation of ideas that have been cultivated elsewhere. This is an untenable project because the practices that he hopes to introduce are foreign to the heath. They are environmentally unsuitable. The narrator recognises Clym Yeobright's fundamental problem: 'the rural world was not ripe for him. A man should be only partly before his time' (p. 204). He is not on the same wavelength as the people around him. After his sight fails and he becomes a furze-cutter, he blends in more effectively, at least physically, with his environment. His eventual role as a preacher suggests that he is never wholly reconciled with his community, in which religious observance is only of marginal interest. However, he does enjoy some sympathy in his final vocation, as 'everywhere he was kindly received, for the story of his life had become generally known' (p. 485). The native also returns in *The Return of the Native* in the sense that characters cannot swerve away from their obsessions. Eustacia's thirst for leaving Egdon Heath is insatiable and is one of the main causes of both her initial attraction towards Clym and the subsequent re-awakening of her interest in Wildeve, whose sudden and spectacular inheritance, eleven thousand pounds from an uncle, is seen as a blessing, as he 'had been seized upon by destiny and placed in the sunshine once more' (p. 355). In a similar fashion to the gambling scene, an unexpected reallocation of wealth impacts significantly upon subsequent events, as Wildeve's riches facilitate his desire to travel, a wish that connects with Eustacia's obsession with escaping from the heath. The native returns, as deep-rooted predilections refuse to be thwarted, but the native is also non-returnable, as a substantially altered body cannot meld smoothly back into its former environment. The title of the novel has paradoxical implications.

A Laodicean (1881)

A Laodicean[18] is one of Hardy's minor novels and is generally not highly regarded, but it is relevant to the present discussion because of the extent to which gambling features in the text. A *Saturday Review* article in 1892 described *A Laodicean* as, 'very queer people doing very queer things'.[19] Such a view is attributable in part to the fact that much of it was written while Hardy was unwell. He was, in fact, obliged to dictate much of the novel, a rough draft of which was completed by May 1881.[20] Much more recently, Peter Widdowson (1996) has suggested that *A Laodicean* is written in a satirical mode.[21] However, the present interest is not in its explicitly stylistic qualities, but rather its characterization and the importance of gambling in the construction of its personalities. The novel was first published in *Harper's Magazine* between December 1880 and December 1881. *A Laodicean* is subtitled, *A Story of To-day*. Its contemporaneity is apparent in the fact that, in the early part of the novel, George Somerset is guided to Castle De Stancy by telegraph poles. Furthermore, they are clearly a recent addition to the landscape: 'a glance at the still ungrassed heap of earth round the foot of each post was, however, sufficient to show that it was at no very remote period that they had made their advance' (p. 20). The electric telegraph system emerged in 1850 and was a significant factor in the growth of off-course betting on horse racing (see chapter one).

The novel is therefore set at some point after 1850, 'an age of railway engineering, telegraphy and the romance of scientific achievement, of tourism, photography, and revolvers'.[22] The castle itself is no longer owned by the De Stancys and the landlord of an inn explains the cause of the loss to Somerset, stating, 't'was gay manners that did it' (p. 42). Peter J. Casagrande (1982) has suggested that Castle De Stancy is to the novel what Egdon Heath is to *The Return of the Native*, namely, 'the chief internal source of commentary on human destiny in the narrative'.[23] From one perspective this is a bleak analysis as the castle is crumbling and decrepit, a relic from a bygone age. However, as Somerset is commissioned to restore and develop the castle, it also suggests the possibility of renewal.

The last of the De Stancys to own the castle was Sir William De Stancy. He is eager to give advice to Somerset, stressing the importance of luck over ability. This is a form of self-justification, with the old man implicitly attributing the demise of himself and his family to the caprice of fortune, thereby evading personal responsibility. More interestingly, when the character of Will Dare (the gambler) enters the novel, he tries to resolve the distinction between luck and ability outlined by Sir William, by seeking to employ his own talent in order to harness luck. In *The Literary Notebooks of Thomas Hardy, Volume 1*, a particular note, written in the late 1870s, foreshadows the position adopted by Sir William: 'leave off the game with fortune while you are in luck.- That is what all the best players do'.[24] Another note by Hardy, headed, 'know the star of your fortune', is similar to a remark by Sir William: 'it is better to know where your luck lies than where your talent lies' (p. 53).[25] Fortune is posited as a metaphysical entity that visits individuals at certain times. Dare harbours a contrary belief, namely that he has the mathematical means to acquire good fortune.

Sir William De Stancy is remembered by the landlord of the inn as having been involved with horse racing, keeping 'thirty race-horses in training at once'. His ownership of race horses is a telling signifier of his former wealth and status, given the sport's upper-class associations. The landlord then implies that Sir William may have lost the castle in a gamble: 'Mr Wilkins, who was the first owner after it went from Sir William, actually sat down as a guest at his table, and got up as owner' (p. 54). Later in the novel, Captain De Stancy (Sir William's son) echoes the landlord's account of the affair: 'my father sat down as host on that occasion, and arose as guest' (pp. 212–13). It is possible that this transaction was the result of a business deal rather than a gamble, but a gamble is more likely, partly because it is in keeping with the kind of lifestyle practised at that time by Sir William, and partly because it is difficult to conceive of a bargain so unfavourable that it would reduce the former nobleman to such a modest state.

Will Dare, in his first appearance in the novel, is characterized by his indeterminacy.

> His age it was impossible to say. There was not a hair on his face which could serve to hang a guess upon. In repose he appeared a boy; but his actions were so completely those of a man that the beholder's first estimate of sixteen as his age was hastily corrected to six-and-twenty, and afterwards shifted hither and thither along intervening years as the tenor of his sentences sent him up or down. He had a broad forehead, vertical as the face of a bastion, and his hair, which was parted in the middle, hung as a fringe or valance above, in the fashion sometimes affected by the other sex. He wore a heavy ring, of which the gold seemed fair, the diamond questionable, and the taste indifferent. There were the remains of a swagger in his body and limbs as he came forward, regarding Somerset with a confident smile, as if the wonder were, not why Mr Dare should be present, but why Somerset should be present likewise; and the first tone that came from Dare's lips wound up his listener's opinion that he did not like him. (pp. 58–9)

Everything about Dare is uncertain. His age is unclear, his jewellery may be inauthentic. He is, in addition, somewhat androgynous. His physical appearance is the expression of the uncertainty which pervades his whole being. Chance is central to Dare's life and conduct. As an illegitimate child his very existence was unplanned from the outset and, throughout the novel, he takes calculated risks in order to better himself. His name suggests both purpose and chance and his conduct provides an example of the former endeavouring to contain and control the latter. His efforts to unite his father with Paula Power and thereby assure his own material welfare, a calculated piece of romantic engineering, involve imposing his own ideal solution on others, regardless of their wishes.

Dare claims to have lived in 'India, Malta, Gibraltar, the Ionian Islands, and Canada' (pp. 59–60). His country of origin is a point of debate and confusion for the other characters, with Somerset thinking he is Canadian, Paula Power stating he is from the East and Charlotte De Stancy claiming he is Italian (p. 80). Dare describes himself as 'a citizen of the world' (pp. 158–9). Later in the novel, a minor character is unable to say whether he is a boy or a man (p. 111), and, on two further occasions, the narrator calls Dare 'the boy-man' (pp. 144, 358). Paula Power, when she discovers Dare's villainy, states, 'a man has to be given in charge, or a boy, or a demon' (p. 431). Even Dare's own father, Captain De Stancy, when looking at a picture of Dare, is confused by what he sees: 'his eye fell upon the portrait, with its uncertain expression of age, assured look, and hair worn in a fringe like a girl's' (p. 174). Through this series of descriptions Dare emerges as an enigma. His thought processes are generally held back from the reader. As the novel develops his life is shown to be one long gamble which is never resolved because, at the end of *A Laodicean*, he disappears to pursue his destiny elsewhere.

Dare is dependent on chance, but this does not mean that he is acquiescent to fluctuations in his fortune. On the contrary, he consciously seeks to shape chance events for his own purposes. One of the chief tools he employs to this end is a book, Abraham De Moivre's *The Doctrine of Chances*. This is an actual book, first published in 1718, and subtitled, *A Method of Calculating the Probabilities of Events in Play*.[26] The book details methods for winning at card and dice games, raffles, lotteries and investments. It has been described as 'the first modern book on probability theory' and, in addition, it is known that De Moivre used to supplement his income by calculating odds for gamblers.[27] However, *The Doctrine of Chances* offers no strategy for roulette, the game on which Dare eventually gambles most heavily, thus suggesting that Hardy's intention in introducing *The Doctrine of Chances* was to highlight Dare's reliance on chance, rather than illustrate his strategy for gambling. Dare's volume is 'as well thumbed as the minister's bible' (p. 155), indicating the importance of the text to Dare. It is his bible in the sense that it provides him with a system for living. The values espoused therein, however, are mathematical rather than ethical, and this has implications for his conduct and outlook.

Captain De Stancy does not have Dare's guile and he is therefore vulnerable to exploitation by his son. In the captain's first substantial appearance in the novel, he gives a brief recitation to his sister which commences, 'when we have made our love, and gamed our gaming' (p. 170). He is conscious of being past his prime. When he and his son meet at the church in Markton, they are prevented from leaving by the fact that Sir William De Stancy is in the churchyard. At this point Dare suggests a game of cards. He has no respect for the sanctity of the church, neither has he respect for his own father, from whom he is happy to win money. Dare tempts his father into the game, stating, with reference to the cards, 'it was by the merest chance I had them', and adding, 'I won't corrupt you' (p. 183). Captain De Stancy is not unaware of the nature of his son's conduct and he seeks to bring it to Dare's attention. His son, however, is only interested in winning the game: 'De Stancy sighed impatiently. "I wish you were less calculating, and had more of the impulse natural to your years!" "Game – by Jove! You have lost again, captain. That makes – let me see – nine pound fifteen to square us"' (p. 184). Dare is quite willing to compete mercilessly against his father, whom he does not even identify as such in language. He has no conception of the responsibilities arising out of family ties, merely an acute awareness of the personal, material opportunities that arise from them. He directs his father towards the romantic pursuit of Paula Power, with the ultimate aim of securing his own welfare. Having shown Paula to his father, he observes the consequences of his actions: '"a fermentation is beginning in him," said Dare, half pitifully; "a purely chemical process; and when it is complete he will probably be clear, and fiery, and sparkling, and quite another man than the good, weak, easy fellow that he was"' (pp. 196–7). The only emotion Dare feels at this point is a vague sense of pity, and this arises out of condescension, perhaps even contempt, for his father. Dare's comments place him in the role of the scientific observer, noting the results of an experiment. Dare constantly thinks in these impersonal, strategic terms. On a further occasion when he seeks to extort money from his father, his judgment is shown to be excellent: 'De Stancy had walked away; but Dare knew that he played a pretty sure card in that speech' (p. 236). Dare is permanently engaged in a contest, pitting his wits against an opponent. Once he has persuaded his father to pursue Paula, Captain De Stancy, too, is drawn into Dare's games. When he thinks about his rival, Somerset, the captain uses language more readily associated with Dare: 'Somerset, with a little more knowledge, would hold a card which could be played with disastrous effect against himself – his relationship to Dare' (p. 207). Captain De Stancy, having been drawn into complicity with Dare, similarly resorts to secrecy and intrigue. These references to cards in *A Laodicean* create an image of a game in which the players, particularly Dare and, to a lesser extent, De Stancy, are acutely conscious of their rivals and constantly seeking a crucial advantage.

The main gambling episode in *A Laodicean* is set in Monte Carlo. Paula, having originally travelled to Nice in the company of her uncle and Charlotte De Stancy, corresponds with Somerset by letter.

> I wish I could write anything to raise your spirits, but you may be so perverse that if, in order to do this, I tell you of the races, routs, scenery, gaieties, and gambling going on in this place and neighbourhood (into which of course I cannot help being a little drawn), you may declare that my words make you worse than ever. (p. 300)

When Somerset, after hearing that she has been joined by Captain De

Stancy, follows her to Nice, we are already aware of the nature of the surroundings in which Somerset will be placed. In point of fact, Paula and her party have moved on to Monte Carlo, 'the beautiful and sinister little spot' (p. 312), a town which is even more renowned for its gambling. As the chapter concludes, Somerset approaches the casino and we are told that he is 'in a state of indecision' (p. 313). He is taking a gamble by following Paula to this spot, risking exposure as her lover in front of her friends and relatives or, more dramatically, rejection by Paula herself. He is in the middle of a life gamble, the resolution of which is unclear. The final words of the chapter are, 'he then crossed the vestibule to the gaming-tables' (p. 313).

The casino is described as being characterized by 'tainted splendour'. In common with Eliot, Hardy sees the surface opulence of the casino compromised by the activities therein. The narrator describes the scene as Somerset looks for Paula.

> The people gathered at this negative pole of industry had come from all civilized countries; their tongues were familiar with many forms of utterance, that of each racial group or type being unintelligible in its subtler variations, if not entirely, to the rest. But the language of meum and tuum they collectively comprehended without translation. In a half-charmed spell-bound state they had congregated in knots, standing, or sitting in hollow circles round the notorious oval tables marked with figures and lines. The eyes of all these sets of people were watching the Roulette. Somerset went from table to table, looking among the loungers rather than among the regular players, for faces, or at least one face, which did not meet his gaze.[28] (p. 314)

In common with the representation of gamblers in the opening chapter of Eliot's *Daniel Deronda*, the roulette players here are in a state of stupefaction. The roulette table and the casino are mesmerisers. Somerset is removed from this process although, paradoxically, he too is involved in a gamble. His positioning at this point is a metaphor for the state of his own destiny. Whether or not he finds Paula is a matter of chance. If he does encounter her he must passively await her response. Moreover, although he does not gamble, he is not impervious to the atmosphere of the casino. We are told that the gambling, 'had that stage effect upon his imagination which is usually exercised over those who behold Chance presented to them with spectacular piquancy without advancing far enough in its acquaintance to suffer its ghastly reprisals and impish tricks' (pp. 314–15). In common with *The Return of the Native*, space is created for a narrative perspective which signifies a general disapproval of gambling.

Somerset examines closely the gamblers at the roulette table.

He beheld a hundred diametrically opposed wishes issuing from the murky intelligences around a table, and spreading down across each other upon the figured diagram in their midst, each to its own number. It was a network of hopes; which at the announcement, 'Sept, Rouge, Impair, et Manque,' disappeared like magic gossamer, to be replaced in a moment by new. (p. 315)

Having already been informed that the gamblers are entranced, this additional description creates an image of a ritualistic and magical process involving diagrams and incantations. The casino is wholly unlike Castle De Stancy, Somerset's previous environment, but it does strike a chord with the nonconformist chapel featured in the early chapters of *A Laodicean,* in which Paula Power refuses baptism by full immersion. In both situations the participants are predominantly believers, but one individual refuses to be fully committed.

Somerset does not find Paula at the casino, but he does encounter a dehumanized Will Dare, whose 'face was as rigid and dry as if it had been encrusted with plaster, and he was like one turned into a computing machine which no longer had the power of feeling' (p. 315). In the presence of a chance event in one of its more obvious forms, Dare's tendency to base his conduct on an assessment of the odds reaches a new height. However, Dare is losing at roulette. This is not surprising. Typically, a roulette wheel features thirty-seven numbers and pays odds of thirty-five to one on the winning number. Therefore, one thirty-seventh of each transaction finds its way to the house. Dare's extraordinary faith in the power of calculations leads to his being unable to see that the game operates with a built-in percentage in favour of the house. The effect that roulette has on Dare is noteworthy, as his wider scheme, of uniting his father with Paula Power, is 'overwhelmed by a rage for play' (p. 317). Dare does not generally allow his emotions to determine his conduct. The fact that he does so on this occasion suggests that the apparent failure of his system has exposed the wider possibility that his methods as a whole may not be infallible. He tries to convince Somerset that his system will prove true, but Somerset responds with cold reasoning: 'just imagine for the sake of argument that all the people who have ever placed a stake upon a certain number to be one person playing continuously. Has that imaginary person won? The existence of the bank is a sufficient answer' (p. 318). The simplicity of Somerset's arithmetic contrasts markedly with the complexity of Dare's, which is distilled through *The Doctrine of Chances*. Roulette is, finally, a mathematically unwinnable game. Dare, with his blind faith in his ability to shape events through calculation, finds this fact impossible to accept.

The greatest paradox in *A Laodicean* with regard to gambling is that Dare eventually wins at roulette, thereby restoring his faith and equanimity, although, in fact, his success is undoubtedly fortuitous. His win prompts concern in Captain De Stancy, who seeks to caution his son: 'you will be for repeating and repeating your experiments, and will end by blowing your brains out, as wiser heads than yours have done' (p. 347). De Stancy's concern for Dare is genuine, but Dare's conduct towards his father is repeatedly parasitic. The ordinary ties of kinship are of no consequence to him, possibly because, as an illegitimate son, he has never benefited emotionally from familial protection. He is clearly the master of his father, as De Stancy's acquiescent nature is ill-matched against his son's guile, but Dare can also raise the stakes when his opponent is more substantial. He is found out by Paula's uncle, Abner Power, and discovers that a gun is being pointed at him, but it transpires that Dare has his own gun which he directs back at his opponent. Thus, one of the by-products of Dare's incessant scheming is that he is rarely outwitted. However, in the final analysis he does not succeed because his most significant speculation, his attempt to marry his father to Paula Power, fails at the last moment.

When Dare is finally and completely uncovered the most serious casualty is Captain De Stancy (now Sir William De Stancy following the death of his father), as his imminent marriage to Paula is brought to a halt. The manner in which he accepts her refusal restores his honour, which had been compromised by his complicity in Dare's plans.

> De Stancy walked a few paces, then said in a low voice: 'Miss Power, I knew – I guessed just now, as soon as it began – that we were going to split on this rock. Well – let it be – it cannot be helped; destiny is supreme. The boy was to be my ruin; he is my ruin, and rightly. But before I go grant me one request. Do not prosecute him. Believe me, I will do everything I can to get him out of your way. He shall annoy you no more. .... Do you promise?'
> 'I do,' she said. 'Now please leave me.'
> 'Once more – am I to understand that no marriage is to take place to-day between you and me?'
> 'You are.' Sir William De Stancy left the room. It was noticeable throughout the interview that his manner had not been the manner of a man altogether taken by surprise. During the few preceding days his mood had been that of the gambler seasoned in ill-luck, who adopts pessimist surmises as a safe background to his most sanguine hopes. (p. 434)

De Stancy is a losing gambler, accustomed to seeing his hopes come to nothing. He has adopted both his father's name and his father's fortune. Following this incident, Paula goes in pursuit of Somerset and catches a fleeting glimpse of him: 'Somerset crossed her front along this street, hurrying as if for a wager' (p. 445). This simile reflects back upon Paula with some irony, as she, at an earlier point in the novel, had been encouraged to believe (by Dare) that Somerset had lost all his money gambling. Somerset and Paula marry, but Castle De Stancy is decimated by fire. The arsonist is Dare, whose actions are described by the narrator: 'a figure flitting in and about those draughty apartments, and making no more noise in so doing than a puff of wind. Its motion hither and thither was rapid, but methodical' (p. 474). To the last, Dare works strategically. He is also now simply a figure, having been an elusive character throughout the novel. He is at his most animated in *A Laodicean* when he gambles, especially when he loses. He lacks a social existence in the normal sense, so gambling imbues him with a sense of purpose and indeed a sense of belonging: he is the embodiment of chance and is at home where chance is dominant. Dare is the complete gambler, constantly assessing, constantly manoeuvring, constantly speculating. He comes alive in the casino, where his essential qualities are reflected in the immediate environment.

In *The Mayor of Casterbridge* (1886), gambling features in the opening of the novel.[29] In common with *Far from the Madding Crowd*, Hardy again presents us with the environment of a fair. The first chapter is set in the early-nineteenth century, and Hardy describes the atmosphere at the fair towards the end of the day: 'the peep-shows, toy-stands, waxworks, inspired monsters, disinterested medical men who travelled for the public good, thimble-riggers, nick-nack vendors, and readers of Fate' (p. 4). The gambling enterprise is based on cheating, thus helping to create an appropriate context for Michael Henchard's betrayal of his wife by selling her at auction. Similarly, in Hardy's final novel, *Jude the Obscure* (1896), gambling contributes briefly to the atmosphere.[30] Following Jude Fawley's rejection from the Master of Biblioll College, he visits a tavern in Christminster in a state of despair. There he notices the other customers.

> Tinker Taylor, a decayed church-ironmonger who appeared to have been of a religious turn in earlier years, but was somewhat blasphemous now; also a red-nosed auctioneer; also two Gothic masons like himself, called Uncle Jim and Uncle Joe. There were present, too, some clerks, and a gown-and surplice-maker's assistant; two ladies who sported moral characters of various depths of shade, according to their company, nicknamed 'Bower o'Bliss' and 'Freckles'; some horsey men 'in the know' of betting circles; a travelling actor from the theatre, and two devil-may-care young men who proved to be gownless undergraduates; they had slipped in by stealth to meet a man about bull-pups, and stayed to drink and smoke short pipes

with the racing gents aforesaid, looking at their watches every now and then. (p. 142)

Along with the horse racing gamblers there is disillusionment and immorality. Jude and his companions are, at best, low-life tourist attractions for the students. Gambling in these two novels provides colour rather than making any thematic contribution, but in both case it illuminates character and situation.

At a time when the anti-gambling feeling in the country as a whole was rising, Hardy's representations of it resist the dominant ideology and focus instead on the importance of gambling as a chance event with significant consequences. In this respect, gambling for Hardy was a trope for the universe itself. It is further significant that Hardy was writing in the aftermath of Darwin, and indeed acknowledged the influence of Darwinian thought in his work. His representations of gambling clearly tie-in with this influence.[31] However, in the two novels considered in detail in this chapter, there are distinctions to be drawn with regard to the way the texts present gambling. In *The Return of the Native* it becomes the focal point of a struggle between individuals. The game of dice is combative and adversarial. This kind of gambling is intensely active. Conversely, in *A Laodicean*, the main form of gambling is roulette, which is passive. However, the gambler, Dare, is an enigmatic but not passive character. He is in opposition to society and indeed fate, and he fights against the stigma and consequences of his illegitimacy, using his wits and his considerable resourcefulness. His strategy, however, is ultimately unsuccessful because it is predicated on the false assumption that events can always be managed by calculations. It is further significant that Dare, when he is first encountered in the casino, is effectively dehumanized. He is, in this respect, similar to Venn gambling on Egdon Heath in *The Return of the Native* when he is referred to as an automaton. However, they are very different kinds of gamblers. Dare is a strategic player, using guile to achieve his ends. Venn relies solely on moral force. In actual gambling this would be of no consequence, but within fiction it is possible to use gambling to engineer a desired moral configuration. Hardy's representation of gambling is not generally polemical, although, as has been shown, the narrator steps forward at one point in both novels to express some disapproval concerning gambling. Moreover, Hardy is not interested in relating his depictions of gambling back to their social context, although in *A Laodicean* the casino episode has to take place on the continent because of the abolition of gaming-houses at home. Furthermore, the presence of gambling at the fair in *The Mayor of Casterbridge* bears some relation to actual modes of gambling in the early-nineteenth century. Ultimately, gambling in Hardy often functions as an abbreviation, whether of conflict between individuals or conflict between an individual and his situation, and in either situation chance is an important element. Venn's struggle with Wildeve, and Dare's struggle with his life chances, both come into focus when they sit down to gamble.

———————— *chapter seven* ————————

'A real Gentleman should never want the Money out of another Man's Pocket

Anthony Trollope, Gambling and Class Contamination

Anthony Trollope was a friend and admirer of William Makepeace Thackeray. Like Thackeray, he got into debt in his youth. Between 1834 and 1841 Trollope was continually in financial trouble, and anxieties over a lack of money feature in *The Duke's Children* through the character of Francis Tregear.[1] Trollope himself said of this period in his life, 'how I got my daily bread I can hardly remember'.[2] Unlike Thackeray, however, Trollope's money worries were not the result of a spectacular gambling misadventure. In fact, on the basis of the available evidence, Trollope's own gambling was modest and controlled. However, within his fiction Trollope's gamblers are often reckless and destructive. This chapter explores the gap between gambling in Trollope's life and in his novels, examining closely some of Trollope's representations of gambling; it focuses on two novels from the Palliser series and two non-fiction articles.

In an article published in 1868, 'On Horse Racing', Trollope felt able to defend horse racing as a qualitatively different and superior form of gambling to all others.

> Man is unquestionably a gambling animal, and the very energy which makes us strive to rise in life is twin-born brother to the spirit which makes men gamblers. (. . .) The only open gambling which exists among us is that which is enacted on racehorses. Nor is betting upon races an unmitigated evil, – least of all in the eyes of those who have seen trente et quarante played in Germany, baccarat in Paris, monte in Mexico, and faro in New York or Washington. Betting about the speed and endurance of a racehorse is unquestionably the noblest gambling in existence.[3]

The English form of gambling was supreme, concerned with performance rather than mere money. Again we notice particular hostility towards foreign modes of gambling, an attitude shared by Trollope's contemporary, Andrew Steinmetz (see chapter one) and thus attitudes to gambling reflect a broader, xenophobic position. In addition, Trollope's account contains a reference to the contemporary legal position of gambling. Betting on horses at race courses was the only 'open' form of gambling, but this description recognizes implicitly the existence of other forms of gambling, legal restrictions notwithstanding. The preface to the article indicates Trollope's concern with a perceived decline in the morality of the Turf: 'if care be not taken to prevent it, an English horse-race will become as little desirable an amusement as an English prize-fight' (p. 7). The root of the problem appeared to be the commercialization of horse racing and the intrusion of the working classes, both as spectators and as participants, into the pastime of the aristocracy. While commercialization improved the integrity of horse racing (see chapter one) it also diluted its exclusivity as the sport reached out to new customers in order to increase its revenue. Trollope's article criticizes 'nameless professional racing men' (p. 48), and he is particularly offended by the social elevation of jockeys.

> That a young, raw, uneducated Yorkshire or Newmarket lad, who can ride seven stone, but who cannot pen a letter of which a milkmaid would not be ashamed, should be welcomed to the homes of dukes and marquises, – that he should be encouraged to smoke cigars, play billiards, and volunteer opinions without restraint in the presence of his betters of either sex, – is one of the saddest anomalies of our modern civilisation. (p. 41)

For Trollope, this phenomenon is symptomatic of the malaise in horse racing as a whole. His position is an echo of the 1844 Select Committee on Gaming, to the extent that he differentiates between betting on horses and other forms of gambling. Furthermore, this division is made along class lines. 'On Horse Racing' highlights the social stratification inscribed in perceptions of gambling, and how this worked to the advantage of the upper classes. Trollope's anxiety also reflects a wider concern about leisure and the working classes, particularly the extent to which popular leisure practices trespassed on the literal and cultural territory of the upper classes.

The Way We Live Now (1874–5)

The distinctive feature of 'On Horse Racing' is that it is uncomfortable with class interaction, implying that the upper classes were abrogating their responsibilities by mixing with working-class jockeys. However, Anthony Trollope was far from being an unqualified admirer of the aristocracy. In *Sir Harry Hotspur of Humblethwaite* (1870), the potential inheritor of a baronet's estate, George Hotspur, is 'a gambler, a swindler, (. . .) a forger and a card-sharper' (ch. 16).[4] Here Trollope uses gambling in an orthodox way to signify villainy in an individual. The idea of the upper classes not living up to their role and responsibilities is a theme of Trollope's *The Way We Live Now*, which first appeared in serial form, from February 1874 to September 1875.[5] The novel addresses explicitly its own moment in history; the chapter headings inform us of the month and the year as it moves from 1874 into 1875. *The Way We Live Now* is thus very interested in the state of contemporary society, which is explored through a narrative focus on financial speculation and its consequences.

The main gambler in the novel is Sir Felix Carbury. However, his conduct (characterized by deceit and recklessness) prompts comparison with another central character in the narrative, Augustus Melmotte, who is a financier on the largest scale, speculating (in effect, gambling) on extraordinary projects with colossal amounts provided by gullible investors. According to N. John Hall (1991) the character of Melmotte is moulded partly on George Hudson (see chapter two) and partly on John Sadleir (see chapter three).[6] The fact that the first of these characters is mentioned by name in Disraeli's *Coningsby* (1844), and that the second is thought to have been the model for Dickens's character of Mr Merdle in *Little Dorrit* (1855–57), is clearly significant. All three novels feature financiers and also feature gamblers, suggesting that, in the popular imagination, there was still a perception that there was a strong connection between the two practices, despite the Stock Exchange's quest to redefine itself as commerce. Trollope, according to Michael Sadleir (1927, no relation), 'was later accused of having copied Melmotte from Merdle in *Little Dorrit*, but he asserted that he first read that novel in 1878'.[7] However, while Trollope may not have read of Merdle he would certainly have heard of John Sadleir and his financial exploits. There is thus a connection between Trollope's fictional character and the wider social and commercial, if not literary, environment, which signifies that Trollope was using *The Way We Live Now* as a means of passing comment on his society (a point underlined by the novel's manifesto-style title).

The main arena for gambling in *The Way We Live Now* is the Beargarden, a private member's club 'in a small street turning out of St James's Street', which consists of 'dining-rooms, billiard rooms and card rooms' (1, 24). The Gaming Act of 1845 prohibited hazard, a large-scale, theatrical form of betting, but this did not mean that all gambling ceased in all clubs. Instead, other, less spectacular activities became the focal point of gambling. While clause two of the 1845 Act had banned games with a built-in percentage in the house's favour, cards and billiards encouraged contests between individuals. Kitson Clark wrote of Victorian England being an era in which gentlemen commenced by dueling and ended up playing golf and we can locate gambling within this pattern as the spectacular gives way to the sedate and open hostility is displaced into commercially and culturally regulated practices.[8] The gamblers at the Beargarden are predominantly upper-class: as well as Carbury there is Lord Grasslough, Miles Grendall (son of Lord Alfred Grendall) and Dolly Longestaffe (son of the squire of Caversham). The narrator, when speaking of Longestaffe, says 'he was willing to play at any game whether he understood it or not, and for any stakes' (1, 27). This is a circle of irresponsible young men with whom Trollope will have little sympathy. When a genuinely intelligent character, Hamilton K. Fisker, plays against the young men he wins from them all, and especially from Sir Felix Carbury (ch. 10). The shortcomings in their guile and skill, in gambling and in other areas of life, are exposed by a character who possesses both qualities.

Sir Felix Carbury, in addition to being the most significant gambler in the novel, is also a reprobate. He exploits his mother and he hopes to marry Marie Melmotte for wholly mercenary reasons. Having said this, it is worth noting that Lady Carbury facilitates and indeed fuels her son's ambition, as noted by Meredith White Townsend, a contemporary reviewer in the *Spectator*: 'she helps this son to run off with the heiress solely to get her money'.[9] Lady Carbury, like many other characters in *The Way We Live Now*, places material wealth above all other considerations, enabling Trollope to pass comment on the avaricious nature of contemporary society.[10] Her son's villainy is compounded by his attempts to seduce a working-class woman, Ruby Ruggles, by encouraging her to believe that he will marry her. His gambling, therefore, is an expression of his personality: irresponsible and callous. His pursuit of Marie Melmotte brings him into conflict with her father, who gives him money in exchange for a promise from Felix that he will cease his quest. Having accepted the money while simultaneously planning an elopement with Marie, Felix loses all of the money gambling. It can easily be argued that this is entirely consistent with his personality. However, it is also fair to suggest that, on an unconscious level, he loses the money deliberately. His pursuit of Marie is rarely more than half-hearted; by losing the money he creates the conditions in which the elopement is impossible and, moreover, he is saved from having to make a conscious decision, an act which would imply a level of personal maturity unavailable to him. In addition, Carbury's loss implies a narrative comment on his ill-gotten gains: he will not be allowed to keep this income because of its origin in a dubious source.

However, gambling in *The Way We Live Now* is much more than simply a signifier for Sir Felix Carbury's irresponsible personality. The language of gambling features repeatedly in relation to Felix's pursuit of Marie Melmotte and, in view of the fact that his interest in her is predicated on her status as Melmotte's prospective inheritor, she is the fortune and his wooing of her is a gamble. In chapter ten the pursuit of Marie is described as a horse race. Felix does not regard himself as the favourite, stating, 'it's ten to one against me' (1, 111). Later, the narrator tells us that Georgina Longestaffe 'understood that the two horses in the running were Lord Nidderdale and Sir Felix' (1, 163). When Felix assesses his own marriage prospects in the face of Marie's father's opposition, he comes to the following conclusion: 'as far as he could see, the game was over (. . .). But romance was not the game he was playing' (1, 223). Gambling is a significant presence in this situation, just as love is a significant absence. Trollope uses gambling to highlight a loveless character taking a gamble by engaging a woman's affections without a father's consent. Felix is aware of the size of the stakes, stating 'the game to be played was too full of danger!' (1, 384), though he finally comes to a decision voiced in explicitly commercial language: 'I'll venture it' (1, 386). His eventual withdrawal from the betrothal is undertaken without any consideration of Marie's feelings. The whole project was a piece of speculation for Felix, in which his emotions were simply not engaged.

The Way We Live Now also features a parliamentary election in the constituency of Westminster, for which Melmotte is a candidate. In common with his representation of marriage, Trollope shows us that gambling is bound up with the political process. In an early stage of the contest we are told that 'the odds are ten to one on Melmotte' (1, 327). His fortunes decline as the election approaches, and 'Melmotte's name had continued to go down in the betting' (2, 116). There is clearly no activity in *The Way We Live Now* which is immune from gambling and speculation. However, Melmotte's opponent, Mr Alf, attacks Melmotte by focusing on his status as a speculator and gambler.

> How great would be the disgrace to such a borough as that of Westminster
> if it should find that it had been taken in by a false spirit of speculation and
> that it had surrendered itself to gambling when it had thought to do honour
> to honest commerce. (1, 418)

Alf makes a firm distinction between business and gambling, but he
loses the election. This may be passing a comment on contemporary
society and its willingness to speculate. However, Alf's analysis is
shown eventually to be accurate as Melmotte falls spectacularly.

Augustus Melmotte is not a gambler in the very strictest sense of
the word. When he plays whist with Lord Alfred Grendall we are told
that, 'he did not gamble, never playing for more than club stakes or
bets' (1, 36). Significantly, he loses money deliberately to Lord Alfred
in order to ingratiate himself with him. The games at the card table are
too small and inconsequential for Melmotte; he is a gambler on a much
larger scale. A defeat at the card table is a skilful move in the context
of a larger project. Melmotte heads the English arm of a railway company, the Great South Central Pacific and Mexican Railway. A
number of the upper-class characters are drawn into the company,
either as investors or as directors whose names lend respectability to
the enterprise. When Sir Felix Carbury wins money at cards he uses
the proceeds to buy shares in Melmotte's company. He therefore does
not withdraw from gambling but instead moves upward in order to
gamble on a larger scale. However, he regards this money as invested,
not speculated. He fails to see that it is another game, but Melmotte
does understand this and he uses this knowledge to exploit the other
characters. However, not everybody is beguiled by Melmotte. Roger
Carbury is reliable and steadfast, and he says of Melmotte: 'he amasses
his money not by honest trade, but by unknown tricks, – as does a
card sharper' (1, 138). The simile is apt and, moreover, it degrades
Melmotte by likening him to a lower-class gambling cheat. It is further
significant that Roger Carbury, like Mr Alf, assumes a distinction
between 'honest commerce' and gambling. This assumption is not
shared by Felix's mother, Lady Carbury, who considers her son in
relation to Melmotte.

> And then again, it was indispensable that he should abandon the habit of
> play – at any rate for the present, while his prospects depended on the good
> opinion of Mr Melmotte. Of course such a one as Mr Melmotte could not
> like gambling at a club, however much he might approve of it in the City.
> Why, with such a preceptor to help him, should not Felix learn to do his
> gambling on the Exchange, or among the brokers, or in the purlieus of the
> Bank. (1, 112–13)

Lady Carbury accepts that the appearance of gambling is problematic, but in substance she does not differentiate between gambling and other forms of speculation. The persistence of this attitude demonstrates the partial failure of the Stock Exchange in its quest for respectability. Alternatively, Trollope may be using Lady Carbury as a mouthpiece for his own views in the context of a novel which identifies a gambling spirit prevalent in and degrading all forms of contemporary human activity. Melmotte's fall and eventual suicide is not lacking in poignancy, partly because the reason for his demise is rooted in his ambition to be a gentleman. This desire causes him to over-extend himself financially. Trollope shows he is not a gentleman by birth, and that this status is not to be bought. In condemning the ubiquitous commercialism of his society Trollope clings to the notion of the gentleman which becomes a signifier for decency uncontaminated by monetary considerations. Whether such a status existed in reality is a moot point. Sir Felix Carbury's villainy is exacerbated by the fact that he is a gentleman yet he fails lamentably to live up to a gentleman's code of conduct.[11]

Gambling in *The Way We Live Now*, in all its forms, is not a fair process. In chapter twenty-four Sir Felix Carbury sees Miles Grendall cheating by putting an ace up his sleeve. He discloses this piece of information confidentially to Dolly Longestaffe, who states his intention to carry on playing. This manifestly foolish position can only be understood by referring to Felix Carbury's justification of his own actions taken as a whole: 'he had eaten and drunk, had gambled, hunted, and devoted himself generally after the fashion considered to be appropriate to young men about town' (2, 154). Gambling is a component part of the upper-class young man's lifestyle. Although legislation had criminalized various forms of gambling, it had rarely sought to interfere with the upper classes, for whom gambling continued to be a popular form of recreation which was carried on more or less openly. The cheating at the Beargarden is replicated on a much larger scale by the business practices of Melmotte and thus Trollope presents a society in which cheating as well as gambling is endemic.

When Trollope moves away from the central characters in *The Way We Live Now*, gambling continues to be present. Sir Damask Monogram's social rise from the grandson of a butcher is symbolized by his having 'a box at every race-course' (1, 299). Contemporary attitudes towards women are reflected in Lady Carbury's statement to her daughter, Hetta: 'you do not drink and gamble, – because you are a woman' (2, 14). Mrs Hurtle, another character who fails in a romantic quest, considers her situation thus: 'the game had been played and the

[175]

stakes lost' (2, 379). Lord Nidderdale, claiming to adopt a more mature stance in life states, in relation to his performance in Parliament, 'I'll bet anybody a fiver that I make a speech before Easter' (2, 437). *The Way We Live Now* presents a disquieting picture of England in the 1870s. Gambling is no longer a pastime and instead has become a governing principle of social life. Furthermore, gambling is not a fair contest between individuals, or an aspect of leisure contained within a commercial framework. Instead, the dice are always loaded in favour of the player with the most guile and the most finely-honed capabilities for deceit. The good characters in *The Way We Live Now* are either flawed or unsuccessful. Roger Carbury has to accept that the woman whom he loves does not love him. Paul Montague gambles in the early part of the novel, and his conduct towards Mrs Hurtle is open to question. Trollope, writing about Montague in a letter of October 1874, stated, 'he is not a hero, but men are seldom heroes'.[12] *The Way We Live Now* has low expectations of human beings and the societies they construct.

Paradoxically, Trollope's own gambling in the 1870s was solely recreational. Furthermore, it too was centred in clubs, though they were very different to his fictional Beargarden. In the 1860s he had become a member of both the Garrick and the Athenaeum, and club life clearly meant a lot to him, as evidenced by this quote from his autobiography: ' the Garrick Club was the first assemblage of men at which I felt myself to be popular'.[13] He became a Committee member of the Garrick after the death of Thackeray. It is thus apparent that clubs were valuable to Trollope primarily as places of social congregation rather than as arenas for gambling. He was also a member of the Cosmopolitan, along with Lord Stanley and George Bentinck (leading figures in horse racing circles), and a member of the Turf Club, concerning which he stated, 'I found (the club) to be serviceable – or the reverse – only for the playing of whist at high points'.[14] His game of choice was whist, which was attractive to him 'chiefly because I like the society of the men who played'.[15] He gives an account of his card playing in the article 'Whist at our Club', published in *Blackwood's Edinburgh Magazine* in May, 1877.[16] From the outset Trollope is keen to establish the nature and atmosphere of his club.

> At our club, which is a most respectable club, a good deal of whist has been played during the last ten or twenty years. The time was when men used to meet together o'nights for the sake of cards and gambling. It was thus that Fox and his friends used to – I was going to say amuse themselves, but I fear that with them the diversion went beyond amusement. But with us at our club there is nothing of that kind. There are perhaps a dozen gentlemen, mostly well stricken in years, who, having not much else to do with their

afternoons, meet together and kill the hours between lunch and dinner. (p. 597)[17]

Trollope deliberately distances his gambling from that of a previous generation which is characterized by recklessness. Whist is a sedate hobby for the mid-afternoon: 'between three and four the party is assembled, and the delight is reached which, for us, makes easy the passage to the grave' (p. 597). This kind of gambling is referred to briefly in the very early stages of *The Way We Live Now*, with Trollope describing a late-afternoon in winter, a time when 'idle men (were) playing whist at the clubs' (1, 21). The sums won and lost in Trollope's club are insignificant; the players are mainly retired professional gentlemen. The idea that the games might provide an opportunity to win substantial sums is frowned upon by Trollope: 'of that stain there is, I think, nothing at our club' (p. 604). Such was the gambling with which Trollope was personally familiar, but it is not the kind of gambling that we tend to encounter in his novels. This may be because genteel whist playing was hardly dramatic. Alternatively, Trollope may well have been responsive to the prevailing perception of gambling at the time he was writing, and thus he uses it signify degeneracy of character within individuals as well as using it to comment upon a perceived decline in moral standards and the hazards of unfettered commercial speculation. This latter phenomenon was a recent memory for Trollope and his readership. A serious commercial crisis had arisen in 1866 following the emergence of a number of finance companies selling shares in concerns which had yet to come into existence.[18] According to Michael Sadleir, Trollope felt that England in 1873 was 'in the grip of evil and transforming powers. The international financial adventurer had settled on London in his swarms'.[19] This kind of speculation was not honest commerce: it was, for Trollope, a threat to national stability.

The Duke's Children (1880)

In 1880 Trollope published *The Duke's Children*.[20] Gambling is a significant theme in the novel. One of the central characters is Lord Silverbridge, who is subject to two main influences: Francis Tregear, who is mature and honourable, and Major Tifto, whose origins are uncertain and who is clearly of a lower class. Tifto's actions through the novel compromise and damage Lord Silverbridge. In common with his 'On Horse Racing' article, Trollope shows the lower classes having a contaminating effect on the respectability of horse racing.

Comparisons may be made between Trollope's representation of gambling in *The Duke's Children* and Disraeli's in *The Young Duke* and *Sybil*. Both authors focus on upper-class gamblers and both feature race horses with loaded names; Lord Silverbridge's horse in *The Duke's Children* is called Prime Minister (his father, Lord Omnium, is a former prime minister). The political aspect of horse racing in *The Duke's Children* is enhanced when a horse named Coalition loses, costing the Duke £400 in the process. Chapter seventeen of *The Duke's Children* focuses on the night before the Derby in a private club, as does the opening chapter of *Sybil*. Both Lord Silverbridge and the Duke of St James lose vast sums taking bets at major horse races. However, despite these points of comparison Trollope and Disraeli are very different novelists. Michael Sadleir states, 'Trollope, in his role of anti-humbug, detested Disraelian fiction for rococo unreality'.[21] Notwithstanding this antipathy, and in spite of the fact that *The Duke's Children* and the first edition of *The Young Duke* are separated by a gap of nearly fifty years, they use gambling in similar ways. This shows that gambling as a signifier for upper-class irresponsibility persisted through the nineteenth century; the same idea is also to be found in the work of Dickens, Thackeray and Eliot. Interestingly, when Melmotte arrives at the Houses of Parliament as a Conservative member in *The Way We Live Now*, he is conveyed by his party leader, who happened to be Disraeli. Trollope may not have liked Disraeli but he was unable to ignore him.

For Lord Silverbridge in *The Duke's Children*, his involvement in horse racing evolves out of his wealth and privilege. In chapter seven we hear that 'racing was an amusement to which English noblemen had been addicted for many ages, and had been held to be serviceable rather than disgraceful, if conducted in a noble fashion' (p. 56). Furthermore, and on a much grander scale, Silverbridge sees one of the primary elements of gambling pervading his very existence: 'chance had made him the eldest son of a Duke and heir to an enormous fortune' (p. 108). He sees himself as having been treated favourably by chance and it is therefore no surprise that he is optimistic with regard to his actual gambling. It is also fair to say that he takes his wealth and status for granted and therefore his gambling losses do not impact on him to the extent that they would otherwise.

Silverbridge is aware of the social compromises involved in patronizing the race course.

> Half the House of Lords and two-thirds of the House of Commons were to be seen at the Derby, but no doubt there were many rascals and fools,

and he could not associate with the legislators without finding himself among the fools and the rascals. (p. 147)

Later, he describes how 'the feeling of being in the power of a lot of low blackguards is so terrible' (p. 412). Silverbridge appears to accept, grudgingly, the dilution of class boundaries at the races, but in real life a number of nineteenth-century observers suffered great anxiety over some of the social consequences of attending the race course. We have already seen, in chapter one, how Joseph Charles Parkinson was appalled by the behavioural excesses which prevailed among working-class race goers at Epsom on Derby Day.[22] We have also seen the concluding remarks of the judge at the trial following the fixing of the 1844 Derby. Further evidence of middle and upper-class anxiety over the blurring of class boundaries occasioned by betting on horse races may be found in *The Greville Memoirs*, in which Charles Greville writes about 'the degrading nature of the occupation'.[23] On a separate occasion he writes about horse racing being 'a pursuit so replete with moral mischief to me'.[24] He also describes his 'remorse and shame at the pursuit'.[25] Trollope himself appears to have been uncomfortable with the explicit nature of Greville's revelations, as he stated in a letter: 'what a blackguard book is that collection of Greville Memoirs!'.[26] From these various commentaries on horse racing we may suggest that class stratification was less flexible in the nineteenth century than it had been in the eighteenth, when it was generally accepted that holidays involved a significant suspension of the social distinctions which otherwise prevailed. It also shows how recreation itself had become a source of anxiety in the context of an industrial economy in which social classes and class interests had become polarized. The scale of class intermingling at the largest race meetings is highlighted in William Powell Frith's painting, *Derby Day* (Plate V, 1858), in which the whole cross-section of contemporary society is shown to be immersed in the festivities.

Silverbridge is undone through his association with Major Tifto. A contemporary reviewer stated that the character of Tifto was 'drawn with knowledge', which carries the implication that Trollope had had first-hand experience of betting on horse racing.[27] One of the first things we learn about Tifto is that he cannot maintain eye contact (ch. 6), which helps to establish the fact that he is untrustworthy, though it may also signify class deference. Silverbridge helps him get elected to the Beargarden, representing a significant piece of social climbing. This is important to Tifto; when he imagines his and Silverbridge's horse winning the Derby, the social elevation which will ensue is the most

Derby Day (William Powell Frith)
Courtesy of Tate Picture Library.

important consideration for him (ch. 17). In a society where class mobility was limited, the world of gambling provides Tifto with his opportunity to make headway through his specialist knowledge of horse racing. However, Silverbridge does his best to keep Tifto at arm's length and thus to keep the class boundaries up. Tifto becomes involved in race fixing, assisted by an even lower-class character, Captain Green. Silverbridge is aware of Green and states, 'I won't have him standing alongside of me on the Heath' (ch. 43). Gambling may blur class boundaries but it does not eradicate them. Tifto, spurred on by Green and offended by Silverbridge's disregard for himself, injures the Duke's horse, which had been entered for the St Leger. In the aftermath of the race Silverbridge considers his position: 'what good would the money have done him had he won it? What more could he have than he now enjoyed? But to lose such a sum of money! With all his advantages of wealth he felt himself to be as forlorn and wretched as though he had nothing left in the world before him' (pp. 351–2). In common with Disraeli's Young Duke, a spectacular gambling loss forces Silverbridge to face his own conduct and mend his ways. In total, he has lost around seventy thousand pounds, and the fixers make a substantial sum. However, this act of villainy does not bring success or happiness to Tifto. On the contrary, his fortunes decline to the extent that Dolly Longestaffe says he 'looked awfully seedy' (p. 593). Tifto makes a full confession to Silverbridge, which is characterized by humility and subservience. He states 'for though you could be rough you was always kind', and adds, 'it was the devil got hold of me, my Lord' (pp. 594–5). Silverbridge grants him a financial allowance, thus highlighting his innate, upper-class decency. Moreover, Tifto finally shows subservience as the natural condition of the lower orders. Class boundaries are threatened in *The Duke's Children* but are finally reinforced.

Silverbridge's younger brother, Gerald, also becomes involved in gambling. In his case his undoing is card-playing. The demise of both brothers highlights the extent to which gambling was thought to pervade the upper classes. The exposure of Gerald's losses provokes an impassioned response from his father: "how can I wash your young mind clean from the foul stain which has already defiled it? (. . .) On my word, Gerald, I think that the so-called gentleman who sits down with the deliberate intention of extracting money from the pockets of his antagonists (. . .) is worse, much worse than the public robber!"' (pp. 516–17). The Duke himself is likely to have been part of a generation that gambled in the exclusive clubs of St James's. However, the Duke of Omnium is a sober and serious character, never tempted by the world of gambling. In an earlier Trollope novel, *Can You Forgive*

Her? (1864), we hear of the Duke that, 'if he was dull as a statesman he was more dull in private life' (ch. 24). *Can You Forgive Her?* also features a game of whist in chapter sixteen, in which a Member of Parliament is one of the players, thus implying corruption in the political world. Trollope's readership will have been aware of the Duke's qualities. In addition to his appearance in previous novels, it is also apparent (as noted by a contemporary reviewer) that he represents 'the best and highest type of the surviving aristocracy of the last generation'.[28] Gambling will have no place in his lifestyle. When the Duke is addressing Gerald in *The Duke's Children*, he considers money in relation to gambling:

> to think that it may be got by gambling, to hope to live after that fashion, to sit down with your fingers almost in your neighbour's pockets, with your eye on his purse, trusting that you may know better than he some studied calculations as to the pips concealed in your hands, praying to the only god you worship that some special card may be vouchsafed to you, – that I say is to have left far, far behind you, all nobility, all gentleness, all manhood! (pp. 517–18)

For the Duke, money obtained through gambling is tainted money. In this respect there is a notable similarity between Trollope's representation of gambling and George Eliot's: in *Middlemarch*, Dorothea Brooke voices concern over the 'chance gotten money' won by Mr Farebrother at cards (see chapter five). Both characters construct a distinction between the proceeds of gambling and money obtained through hard work or honest enterprise. This is a sustainable position to the extent that other forms of human activity create wealth whereas gambling simply reallocates it. However, the production of wealth can easily be predicated on exploitation, and it can be argued that Britain as the world's most significant colonial power in the nineteenth century did precisely that. Moreover, venture capitalism is notoriously speculative. The characters in both *Middlemarch* and *The Duke's Children*, therefore, make assumptions about methods of wealth creation which are clearly open to debate. The Duke's tirade against Gerald is rooted in a moral objection rather than in stern, economic analysis. Gerald has, in the Duke's eyes, betrayed his class.

There is nothing surprising about the Duke's objections to his sons' conduct. At an early stage in the novel he states, 'races! a congregation of all the worst blackguards in the country mixed with the greatest fools' (p. 144). Nor is he the only character in *The Duke's Children* to be opposed to gambling. Lady Mabel Grex declines an offer of marriage from Lord Silverbridge, in spite of the material security it would bring.

This may be partly because her own father and brother are heavy gamblers. Earl Grex's main interests are 'cards and racing' (p. 73), and her brother Percival is the chief beneficiary of Gerald's gambling losses. Her own view of gambling anticipates the Duke of Omnium's outburst later in the novel.

> Of all things that men do this is the worst. A man who would think himself disgraced for ever if he accepted a present of money will not scruple to use all his wits to rob his friend of everything that he has by studying the run of cards or by watching the paces of some brutes of horses! And they consider themselves to be fine gentlemen! A real gentleman should never want the money out of another man's pocket; – should never think of money at all. (p. 159)

Lady Grex's personal experience has caused her to see the full consequences of excessive gambling: her family's wealth and prestige is being eroded through profligacy. Trollope is showing the most grave effects of upper-class gambling, although her comments are self-delusional because they assume that social status can be separated entirely from economics. However, Lady Grex is not rewarded in the novel. Silverbridge's affections are transferred elsewhere, and we hear of Lady Grex that, 'she had played her cards so badly that the game was now beyond her powers' (p. 318). In common with *The Way We Live Now*, Trollope is using gambling in *The Duke's Children* in relation to affairs of the heart. The Derby is the first topic of conversation between Lord Silverbridge and Isabel Boncassen, his eventual wife. This highlights the social pervasiveness of gambling while also introducing the ideas of risk and a contest, both of which are applicable to the relationship as it develops. On a further occasion, a conversation between Silverbridge, Isabel and Dolly Longestaffe becomes animated when they talk about the St Leger (ch. 33). Dolly Longestaffe is a rival for Isabel's affections, but he tells Silverbridge: 'I'm not going to enter myself to run against you' (p. 549). The crossover in language from gambling to relationships may involve a cheapening of love, reducing it to a contest and the pursuit of a prize. However, it is significant that, in another relationship in *The Duke's Children*, Francis Tregear's rival suitor for the hand of Mary (Lord Silverbridge's sister) is Popplecourt. He does not gamble. However, he is also dull and lifeless. Trollope is returning to the position outlined in 'On Horse Racing', in which the desire to gamble is associated with vitality. *The Duke's Children* presents some of the worst consequences of gambling but it does not necessarily lambast gambling itself. Instead it criticizes the corruption of gambling which arises out of individual faults. In *The Duke's Children* these faults are located in lower-class characters who, through their actions, compromise upper-class characters who are foolish without being evil.

Trollope used gambling again in *Mr Scarborough's Family* (1883), in which Mountjoy Scarborough, heir to a significant estate, gambles away his inheritance. Again we see a character of wealth and privilege exploiting his rights and failing to live up to his responsibilities. The kind of gambling in which Trollope himself engaged was limited in terms of its signifying potential within fiction. 'Whist at our Club' shows card games as a pastime for elderly gentlemen. In fiction there was much more to be said about spectacular gambling losses within the aristocracy. The profligacy of Sir Felix Carbury and Lord Silverbridge does not disappoint on a dramatic level. This authorial choice enabled Trollope to talk about upper-class irresponsibility and the extent to which this was an abrogation of responsibilities which, for Trollope and some of his characters, were almost sacred. Gambling in Trollope's novels is also located firmly in its social context. In this respect he is very unlike Thomas Hardy, although they were writing around the same time. Trollope directs his reader's attention towards the contemporaneity of the text in *The Way We Live Now*, both in the title of the novel and in the individual chapter headings. In both *The Way We Live Now* and *The Duke's Children* gambling expresses the *modus operandi* of society as Trollope perceived it. Marriages pursued for the financial advantages that might ensue therefrom, unfettered speculation pandering to a 'get rich quick' mentality, the absence of any informing moral principle in all but a few characters: all this is representative of the gloomy sub-text of Trollope's vision of England in the last quarter of the century. Everybody is now a gambler in some way, shape or form, and it is the actual gamblers themselves who are often playing for the smallest stakes. All around them people are gambling with their lives in marriages which threaten to be loveless (Marie Melmotte acquiesces to this very prospect in the aftermath of her romantic disappointment with Sir Felix Carbury), or gambling with the lives of others in extraordinarily irresponsible, large-scale speculations. In a social and economic context in which money now meant at least as much as breeding, the gamblers (who at their worst were, like Captain Green, unqualified villains) were now knocking at the door of respectable society.

chapter eight

'One Law for the Rich and another for the Poor'

George Moore's Working Gamblers

Horse racing and gambling saturate George Moore's *Esther Waters* (1894), which follows the life of a female servant who lives, often involuntarily, off the proceeds of gambling. The novel was received as a vitriolic anti-gambling text at a time in which gambling was being roundly attacked by the National Anti-Gambling League. The editor of the *Sporting Times* went so far as to call Moore 'a Puritan killjoy'.[1] However, although *Esther Waters* clearly does condemn gambling, it also attempts to understand, often sympathetically, the circumstances underlying gambling. These circumstances determine the conduct of the gamblers in the novel to a significant extent. Moore's own knowledge of horse racing was extensive, hence his representations of horse racing and gambling are both insightful and technically accurate.

George Moore came from a family in which horse racing played a significant part. His father had a stable of race horses in Ireland, the success of which enabled him to send his son to an expensive school. Furthermore, George Moore's uncle died following a horse racing accident, and this may have been the reason why Moore's parents discouraged him from riding race horses himself.[2] In the mid-1860s, however, Moore's father was forced to give up his stables following a run of bad luck, and the family moved to London in 1869.[3] Some time later, in 1883–84, Moore went back to Ireland on a visit and found that the stables were all empty, an event similarly experienced by Esther at the end of *Esther Waters* when she returns to Woodview. George Moore himself was involved directly with horse racing and gambling in his teenage years. In his autobiographical *Confessions of a Young Man* (1888), he states, 'I read the racing calendar, stud-book, latest betting, and looked forward with enthusiasm to the day when I should be known as a successful steeplechase rider' (p. 3).[4] He also recalls 'small bets made in a small tobacconist's' (p. 4). Given that these events occurred in the late 1860s, it is clear that Moore must have been frequenting an illegal off-course bookmaker, a world he was later to revisit in *Esther Waters*. Moore combined his interest in horse racing and gambling with more erudite pursuits, and once took a copy of Kant's *Critique of Pure Reason* to the Derby at Epsom.[5] By this time he seems to have turned away from gambling, stating, in *Confessions*, 'I neither betted nor drank' (p. 9). He rejected gambling in favour of the entirely different world of the visual arts. However, he formed, albeit without much exploration, connections between his different experiences in *Confessions*, when he stated, in reference to the perceived malaise in contemporary life, 'the duke, the jockey-boy, and the artist are exactly alike' (p. 116). Such a view does not bear a great deal of scrutiny, but it does show that Moore remained conscious of the world of horse racing after he ceased to be involved personally with racing and gambling. Furthermore, the position he adopts regrets the blurring of social boundaries. He had wanted to be a steeplechase rider yet he seems to have accepted the low social status nominally accredited to a jockey boy. He thus accepted the ideology of his own time, such as that expressed in the *Quarterly Review* article of 1889 (see chapter one) which saw gambling as a degrading and belittling process.

Spring Days (1888)

Both horse racing and gambling are featured, though not foregrounded, in two of Moore's early novels, *Spring Days* (1888) and *Mike Fletcher* (1889).[6] Neither book is especially highly-rated, and neither features in the Ebury edition of Moore's works (London: Heinemann, 1937). However, both are interesting because they treat gambling differently to the more analytical approach adopted in *Esther Waters*. In *Spring Days*, gambling features in the opening chapter, with Mr Brookes referring to his son's losses in business in the West End as 'mere gambling'. He distinguishes these transactions from 'legitimate city business' (p. 10). In common with Roger Carbury in Anthony Trollope's *The Way We Live Now*, Brookes emphasizes the distinction between commerce and gambling.

Elsewhere in *Spring Days*, Frank Escott sees 'a splendid young man' with 'embroidered waistcoats' who states, 'he would have to run up to London, then he must have a shy at *trente et quarante* at Monte Carlo, then he must get back for the spring meeting at Newmarket' (p. 171). Here, gambling signifies the ostentatious wealth of the character, who is interested in being seen in all the right places. He is quite similar to the figure of the upper-class young man of the early-nineteenth century who frequented exclusive gaming houses in the West End. If the example of the Prince of Wales was anything to go by, this figure was enjoying a late-century revival. As discussed earlier, the future Edward VII's attendance at race meetings attracted adverse comment from the National Anti-Gambling League, and the Tranby Croft case suggested that his involvement with gambling was not controlled and recreational.

In *Spring Days*, when Frank Escott first encounters Charles Stracey, an unacceptable suitor for one of Mr Brookes's daughters, Stracey is lying in the bath reading *The Sporting Times* (ch. 11), thus identifying him as a slightly raffish figure. In chapter fifteen, General Horlock recalls some of the excesses of his past: 'I won five hundred pounds with that horse; but I wouldn't be satisfied, and I ran him again the following day and lost it all and five hundred more with it' (pp. 336–7). The story is told by the General as a comic anecdote, which indicates his wealth and status. He is sanguine about losses which, had they happened to someone else, may well have been calamitous. It further underlines the fact that gambling had been acceptable for some classes in society, but that its association with irresponsibility had overpowered its connotations of glamour by the late-century.

Following various business failures, Willy Brookes starts breeding racehorses. He soon exhibits a thorough knowledge of the subject.

> 'I have bought Blue Mantle, the winner of the Czarewitch, and only beaten by a length for the Cambridgeshire, a three-year-old, with eight stone on his back; a most unlucky horse – if he had been in the Leger or Derby he would have won one or both. He broke down when he was four years old. By King Tom out of Merry Agnes, by Newminster out of Molly Bawn.' (p. 326)

Willy further recounts the minutiae of racehorse breeding in chapter seventeen. His technical knowledge of the lineage and performance of race horses is surprising, given that, up to this point in the novel, he has been portrayed as a feckless and flighty character, unable to sustain any business in which he is involved. His explanation for his suddenly heightened awareness, 'I know more than you think' (p. 326) is unconvincing. Moore is, it seems, feeding his own knowledge of horse racing into the text. He gives the personality of Willy a further dimension and creates a successful character. In the final chapter of the novel Frank Escott sees one of Willy's horses: 'the horse came towards them, his large eyes glancing, his beautiful crest arched. His coat shone like satin, his legs were as fine as steel, and with exquisite relish he drew the carrots from their hands' (p. 370). In a novel in which Frank rejects youthful infatuation for the possibility of a more lasting relationship, this encounter symbolizes his new strength and maturity. Moore employs this technique again in *Esther Waters*, when Esther, at a crucial point in her life, sees a horse whose situation bears a distinct similarity to her own. The image also functions as a reminder of the elevated social status ascribed to horse racing. It would be hard to imagine an illegal street-bookmaker being afforded the same, luxurious description.

Mike Fletcher (1889)

The character of Mike Fletcher is introduced in chapter six of *Spring Days* as an Irish journalist. In the novel *Mike Fletcher*, gambling forms a substantial part of Fletcher's generally dissolute existence.[7] Initially, his gambling illustrates his abilities as much as his shortcomings: 'he was naturally clever at cards, and one night he won three hundred pounds' (p. 22). He is clearly a good gambler, in the sense that he is successful, a point highlighted in chapter five when Fletcher's success playing baccarat is mentioned, although it is also suggested that he does not pay up when he loses, and thus his fundamental untrustworthiness is made apparent. Furthermore, Fletcher wins money by cheating at cards (ch. 8), and he continues to spend much of his time playing cards even after he has been elected as a Member of Parliament (ch. 10). Fletcher thus expresses political as well as personal degradation. Frank Escott, who also appears in *Mike Fletcher*, sees Fletcher holding a hand-kerchief formerly belonging to Lady Helen Seymour, who has recently committed suicide. Escott states, 'you blackguard (. . .) you are taking that handkerchief to a gambling hell' (p. 105). Escott sees Fletcher's conduct as highly indecorous, but Fletcher is unconscious of the impropriety, being focused solely on his own appearance and desires. The fact that he is on his way to a gaming house suggests that they survived during prohibition although, for obvious reasons, their history is not recorded.

As *Mike Fletcher* develops, Fletcher feels the first pangs of conscience with regard to his lifestyle: 'in full revulsion of feeling his mind turned from the long hours in the yellow glare of the lamp-light, the staring faces, the heaps of gold and notes, and the cards flying silently around the empty spaces of green baize' (p. 121). Moore's use of imagery in this sentence is highly effective as it focuses on light, space and silence. The description, however, is virtually devoid of any emotional input. Fletcher is slowly becoming aware of the spiritual vacuity of his own existence. However, gambling is still valuable to him, for its psychological as well as its material benefits. At one point Fletcher states, 'I'm dying for a gamble; I feel as if I could play as I never played before' (p. 141). His skill at card playing, along with his womanising, becomes his main source of self-esteem. Furthermore, he forms connections between these areas of his life, and expresses his affection for a particular woman by stating, 'I would sooner see her than green cloth' (p. 141–2). By explicitly forming a connection between a potential love affair and a context for gambling, Fletcher exposes his own inability to engage seriously with other people. This character trait is further apparent when he plays ecarté to determine the fee to be paid for a manuscript he has written (ch. 8). Gambling takes the place of proper business negotiation: Fletcher would rather trust to a combination of chance and his own skills as a gambler than participate in a serious, mature discourse. In certain respects he is like Trollope's character of Sir Felix Carbury (*The Way We Live Now*). When faced with a serious decision, both prefer gambling. In addition, both of them exploit women. However, both of these fast young gentlemen are brought down, thereby passing comment on their callousness and lack of principle.

Fletcher's behavioural excesses fail to bring him happiness: 'he sought to tempt his jaded appetite with many assorted dissipations, but he turned from all in disgust, and gambling became his sole distraction' (p. 261). One by one, his various vices cease to satisfy him until, finally, even gambling fails to nullify his gnawing discontent. Fletcher then heightens his level of risk: 'Mike played several games of ecarté, cheating openly, braving detection. He did not care what happened, and almost desired the violent scene that would ensue' (p. 276). At this point Fletcher is like George Eliot's Gwendolen Harleth: 'since she was not winning strikingly, the next best thing was to lose strikingly' (*Daniel Deronda*, 1874). Gambling here articulates a protest: either against one's fixed position in life or, in Fletcher's case, in a self-directed protest against his own lack of principle. He defies those around him while simultaneously seeking chastisement. For Fletcher, the risk element of gambling is no longer sufficient to produce excitement, and he thus increases his personal stake by cheating. At the end of the novel Fletcher confronts the shallowness of his existence and, prior to his suicide in the final chapter, he concludes that 'man may not live without wife, without child, without God' (p. 261).

Mike Fletcher is perhaps the least artistically successful of all Moore's novels and, most significantly, it is the only one of his novels that he never revised, having lost faith in it entirely. However, it does show that, prior to the more thoughtful strategy of *Esther Waters*, Moore was willing to use the more obvious significance of gambling. Furthermore, the conclusion of the novel rejects wholeheartedly Fletcher's self-serving hedonism and, through his despairing suicide, advocates implicitly a philosophy of responsibility and duty.

Esther Waters (1894)

Esther Waters is full of references to horse racing and gambling.[8] It was written at a time when betting on horse racing was perceived to have risen sharply, particularly among the working class. A contemporary commentator spoke in 1891 of racing having become 'a popular passion'.[9] Another observer, in 1894, noted 'how all pervading is the gambling instinct among the working classes'.[10] The first mention of gambling in *Esther Waters* occurs in chapter one, when William Latch speaks of a servant dismissed for passing information from the stables at Woodview when he was drunk. He mentions this point briefly in his first conversation with Esther, without feeling the need to explain the significance of the event, namely that the servant would have aided other gamblers and, furthermore, his information would have affected the odds offered by bookmakers on horses from Woodview. Gambling is such a prominent feature of life at Woodview that it is presupposed (wrongly) that Esther will understand the story and its meaning.

Esther is a 'fish out of water' at Woodview. In an environment in which almost everyone, servants as well as masters, is obsessed with gambling, her stern religious upbringing provokes reactions of fear and mistrust within her: 'she had heard of racecourses as shameful places where men were led to their ruin, and betting she had always understood to be sinful, but in this house no one seemed to think of anything else. It was no place for a Christian girl' (p. 20). Here, *Esther Waters* introduces a recurrent theme in the novel, namely the tension between Esther's religion and the gambling in which she is increasingly enmeshed. Gambling pervades life at Woodview to the extent that the most unexceptional matters can become the subject of a wager, with another servant, Sarah, being willing to bet on the opinion that Esther is illiterate (ch. 2).

Esther's first direct involvement in gambling occurs when she is persuaded by William to participate in a sweepstake. The act is part of the developing intimacy between William and herself, and in this respect gambling facilitates the progress of their relationship. William docs not in any way believe that he is compromising Esther morally by encouraging her to take part. His immersion in gambling on horse racing is so deep that he fails to identify the sweepstake as a gamble. His mother, however, is sensitive to the potentially corrosive effects of gambling. It transpires that the Latch family has been reduced to earning its living in service because its former prosperity has been destroyed by gambling. The first prize in the sweepstake is won by Esther, but the division of the prize money creates friction among Esther, William and Sarah, to whom William was formerly attached. Gambling becomes the focal point for the playing-out of personal favouritism. Moore, in common with Thomas Hardy at this point, uses gambling to abbreviate a conflict between individuals. William's desire to give more of the money to Esther denotes his romantic inclination towards her and his rejection of Sarah. More generally, the sweepstake was a popular transitional form of gambling between the end of the state lottery and the closure of the gaming-houses on one hand, and the growth of horse racing on the other. Its peak, therefore, was in the 1840s, before the period in which *Esther Waters* is set. However, Woodview is so absorbed by gambling that it features in every aspect of life in the house. The sweepstake for modest stakes is socially inclusive in *Esther Waters*, allowing all the servants to share in the excitement of the race.[11]

As the relationship between William and Esther develops, they go for a walk.

> The sheep had been folded, and seeing them lying between the wattles, the greyness of this hillside, and beyond them the massive moonlit landscape and the vague sea, Esther suddenly became aware, as she had never been before, of the exceeding beauty of the world, Looking up in William's face, she said:
> 'Oh, how beautiful!'
> As they descended the drove-way their feet raised the chalk, and William said:
> 'This is bad for Silver Braid; we shall want some more rain in a day or two.' (p. 43)

Whereas Esther is receptive to the landscape, William can only understand its effect on a race horse. His ambition is to acquire sufficient money through gambling to become a bookmaker himself. His business plan is, in certain respects, sensible enough as he realizes that the real money in gambling is made by the operators rather than the punters. However, his plan requires capital which he can only gain through gambling. He is thus in a logically flawed position, as an act (betting) which he knows to be fundamentally unprofitable is the very act from which he hopes to derive a profit. His belief in his own acumen with regard to horse racing creates the conditions in which he feels that he can prosper where others have failed.

At an early stage in the novel, Esther sees the effects of excessive gambling. She meets Mrs Randal, whose husband is obsessed with betting on horses, and notes that hers, 'was the leanest house she had ever been in'. Mrs Randal tells her that, 'the sufferings of a gambler's wife cannot be told' (p. 52). Mrs Randal defines her husband's obsession as an addiction: 'he can't resist having something on any more than a drunkard can resist the bar-room' (p. 53), thereby partly absolving Mr Randal, as he is seen as being in the throes of an illness more than he is shown to be personally irresponsible. Esther's encounter with Mrs Randal has additional significance. First, it occurs as Silver Braid competes for the Stewards Cup at Goodwood. The narrator, however, rather than describing the race, around which so much of the conversation and action in *Esther Waters* has revolved, describes instead the meeting between Esther and Mrs Randal. The emphasis, therefore, is not on the spectacular event of the horse race, but on the human cost of excessive gambling. Secondly, Esther's witnessing of Mrs Randal's plight foreshadows her own fate when she is married to William.[12]

The victory of Silver Braid provokes a celebration. Almost everyone around Woodview benefits, through gambling, from the success of the horse. We hear how 'the flood of gold continued to roll into the little town', and then the narrator goes even further: 'the dear gold was like an opiate; it wiped away memories of hardship and sorrow, it showed life in a lighter and merrier guise, and the folk laughed at their fears for the morrow and wondered how they could have thought life so hard and relentless' (p. 63). Gambling brings prosperity and happiness to the town, but it is a temporary respite which makes people oblivious to their actual conditions. A servants' ball is held as part of the celebrations, in the aftermath of which Esther sleeps with William. The success of the community, brought about through the bets on Silver Braid, creates an atmosphere of gaiety in which the normal rules governing behaviour are in suspension. Gambling is thus indirectly responsible for a major event in Esther's life, namely becoming a mother.

The breakdown of William and Esther's relationship is also connected with gambling, as William cites his ill fortune in gambling as the reason why he does not have enough money to marry Esther (ch. 11). However, this is a spurious argument as he soon elopes with another woman. Esther thinks how, 'he had gone where the grand folk lived in idleness, in the sinfulness of the world and the flesh, eating and gambling' (p. 77). She falls back upon her religious upbringing to understand his desertion of her. Shortly thereafter, the narrator describes the moment at which Esther realizes that she is pregnant.

> It was one afternoon at the beginning of December; Mrs Latch had gone upstairs to lie down, and Esther had drawn her chair towards the fire; a broken-down racehorse, his legs bandaged from his knees to his fetlocks, had passed up the yard; he was going for walking exercise on the downs, and when the sound of his hoofs had died away Esther was quite alone. She sat on her wooden chair facing the wide kitchen window. She had advanced one foot on the iron fender; her head leaned back, rested on her hand. She did not think – her mind was lost in vague sensation of William, and it was in this death of active memory that something awoke within her, something that seemed to her like a flutter of wings; her heart seemed to drop from its socket, and she nearly fainted away, but recovering herself she stood by the kitchen table, a deathlike pallor over her face, with drops of sweat on her forehead. The truth was borne in upon her; she foresaw the drama that awaited her, from which nothing could free her, which she would have to live through hour by hour. (p. 82)

Immediately prior to the moment of revelation, Esther sees a broken-down racehorse. She sees a creature that is damaged, injured, unable to perform, a reflection on her own situation and her own experience. She, too, is injured, by William's desertion, and the fact of her pregnancy further worsens her situation. However, the difference between her position and that of the horse is that the horse will be nurtured back into prime condition, whereas Esther will be excluded from the community.

When William disappears from *Esther Waters*, so does gambling. His return to the novel marks the re-emergence of gambling as a central theme. When he accidentally meets Esther he is thinking about the prospects of a particular race horse, and one of his first comments to Esther is that he has been 'backing winners all this year' (p. 194). His attitude towards gambling differs markedly from Esther's: "'racing don't seem to bring no luck to anyone. It ain't my affair, but if I was you I'd give it up and get to some honest work." "Racing has been a good friend to me. I don't know where I should be without it to-day"' (p. 212). Having been steeped in a culture of horse racing and gambling, William is unable to envisage any other means of making a living. The text, however, has already unseated his position by showing how the Barfields of Woodview have been ruined by horse racing (ch. 21). *Esther Waters* repeatedly signposts the fact that gambling ultimately delivers poverty rather than prosperity.

In William's absence, Esther has developed a relationship with Fred Parsons who, like Esther, is religious. Her rejection of Fred in favour of William involves gambling, as she believes that her son, Jackie, would ultimately reject Fred and thereafter seek out his own father, with whom he would become involved in betting and drinking (ch. 26). She tries to defend her position to Fred in chapter twenty-nine: "'ah, yes; he'd have liked you well enough if he'd never seen his father. But he's so taken to his father, and it would be worse later on. He'd never be contented in our 'ome. He'd always be after him, and then I should never see him, and he would be led away into betting and drink'" (p. 235). Esther's reasoning at this point is most questionable. There is no truly compelling argument to the effect that her union with Fred would alienate her son. There is, however, an alternative reason (notwithstanding personal preference) to explain why Esther opts for William instead of Fred: 'if she took the road to the public-house and the racecourse she did not know what might not happen. But William had promised to settle £500 on her and Jackie' (p. 238). Throughout her life, Esther has to struggle against poverty. As a single mother in the second half of the nineteenth century, her prospects of economic survival are never encouraging.[13] William's financial situation appears to be good, and this has to be a significant consideration for Esther. In point of fact, he states that he will give her money irrespective of her decision, but his commitment is not tested and, at this point in the novel, William has done nothing to suggest that he is a reliable character. Esther has to consider the financial consequences of her decision. William's apparent prosperity is a key factor in her choice as, by opting for him, she believes that she is securing Jackie's material welfare. She is propelled by economics into making the choice that she makes, in much the same way that William's subsequent illegal bookmaking is born of necessity rather than choice. Esther, like Gwendolen Harleth, gambles in a relationship when the alternative is poverty. These particular women gamblers are in a state of quiet desperation. Forced into a corner by a society which does not allow them the possibility of forging their own destiny, they have no alternative but to throw the dice.

After Esther moves in with William at the Kings Head pub, he continues to make money through gambling, leading Jackie to form a direct connection between gambling and prosperity when he talks to his mother: 'there's a new shop open in Oxford Street. The window is all full of boats. Do you think that if all the favourites were to be beaten for a month, father would buy me one?' (p. 242). Esther is surprisingly sanguine about this statement. His words and her response indicate the extent to which she and her son are already immersed in a gambling culture. They have assimilated quickly into their new environment. However, the text drops increasingly heavy hints with regard to the future direction of the plot. William starts to lose money and the character of Mr Randal is reintroduced. He is now emaciated, but still obsessed with gambling. The narrator states, 'old John listened with the indifference of a man whose life is absorbed in one passion and who can interest himself with nothing else' (p. 246). Horse racing and gambling have sapped his energies. The Kings Head is patronized by different kinds of gamblers who employ different strategies, but all of them are ultimately losers as the text again demonstrates the end product of gambling. The only exception to this rule is a gambler spoken of in the Kings Head, named Mr George Buff (ch. 30). He is the legendary lucky gambler, whose strategy is an enigma, but, significantly, he does not appear personally in the text. He exists as a kind of talisman to the other gamblers but his actual level of success is never made known and, given the fact that, in the final analysis, gambling simply redistributes wealth upwards, it seems likely that his fortune is less spectacular than his reputation. However, gambling in *Esther Waters* can be benign, albeit temporarily, as it instils hope and expectation into the lives of many of the characters, a point emphasized by the narrator in the concluding words of chapter thirty: 'a bet on a race brings hope into lives which otherwise would be hopeless' (p. 257).

Chapters thirty-one to thirty-three are set at the Derby. William dresses ostentatiously in order to attract custom. The bookmakers resort to a variety of strategies to further their business. The narrator describes them as 'so many challenging cocks, each trying to outshrill the other' (p. 268), an accurate description of the actual conditions in which many on-course bookmakers operated from the mid-century onwards.[14] The narrator describes the crowd at the race, and Sarah's attention is held by 'a boy walking through the crowd on a pair of stilts fully eight feet high' (p. 267). A very similar scene is depicted in Gustave Doré's drawing, 'At Lunch', which was also based on the Derby and published in *London: a Pilgrimage* (Plate VI, 1872).[15] In the illustration, the race is in the background, with the focus more on the dense crowd, a fire-eater and a figure on stilts. Like Doré, Moore seems more interested in the spectacle of the Derby than in the actual race itself, a point made explicit in a letter from Moore to his brother, dated 31 July 1893: '30 or 40 pages: no racing, only the sweat and boom of the crowd – the great Cockney holiday'.[16]

Esther meets Fred Parsons at the Derby. He is preaching at a mission tent against the evils of gambling. His companions are handing out

The Derby – At Lunch (Gustave Doré)
From 'London, a Pilgrimage', written by William Blanchard Jerrod (1826–84,
engraved by Paul Jonnard-Pacel (d. 1902), pub. 1872 (engraving) by
Gustave Doré (1832–83). Courtesy of Central Saint Martin's
College of Art and Design, London, UK/Bridgeman.

material headed, 'The Paradise Plate, for all comers' (p. 271). Fred is now involved in organized opposition to gambling, a phenomenon which (given the emergence of the National Anti-Gambling League) grew in size towards the end of the century. Having left Fred, Esther goes on a mechanical horse ride, on which she wins a prize. She chooses a china mug with the word 'Jack' written on it.

William also has a successful day at the Derby, whereafter he holds a drunken and expensive celebration. It is significant that, when Esther enjoys a modest success, she looks for a gift for her son, whereas William opts for something more self-centred and hedonistic. As *Esther Waters* develops, William and Esther enjoy a generally happy, if financially insecure, marriage, but there is always a qualitative difference between Esther's selfless devotion to her son and William's more worldly perspective. It is further significant that, as the horse races are in progress, Esther opts instead for a mechanical horse ride, offered as part of the amusements at the race course. Despite the role that horse racing and gambling comes to play in her life, she is always slightly removed from the practice and is never immersed in gambling in the way that her husband is. This applies both at the beginning of the novel, when she is a religiously-minded servant with no particular awareness of gambling, and when she is a married woman effectively supported by the proceeds of gambling. Esther's horse ride also works on a metaphorical level: in her life she is being carried along by the machinery of the horse racing industry, but she is merely travelling around in circles, not getting anywhere.

William's constant attendance at horse racing meetings leads him into ill-health. He is forced to give up bookmaking at race meetings and resorts instead to running an illegal bookmaking operation at the Kings Head. Gambling thus creates both the problem (ill-health) and its solution (off-course bookmaking), even though the solution itself is problematic, owing to the fact that it was criminalized in the 1853 Gaming Act. Wray Vamplew (1976) estimates that there were between one hundred and one hundred and fifty betting houses in London in the 1850s catering to working-class customers.[17] William's trade in *Esther Waters* is thus rooted in a broadly contemporary social reality. A commentator in 1889 described bookmakers operating in pubs.

In the corner of a smoking-room you may see a quiet, impassive man sitting daily in a contemplative manner; he does not drink much, he smokes little, and he appears to have nothing in particular to worry him. If he knows you well, he will scarcely mind your presence; men (and boys) greet him, and little gentle colloquies take place from time to time.[18]

In this instance the bookmaker is a customer rather than the landlord, but the essential quality is the same, as emphasis is placed upon the unobtrusive and discreet behaviour of the bookie. In *Esther Waters*, the fact that William is operating outside the law makes him increasingly vulnerable. When a young man accuses him of refusing to pay a bet, William threatens to call a policeman, but this would draw attention to his illegal business (ch. 34). William's situation is further worsened by Fred Parsons, who is by now a captain in the Salvation Army. Fred makes his position known to Esther: '"the whole neighbourhood is demoralised by this betting; nothing is thought of but tips; the day's racing – that is all they think about – the evening papers, and the latest information. You don't know what harm you're doing. Every day we hear of some new misfortune – a home broken up, the mother in the workhouse, the daughter on the streets, the father in prison, and all on account of this betting. Oh, Esther, it is horrible; think of the harm you're doing"' (p. 292). Fred also speaks of a fourteen-year-old boy ruined through gambling, and he reminds Esther that he will need sworn testimony prior to the instigation of a police raid, showing how a problem highlighted by the 1844 Select Committee on Gaming still persisted at least a generation later. Fred's warning also highlights his compassion, as he is, in effect, offering Esther a stay of execution, giving her the opportunity to put a stop to the bookmaking before the raid takes place.[19] Fred's general position echoes a series of anti-gambling arguments, from 'A Fashionable Gaming-House' from *Bentley's Miscellany* in the 1840s, through to Andrew Steinmetz *The Gaming Table* in the 1870s and The National Anti-Gambling League's *The Bulletin* in the 1890s. Gambling is shown to be destructive, corrupting and parasitical. However, there is no analysis of the causes of gambling. William runs an illegal bookmaking operation because it is his sole means of support. His custom at the Kings Head is conditional upon the gambling facilities offered there. William is very sensitive to the injustice of his position.

'It is the betting that brings the business; we shouldn't take five pounds a week was it not for the betting. What's the difference between betting on the course and betting in the bar? No one says nothing against it on the course; the police is there, and they goes after the welshers and persecutes them. Then the betting that's done at Tattersall's and the Albert Club, what is the difference? The Stock Exchange, too, where thousands and thousands is betted every day. It is the old story – one law for the rich and another for the poor. Why shouldn't the poor man 'ave his 'alf-crown's worth of excitement? The rich man can have his thousand pounds' worth whenever he pleases. The same with the public-'ouses – there's a lot of hypocritical folk that is for docking the poor man of his beer, but there's no one that's for interfering with them that drink champagne in the clubs. It's all bloody rot, and it makes me sick when I think of it.' (p. 296)[20]

William identifies the class prejudice which pervaded nineteenth-century legislation on gambling. Tattersall's was respectable, and the police generally protected the integrity of on-course betting on horse races. Those who wished to bet but could not afford to participate in these forms of gambling were automatically criminalized. William further forms a link between betting and alcohol, as alcohol and the drinking place were, like gambling, stigmatised in the second half of the nineteenth century.[21] In addition, and in spite of all the commentators who linked gambling to personal ruin, it is by no means certain that this connection existed in reality. P. D. Pedder, in an article entitled 'The Tipster and his Trade', published in 1903, stated: 'very likely his (the gambler's) house is *not* broken up, his furniture is not sold, his wife and children never see the inside of the workhouse. He is degraded that is all, and his descent is progressive'.[22] For Pedder, gambling is pernicious morally but not ruinous economically.

However, gambling is wholly responsible for still further misery in *Esther Waters*. Sarah forms a relationship with Bill Evans, by whom she is ill treated and exploited. He attributes his maltreatment of her to his bad luck at gambling (ch. 36). Sarah resorts to stealing from her employer in order to get gambling money for Bill. The money is bet on a horse in the Cesarewitch race, and Bill Evans tells Sarah that he will marry her if the horse wins (ch. 37).[23] Sarah has now staked everything on the race, including her whole future and indeed her personal liberty. Gambling in *Esther Waters* is seldom just recreational: now, yet again for a woman gambler, it is a desperate throw of the dice. The defeat of the horse results in a prosecution against Sarah, in which class prejudice is again present. The judge, 'whose betting transactions were matters of public comment' (p. 317), takes a strong line against Sarah, giving her a custodial sentence of hard labour, even though he had betted on the same horse for the same race. His lengthy speech (pp. 317–21) contains some familiar anti-gambling arguments: 'the vice (of gambling) among the poorer classes is largely on the increase (. . .). Drink and gambling are growing social evils; in a great measure they are consequential, and only require absolute legislation to stamp them out almost entirely'. The judge's fondness for champagne has already been mentioned and thus his hypocrisy is compounded. Gambling is thought to be an increasing menace, but its presence in the higher tiers of society is again disregarded. Sarah is, in effect, convicted for her class status as well as for the theft.

In the last quarter of *Esther Waters*, gambling destroys many of the remaining characters. Mr Randal becomes haggard and decrepit and his wife is reduced to begging (ch. 39). Ketley, one of the gambling regulars of the pub who bases his bets on certain omens of which only he is aware, commits suicide in the King's Head by stabbing himself in the neck (ch. 40). At the inquest, his gambling losses are brought into the open and the foreman of the jury states that 'betting houses were the ruin of the poorer classes, and that they ought to be put a stop to' (p. 332). The Kings Head is raided, the gambling is stopped and William, in order to make a living, is compelled to return to on-course bookmaking in spite of his poor health. Gambling as such is less harmful to William than the anti-gambling legislation which forces him to endanger his health. In real life, there were a number of police raids on illegal betting houses in 1865, the effect of which was to force many bookmakers to conduct their operations in the street.[24] William's trade and expertise, however, is founded on the race course and, unsurprisingly, it is to the race course that he returns. Esther's analysis of their situation is simple: 'horses had won and horses had lost – a great deal of trouble and fuss and nothing to show for it' (p. 334). She further recognizes the seriousness of William's ill health and its implications: 'it was for his very life that her husband was now gambling on the race-course' (p. 342). Like Gwendolen Harleth, Esther and Sarah, William is now a desperate gambler, staking more than just money. Circumstances have increasingly 'raised the ante', to the point at which William has to stake his life merely to stay in the game.[25] In common with women, working-class men in the late-nineteenth century lived in circumstances which they had done little to shape, despite their role as wealth creators in a capitalist economy. Gambling offered a route out of their troubles although, in reality, it simply directed the little wealth they had into the pockets of businessmen, legitimate or otherwise.

William is advised to go to Egypt for his health and he tries to raise the money for the journey by betting on horses. He fully recognizes the seriousness thus imbued in his stake money, calling it 'his very life-blood' (p. 343). Gambling has formerly been his sole means of economic support, now it is the one hope for his very existence. He places a bet and, prior to the outcome of the race, Esther 'knelt down by the bedside and prayed that God would allow the horse to win' (p. 345). The tension between her religious leanings and gambling environment is resolved, and spiritual commitment is subsumed to economic necessity. Her desperate situation causes her to devote a prayer to a gambling success, an act entirely antithetical to the tenets of her faith. However, Esther is less conscious of the contradiction than she is of her husband's plight and she is prepared to do anything to guarantee his welfare. Further gambling losses render William's situation increasingly helpless, until he places one last bet on the outcome of two races, recognizing this gesture as 'my last chance' (p. 346). Esther again prays for success and she identifies the consequences of the victory or defeat of the horse, named Chasuble: 'the race was being run, Chasuble's hoofs were deciding whether her husband was to live or die' (p. 350). Here, then, is the ultimate stake in a gamble and Esther realizes that she is personally powerless. She has yielded all control over her own destiny. Esther and William commit themselves to chance as it is the only option available to them.

Following the horse's defeat, William recognises his fate: 'I shall be under the ground before the next meeting. I shall never take or lay the odds again' (p. 352). Even when faced with death, William articulates his situation using the language of horse racing and gambling. Gambling has been his life and he uses it in an attempt to understand his own imminent death. Significantly, he now starts reading the Bible, which may be regarded as simply part of a continuum. As his business has been criminalized, his health impaired and his increasingly desperate gambling thwarted, he now turns to religion which represents his final prospect of salvation. It may even be seen as his last bet on an outsider. However, it is noteworthy that, whereas Esther seeks to employ her religion in order to assist gambling, William finally rejects gambling in favour of religion. Esther and William reach for each other's values at a time of crisis.

When William addresses his son for the last time he imparts a moral message.

'I want you to promise me, Jack, that you'll never have nothing to do with racing and betting. It hasn't brought me or your mother any luck.'
'Very well, father.'
'You promise me, Jack. Give me your hand. You promise me that, Jack?'
'Yes, father, I promise.'
'I see it all clearly enough now. Your mother, Jack, is the best woman in the world. She loved you better than I did. She worked for you – that is a sad story. I hope you'll never hear it.'
Husband and wife looked at each other, and in that look the wife promised the husband that the son should never know the story of her desertion.
'She was always against the betting, Jack; she always knew it would bring us ill luck. I was once well off, but I lost everything. No good comes of money that you don't work for.' (p. 360)

William has worked hard, but his efforts have been focused on the reallocation of wealth rather than its production. Following William's death, Esther returns to Woodview to find it run down and neglected. Horse racing and gambling has ruined Woodview as it has ruined almost everything else. *Esther Waters* depicts gambling as a kind of parasitical virus which systematically destroys those whom it affects. However, it is also interested in the circumstances underpinning gambling and, more specifically, draws attention to class prejudice and hypocrisy. William's activities are criminalized under the terms of the 1853 Act, but, fundamentally, there is little or no difference between his business and that of a legal gambling operator. Whereas the Act, and non-fiction articles such as Charles Dickens's 'Betting-Shops', labelled and stigmatized off-course bookmakers, George Moore foregrounds the actual personalities involved, showing them to be victims rather than villains.

George Moore's representations of gambling are, prior to *Esther Waters*, fairly straightforward. For example, gambling can signify status, in the case of a rich man laughing off the loss of more than five hundred pounds in *Spring Days*, or nefariousness in the character of Mike Fletcher. In *Esther Waters*, however, we find a more developed understanding of gambling. Gamblers are sometimes at fault in *Esther Waters*, and gambling is consistently destructive, but the environmental factors that produce gambling, and the parliamentary and judicial processes which discriminate between gamblers along class lines, are also exposed. Furthermore, by highlighting the circumstances in which gambling flourishes, and showing the extent to which the main characters are, in effect, compelled to earn a living through gambling, Moore challenges the moral assault on gambling. For Moore, gambling is simply a part of life, particularly working-class life, which is otherwise largely devoid of amusement. It becomes a displaced intellectual activity, with many of the characters at Woodview or in the King's Head having an encyclopaedic knowledge of horse racing. Gambling causes harm in *Esther Waters*, but it is more of a social issue than a moral one. Finally, *Esther Waters*, focusing on working-class people seeking to earn a living through gambling rather than upper-class people dissipating a fortune through gambling, shows, as Moore had intended, an environment in which gambling destroys both servants and masters.[26]

Conclusion

It was hard to avoid gambling in the nineteenth century. Whether one was a gambler oneself, or a reader of novels and journals, or simply exposed to the controversies of the day, the metamorphosis in the perception of gambling through the course of the Industrial Revolution was truly striking. Paradoxically, this change in gambling's status was very useful for those who wielded or aspired to power, as it facilitated a discrimination between an industrious middle class on the one hand and, on the other, a profligate aristocracy and an irresponsible proletariat. Furthermore, the condemnation and attempted legislative suppression of gambling militated against the postulation that gambling *exposed* rather than subverted aspects of the new economic base, which was rooted in speculation (both commercial and marital) as much as individual industry. In this concluding chapter, gambling in the nineteenth-century novel will be considered within each of the three distinct contexts specified in the introduction. There will also be a consideration of the different forms of gambling featured in the study and, finally, some concluding remarks on gambling in the nineteenth-century English novel.

Gambling in the Novels

Benjamin Disraeli employs gambling as a means of commenting on a political malaise. His gamblers are wealthy yet profligate, sophisticated yet socially ignorant. The nobility features numerous gamblers who indulge in the privileges of rank without answering to its responsibilities, thus prompting a cross-reference with Trollope's upper-class gamblers. Disraeli also utilizes the potential of horse racing to symbolise wider contests between individuals, factions and ideas. The rejection of gambling by characters in Disraeli's works involves the adoption of a more mature perspective.

Charles Dickens's representations of gambling share certain features with Disraeli's, as Dickens, in *Nicholas Nickleby*, also depicts gamblers as titled reprobates. One of them, Lord Frederick Verisopht, undergoes a brief yet lucid penance before he dies, implying that the aristocracy, notwithstanding its corruption, is fundamentally decent. The use of this character type by both Disraeli and Dickens demonstrates that the figure of the pleasure-seeking young aristocrat was recognised and understood in the first half of the century. The same licence was not granted to people lower down the social scale. In *The Old Curiosity Shop*, Dickens explores the impact of a gambling mania. Gambling also tests the strength of Little Nell's familial affections. Gambling is the threat which the small child, the personification of moral constancy, resists. Dickens utilises the potential of gambling to express personal irresponsibility and villainy in *Hard Times*, and looks at a less explicit mode of gambling, namely excessive financial speculation, in *Little Dorrit*, which highlights inherent flaws in the 'get rich quick' mentality at the cost of honest endeavour. Significantly, *Little Dorrit* coincides with the emergence of Limited Liability legislation, which boosted commercial and entrepreneurial activity.

In the shorter works of William Makepeace Thackeray examined in this study, gambling can be a tale of ruin or a story of exploitation. In his novel, *Pendennis*, some of the more notorious characters frequent gaming-houses, an action which emphasises their untrustworthiness. In *Vanity Fair*, the main gambler is actually described at a roulette table. Her fortunes are, by this stage, on the decline, but she is still willing to play the game. The scale and nature of Becky's gambling says something about her impropriety and even her desperation, but it also suggests that, in her willingness to keep on trying her luck, she is irrepressible. The conclusion of *Vanity Fair*, in which Becky attains eminent respectability, reinforces the view that she is indomitable. In addition, gambling in the works of Thackeray frequently passes judgment on a whole community, be it callous expatriates in *The Paris Sketch Book*, a debauched upper class in *Pendennis* or a gambling-ridden society in *Vanity Fair*.

In the works of George Eliot considered in this study, gambling primarily signifies irresponsibility. This is certainly the case with regard to Dunsey Cass in *Silas Marner* and Fred Vincy in *Middlemarch*. However, Eliot also uses gambling for other purposes. In the character of Tertius Lydgate, his impetuous bout of gambling reinforces the point that he has an impulsive streak in his character. This personality trait is counter-productive when he gambles and positively destructive in his relationships, where it leads him into making an unwise marriage. In *Daniel Deronda*, through the character of Gwendolen Harleth, gambling comes to express a form of existential protest, although

Eliot also returns to her primary idea of gambling as a signifier for irresponsibility, in the character of Lapidoth.

In Thomas Hardy's *The Return of the Native*, a lengthy bout of gambling is a form of displaced combat. Hardy places gambling under the microscope, focusing on the characters' reactions and excluding the outside world. Gambling in *A Laodicean* is less utterly divorced from its social context, as the main gambling scene takes place in a continental casino. However, the narrator is still less interested in verisimilitude than in using the atmosphere of the casino to reflect George Somerset's position in relation to Paula Power. *A Laodicean* also features the personification of gambling in Will Dare who repeatedly avoids classification through the uncertainty which pervades his whole being.

At the opposite end of the scale to Thomas Hardy is Anthony Trollope, for whom gambling is a means of passing comment on contemporary society. Furthermore, his novels involve the reintroduction of the young, male, aristocratic gambler. In common with earlier writers, Trollope presents this character type as irresponsible and immature. In addition, however, the figure of Sir Felix Carbury acquires a representative status, whereby his mode of living is reproduced on a larger scale by more substantial, though less obvious, gamblers. *The Duke's Children* highlights another aspect of gambling, consistent with the position laid down by Trollope in his non-fiction article, 'On Horse Racing'. Here, gambling is not intrinsically evil, but it is being dragged down by unprincipled, lower-class opportunists.

Comparisons may be drawn between Trollope's representations of gambling and George Moore's in *Esther Waters*, which, throughout, is similarly rooted in its social context. Although Moore's use of gambling in both *Spring Days* and *Mike Fletcher* is fairly orthodox, with gambling being used to signify self-indulgence and irresponsibility, *Esther Waters* offers a much more detailed analysis. Gambling in *Esther Waters* is underpinned by economic factors and social relations. However, Moore also uses horse racing and gambling to say something about his characters, particularly Esther herself whose worth, or lack thereof, at Woodview is made apparent when, at the point at which she discovers she is pregnant, there is a stark contrast between the care offered to a wounded horse and the disregard for the welfare of Esther herself.

Gambling in the Lives of the Novelists

In considering the role of gambling in the lives of the novelists examined in this study and, more specifically, the extent to which their knowledge of gambling fed through into their writings, there is, once again, considerable variation. Benjamin Disraeli patronized Crockford's and eventually became a member. He was therefore well aware of the gambling habits of the upper class in the first half of the century. However, he was less interested in gambling as such than in the opportunity it provided to advance his own political ambitions. Furthermore, although Disraeli is interested in gambling in the public arena of Crockford's, he also describes gambling in private spaces, such as the card game in *The Young* Duke. It is known that Disraeli himself played card games for money in private houses, though at a later stage in his life and for far less significant stakes. It is therefore by no means certain that his knowledge of card games of this kind fed through into *The Young Duke* which, in common with *Sybil*, is interested in showing how gambling was a symptom of irresponsible living within a wasteful upper class.

Charles Dickens's personal knowledge and opinion of gambling is only fully apparent in one or two letters and in the non-fiction article, 'Betting-Shops'. He had clearly seen enough of off-course betting on horse races, and the effects of gambling at horse race meetings, to form the view that gambling was ruinous. However, the only significant reference to gambling and horse racing that I have been able to find occurs in *The Old Curiosity Shop*, when Little Nell is the one spectator at the race meeting not immersed in the experience, and who notes the splendour of the horse in opposition to the greed of the gamblers. She thus reflects her creator's view that gambling is threatening and destructive. This perspective is further apparent in *Nicholas Nickleby* in which Sir Mulberry Hawk is an inveterate gambler who draws Lord Frederick Verisopht into his clutches, and in *Hard Times*, in which gambling debts lead the younger Thomas Gradgrind into committing a burglary and ensuring that the blame falls elsewhere.

Unlike Dickens, William Makepeace Thackeray had extensive personal experience of gambling. His own losses at the hands of two professional gamblers while he was studying at Cambridge are echoed by the experience of Arthur Pendennis whilst he, too, is an undergraduate at Cambridge. Thackeray's losses at cards may also have been an influence in 'Dimond cut Dimond', in which a naive young man is robbed by two wily gamblers at ecarté, the game at which Thackeray was similarly exploited. There are other instances in which Thackeray's experiences of gambling make their way onto paper. In *The Paris Sketch-Book*, Thackeray makes it clear that he is basing his account of a gambler's suicide on an actual incident. Thackeray frequented gaming-houses, as do some of his characters in both *Vanity Fair* and *Pendennis*. Thackeray's own experience of gambling as a whole had shown him that, far from being a level contest, it was often a kind of confidence trick, characterized by manipulation and villainy. This form of gambling, in which the odds are stacked against the guileless player, features in *Vanity Fair*. For example, Becky Sharp manipulates George Osborne through flirtation while her husband wins Osborne's money, various young soldiers lose money to Rawdon Crawley while Becky feigns concern for their welfare, and in Becky's later incarnation in continental Europe she again uses her sexual allure to win money from young men. This is not blatant cheating at gambling and, similarly, it is not known if Thackeray himself was the victim of explicit cheating in his own gambling misadventures. However, both forms of gambling occupy, at best, a grey area, in which the player is lured into the game by a much wilier party who feigns a less expert understanding of gambling than is actually the case.

George Eliot's experience of gambling was limited, but it was enough for her to form the view that it was reprehensible. Her representation of gambling in *Silas Marner* reflects her hostility. Eliot's own perspective on gambling is again apparent in *Middlemarch*, although the novel also contains evidence of movement away from Eliot's personal views. In the characters of both Lydgate and Farebrother, gambling is more than simply a vice as it reflects impulsiveness in the former character and an element of economic necessity (as well as recreational preference) in the latter. This departure from a position of undiluted hostility is further developed in *Daniel Deronda* through the character of Gwendolen Harleth. Eliot was capable of using gambling as more than just a signifier for irresponsibility, being sensitive to the symbolic potential of gambling as an expression of both aspiration and frustration. There is also a paradox in the figure of Gwendolen at the roulette table. On the one hand it stresses chance, with Gwendolen being willing to hazard her future when the occasion demands. However, on the other hand, roulette operates with a built-in percentage operating against the player, and thus Gwendolen is condemned to defeat from the outset.

Thomas Hardy knew as little about gambling as George Eliot. His description of the game of poker dice in *The Return of the Native* is technically accurate without being detailed. His description of roulette in *A Laodicean* is similarly unelaborate, with the focus resting on the players and their collective attitude. Hardy's interest in gambling in *The Return of the Native* is centred on the way in which gambling conducts a conflict at an accelerated pace. Gambling forms the arena for a clash between two characters, for which little direct experience or knowledge of gambling is required by the narrator. In *A Laodicean*, the use of gambling is similarly metaphorical; it is also a key personality trait in the character of Will Dare. However, in common with the representation of gambling in *The Return of the Native*, the gambling of Will Dare is not a matter of meticulous detail, despite the technical knowledge of gambling that Dare acquires through *The Doctrine of Chances*. Instead, gambling says more about the essence of Will Dare as a character.

Anthony Trollope was sufficiently confident about his knowledge of horse racing and gambling to publish his article, 'On Horse Racing'. He also gambled at whist. However, the defining quality of gambling in his life was that it was always recreational and never obsessional. It is clear that this does not feed through directly into his fiction, as his gamblers are often reckless. However, it is hard to imagine that Trollope would have been unaware of the sort of gambling that was taking place on horse racing or at the card table around the time he was writing. His own experiences of gambling lend verisimilitude to his representations of it, as noted by the reviewer of *The Duke's Children* who drew attention to the character of Tifto and the accuracy with which he was drawn (see ch. 7).

George Moore's knowledge of gambling and horse racing was extensive. The level of knowledge he possessed is apparent in *Esther Waters* which contains detailed information about betting on horse races. This strategy also reflects Moore's interest, in the 1880s and 1890s, in the literary techniques of naturalism. Moore's lengthy descriptions of bookmaking in the nineteenth century enhance the realism of *Esther Waters*. George Moore's personal experience of gambling was limited to horse racing and is recorded in *Confessions of a Young Man*. His representations of gambling in his fiction are thus largely confined to horse racing, with only an incidental mention of casino gambling in *Spring Days* and the card playing in *Mike Fletcher* deviating from this general pattern.

Gambling in its Social Context

Benjamin Disraeli wrote *The Young Duke* when Crockford's was in full swing. The main character of the novel is, unsurprisingly, a member of Crockford's. There are also connections to be drawn between Disraeli's Young England trilogy and gambling in Victorian England, as an exclusive gaming-house is featured in *Sybil*. In a novel written and set in the 1840s, Disraeli reflects concern about the gaming-houses by presenting an entire lifestyle of self-indulgence and dissipation with which gambling is associated, centred in an exclusive club. In addition, Disraeli's representations of gambling often involve an adversarial contest between individuals. The aristocrat taking bets on horse races is not the same as the commercial bookmaker. It is a much more personal process, and this aspect of gambling is heightened in the context of a card game around a table. This form of gambling became less common in the second half of the nineteenth century as gambling became more accommodated within a commercial framework. This wider, historical development is recognised by Hugh Cunningham (1980): 'there is widespread agreement that a new phase in the history of leisure opens in the mid-nineteenth century'.[1] The Disraelian gambler is still seeking to forge his own destiny in direct competition with others; he is not the customer of a remote business.

Charles Dickens was clearly aware of the debate surrounding gambling in the early-1850s, as his article about off-course betting shows. However, in his fiction he was generally less responsive to contemporary developments in gambling, although *Nicholas Nickleby* does reflect a common attitude of its time by associating gambling with upper-class excess. In the one Dickens novel in which gambling is a very significant theme, *The Old Curiosity Shop*, it is largely removed from its social context and concentrated in an individual although, through Dick Swiveller's fantasy world, the association of gambling with the lifestyles of the wealthy remains. Elsewhere, Dickens relies on the signifying potential of gambling within the text, rather than relating gambling back to its social context, although the speculations of Merdle in *Little Dorrit* can be related to commercial expansion around the mid-century. When Dickens wished to pass explicit comment on gambling in Victorian society, he did it through the medium of non-fiction.

William Makepeace Thackeray's representations of gambling owe something to their socio-economic context. *Barry Lyndon* focuses on the excesses of the late-eighteenth century, which were realistic enough to attract comment in the report of the 1844 Select Committee on Gaming. Through 1847 and 1848 he published *Vanity Fair*, a novel set in the previous generation. He was thus able to speak of his characters frequenting gaming-houses while simultaneously using this fact to comment on their lack of moral substance. A similar strategy is employed in *Pendennis*, with Sir Francis Clavering's weak character and wasteful habits being typified by the fact that he is an inveterate gambler despite his repeated losses. In the works of Thackeray considered in this study, he has nothing to say about off-course bookmaking. This is partly because his own experiences of gambling had centred on the gaming-house and the card game, but also because, chronologically, his last work to be considered is *Pendennis* which, completed in 1850, just precedes the period in which off-course bookmaking became a matter for widespread social concern.

It is less easy to place George Eliot within the history of gambling in Victorian England. In *Silas Marner* there is no significant gambling episode within the text. We are, however, able to locate Dunsey Cass as a character type, as he is from a family with wealth and influence in the community of Raveloe, and he is a reprobate by nature. He is thus associated with the figure of the irresponsible, upper-class, early-nineteenth-century pleasure seeker alluded to retrospectively in both some of the exchanges in the 1844 Select Committee and in the historical sweep of gambling offered in Andrew Steinmetz's *The Gaming Table*. In *Middlemarch*, Fred Vincy, in his gambling habits, is broadly similar to Dunsey Cass although, unlike Cass, he reforms. In common with *Silas Marner*, the text does not represent Fred Vincy in a specific act of gambling. When this does happen in *Middlemarch*, the gambler is Tertius Lydgate and the action takes place in a pub, which was a recognized arena for gambling in the nineteenth century. *Middlemarch* also features card games at private houses, for relatively modest stakes. The representation of gambling in *Daniel Deronda* does owe something to its historical context, as Gwendolen gambles in a continental casino approximately twenty years after the gaming-houses had been criminalized in England. However, gambling in *Daniel Deronda* is more interesting for its signifying potential with regard to the character of Gwendolen than it is for the realism or otherwise of its portrayal of a European casino in the 1860s. George Eliot's personal hostility to gambling, as evidenced in her letters from the early-1870s, is in accord with the dominant view of gambling of her time.

It is very difficult to productively assess Thomas Hardy's representations of gambling in their wider context. In *The Return of the Native* Hardy excludes the outside world and concentrates solely on Egdon Heath. The gambling scene in *The Return of the Native* is recorded at length but nothing beyond the actual game and the responses of the characters is featured. *A Laodicean* is more responsive to its wider surroundings as Will Dare's attempts to win money at roulette occur in a recognizable environment for gambling. Furthermore, this context also has contemporary significance in relation to the 1845 Act, similar to Eliot's in the opening chapter of *Daniel Deronda*. *Jude the Obscure*, in common with Eliot's *Middlemarch*, reinforces the connection between gambling and pubs. Taken as a whole, Thomas Hardy's representations of gambling pay little heed to parallel developments in gambling in society.

In *The Way We Live Now* Anthony Trollope intended gambling to be seen in its social context. We have the private club as an arena for gambling, although the age of the hazard table was, by that stage, a thing of the past. In *The Duke's Children* Trollope describes betting on horse races, although Lord Silverbridge takes bets himself rather than through the agency of a commercial bookmaker. *The Duke's Children* also articulates grave concern over the involvement of working-class people in betting, although this anxiety has more to do with a perceived lessening in the integrity of the Turf than it has to do with concern over the fact that gambling might have on the working class itself.

George Moore's representations of gambling in his novels are also closely linked to their historical context. *Spring Days* features an ostentatious young man who frequents continental casinos and Newmarket races, thus identifying him as a wealthy pleasure-seeker. However, through the reactions of the characters by whom he is witnessed, the narrator conveys disdain for his shallowness, thereby reflecting a common anti-gambling attitude of his own time. Mike Fletcher, in the novel of the same name, is an adept card player. However, *Mike Fletcher* is also hostile to gambling, as Fletcher's life is characterized by meaningless relationships, owing to his triviality, duplicity and his combative approach to most situations. *Esther Waters* rests substantially on the culture of betting on horse racing in the aftermath of the 1853 Act. It looks at the surface extravagance of on-course bookmaking and also the hard labour by which it was underpinned. It further examines the world of illegal off-course betting on horses, showing how customers and publican conspired to maintain facilities for gambling despite prohibition. *Esther Waters* also explicitly draws attention to the main problem surrounding legislation on gambling in the nineteenth century, namely the extent to which successive parliamentary Acts selectively targeted forms of gambling which were popular amongst the working class. Moore expresses this grievance through the character of William Latch, who finally emerges in *Esther Waters* as a hard-working man struggling against the odds: while the brewing industry had a strong political lobby, off-course bookmakers operated without allies.[2] The hypocrisy Latch highlights is thus imbued with the additional force of his anger, as he is one of those who suffers directly as a result of legislative prejudice. *Esther Waters* is, finally, an anti-gambling novel, as the dying William Latch rejects money that has not been earned although, paradoxically, he works extremely hard in seeking to earn a living through the proceeds of gambling. Furthermore, there is a significant difference between the opposition to gambling expressed in *Esther Waters* and the naked hostility to gambling on moral grounds which became more pronounced towards the end of the century. Although Moore is opposed to gambling in *Esther Waters*, his analysis is mindful both of economic necessity and class prejudice.

Different Forms of Gambling

In seeking to draw distinctions between the various forms of gambling featured in earlier chapters, the first division to be made is between active and passive.[3] For example, gambling on card games is active, as the skill of the player is a key factor in determining the result. Conversely, gambling on roulette is passive, with the player finally trusting to the beneficence of chance. Gambling on horse racing contains both active and passive elements. The player is passive as the outcome is determined by the combination of horse and jockey, but he is active in that he uses his skill and judgement to pick the winner. In Benjamin Disraeli's *The Young Duke*, the Duke of St James samples different kinds of gambling. He patronizes the exclusive clubs and takes a large number of bets at the St Leger horse race, on which he loses spectacularly. From his evident lack of shrewdness at bookmaking it may be suggested that he is less interested in making a profit than in highlighting his own wealth and status and fulfilling the role of the genial aristocrat. However, his main experience of gambling centres on cards. He is thus active in the process which almost effects his own ruin. His own direct, personal responsibility for his huge losses forces him to confront his failings, as there is no one else to whom he can apportion blame. In both *The Young Duke* and the Young England trilogy, Disraeli repeatedly features horse racing, being not only interested in the betting on the race but in the intrinsic and symbolic qualities of the race itself. This is an active and indeed highly competitive process.

Charles Dickens made considerable use of the symbolic potential of card games in his novels. Nell's grandfather, in *The Old Curiosity Shop*, actively seeks out and plays in card games. However, he has a mania for gambling rather than a skilful technique, as evidenced in his marked lack of success. He is never a match for his opponents, whose guile stands in stark contrast to his comparative innocence. Nell's grandfather is ill placed in the combative environment of a card game for money because of his passivity, the degree to which he can be exploited and infantilised by characters whose approach to gambling is strategic rather than obsessional. Card games call for active participation but Nell's grandfather is too easily rendered passive by his opponents. In *Nicholas Nickleby*, Mulberry Hawk is an aggressive card player, like Daniel Quilp in *The Old Curiosity Shop*. In both cases this is a reflection of the character's combative personality. It is not enough for them to gamble: they have to gamble in opposition to others in order to assert their dominance.

In the works by Thackeray considered in this study, card playing is one of the most common forms of gambling. However, whilst this is active, the contest is frequently uneven, with a naive player in opposition to a superior opponent. This is the case in *The Yellowplush Papers* and on more than one occasion in *Vanity Fair*. The game is less competitive than it is exploitative. The game of cards is active but one player, paradoxically, is in a passive position as he is, effectively, at the mercy of his opponent. Thackeray's image of Becky Sharp at the gaming table in *Vanity Fair* is also significant because, although roulette is a passive form of gambling, Becky Sharp is not a passive gambler. Quite simply, she cannot resist taking her chances. When circumstances are propitious she manipulates the game to her advantage, but even when they are not she still spins the wheel.

The figure of the female gambler at the roulette table is repeated in George Eliot's *Daniel Deronda*. The roulette player, Gwendolen Harleth, is passive whereas, in *Middlemarch*, the billiard player, Tertius Lydgate, is active. In Gwendolen's case this is appropriate as, despite her ambitions to the contrary, she is increasingly rendered passive in the novel. Lydgate is active in seeking to determine the result of the game in which he participates. However, prior to his experience of gambling he had been unsympathetic towards it, and therefore his very participation in gambling is an act of submission as he rejects a principle he had formerly held. This is symptomatic of his fate in *Middlemarch* as a whole, as his lofty ambitions are dragged down. Elsewhere in *Middlemarch*, Mr Farebrother plays cards for money. He is active in this process, but he is not combative or exploitative. He, unlike the vast majority of the gamblers featured in this study, is able to maintain personal integrity despite the fact that he gambles. He plays cards for recreational as well as economic reasons and his card playing is thus an experience which is shared rather than adversarial.

The gambling episode in Thomas Hardy's *The Return of the Native* is intensely adversarial. The game of dice occurs between the protagonists whereas, in the environment of a gaming-house, the player ordinarily competes against the bank. The combative nature of the relationship between Venn and Wildeve is reflected in the form of gambling in which they engage. Neither player is able to dictate the outcome of each roll of the dice, and thus they are both passive. The resolution of their mutual animosity is thus left to chance, although the winner of the gamble is by far the better character of the two which suggests that Hardy is using the gamble and its resolution to express something about the moral worth of the characters involved. In *A Laodicean*, Will Dare is quite happy to win money from his father at cards. This shows him to be heedless of family ties when the prospect of gaining a personal, material advantage is at stake. The other form of gambling featured in *A Laodicean* is roulette. Two of the main characters are found in the casino, Dare and Somerset. For Somerset the environment is appropriate because he is passive as he awaits an audience with Paula Power. For Dare the casino is appropriate because his entire existence is connected with chance and he is constantly gambling, either with other people's money or their welfare.

Sir Felix Carbury's card playing in Trollope's *The Way We Live Now* is active. He seeks to win money from his closest associates, signifying his shallowness. The loss of the money with which he planned to elope with Marie Melmotte is, paradoxically, passive, to the extent that the loss allows him to avoid being active in relation to a more serious decision. In *The Duke's Children* Lord Silverbridge tries actively to succeed through the purchase and preparation of a horse and by betting on it for the St Leger. However, his attempts are subverted by the equally active Tifto who harbours a class grievance against Silverbridge. His nefarious conduct, combined with Silverbridge's finally magnanimous treatment of him, expresses the moral worth of these characters and the classes from which they arise.

In George Moore's *Mike Fletcher*, the eponymous main character gambles at card games. This is consistent with his generally competitive personality. His enjoyment of victory at cards is like his delectation in sexual contests; each being used by Fletcher in a finally futile strategy to bolster his self-esteem. In *Esther Waters*, a series of working-class gamblers are ruined by betting on horse racing. Many of them are active in devising strategies for success but, without exception, they are defeated, thereby implying that they are fundamentally passive as the odds are, in the end, too heavily stacked against them. Despite the best efforts of the punters, the bookmakers finally come out on top. This does not apply to the main bookmaker in the novel, William Latch, but he is defeated by a biased legislature rather than by the economics of gambling. The form of gambling foregrounded in *Esther Waters* also says something about Esther herself. She is drawn into the world of horse racing at an early stage in the novel and is thereafter compared and contrasted with a race horse who, unlike Esther, is a prized asset. Although she does not bet on horses herself, she takes a significant risk when she chooses William in preference to Fred Parsons. Her fate thereafter parallels that of the gamblers amongst whom she is placed, largely because, through her husband, she is now integrally connected with the world of horse racing and gambling. Furthermore, she, like the gamblers, watches her fortunes decline. Esther, however, is defeated not by a poor betting strategy but by a legislative climate in which her husband is criminalized, a process which ultimately leads to his death. Esther, though not a gambler herself, is like a gambler as she is constantly working against odds which are, in the final analysis, insurmountable.

When the novelists considered in this study use gambling in a way which reflects orthodox views on the subject, they are able to convey economically substantial information about a character. Rawdon Crawley in *Vanity Fair* is first spoken of as a gambler, which helps to identify him as a rogue. Dunsey Cass in *Silas Marner* is similarly defined as someone with a fondness for gambling when his personality is first discussed, thereby helping to create an image of him as an irresponsible character. When, in *Hard Times*, Mrs Sparsit describes James Harthouse by stating that he looks like a gambler and is therefore quite likely to be immoral, the point is only missed by Bitzer because he has been indoctrinated in an extreme utilitarian system and is therefore not receptive to her metaphor. He sees in betting only an untenable economic principle. Gambling is thus useful as a means of casting doubt on the trustworthiness of a particular personality. Hostility to gambling, especially from the mid-century onwards, in Parliament and in non-fiction writing, created the conditions in which novelists could use the image of gambling and the gambler to express with economy a wealth of information about character and situation.

However, when the novelists featured in this study develop and explore the theme of gambling in their works, the results are even more interesting. For example, gambling reflects on the personality of Tertius Lydgate in *Middlemarch*, but it does not imply that he is an irresponsible character. Instead, it says something about his impulsiveness. Gambling is a more prominent theme in *Daniel Deronda*, and again the development of gambling leads to its being suggestive of existential hunger rather than personal irresponsibility, through the character of Gwendolen Harleth. When George Moore utilises the full potential of the theme of gambling in *Esther Waters*, it leads to a perspective which is hostile to the effects of gambling but which frequently sympathizes with the gambler. This position is substantially different from that adopted in many non-fiction commentaries (particularly the late-century publications of the National Anti-Gambling League) in which gambling is represented as a reprehensible personal weakness and branded as, 'this excrescence on our civilization.'[4] The novels considered in this study differ most fundamentally from non-fiction accounts of gambling through their more exploratory approach to the subject, which enables them to develop the imaginative potential of gambling as a theme. For example, George Eliot immerses the reader immediately in the action in *Daniel Deronda*, with Gwendolen Harleth at the roulette table functioning as a metaphor for her life situation. The irony, however, is that she becomes the stake as well as the player, selling herself in a loveless marriage.

Some representations of gambling are much more technically accurate than others. This may well be a reflection of the respective novelists' personal knowledge and experience of gambling. There are also instances in which the outcome of a gamble in fiction is unlikely. Will Dare in *A Laodicean* finally prospers through roulette, attributing his success to *The Doctrine of Chances*, but this is not a sustainable position mathematically. In *The Return of the Native*, the outcome of the gamble between Venn and Wildeve has more to do with a desired moral configuration than with a likely series of throws in a game of poker dice.[5] However, the dramatic effectiveness of the gambling episode in *The Return of the Native* has little to do with the accuracy or otherwise of its portrayal of a game of dice. Instead, it relies for its effect on the increasing intensity of the conflict between the characters. We can, in general, suggest that some measure of technical accuracy is conducive to the effectiveness of representations of gambling, but that it is not a necessary pre-condition, as, in fiction, gambling can draw upon its symbolic potential for its dramatic impact.

A further consideration is why novelists use a description of a gamble on some occasions and a gambling metaphor on others. The simplest, most reductive answer is that actual gambling focuses conflict. This is especially true of the pre-commercialisation era, when gambles were frequently centred on contests between individuals. We can easily find examples of this in literature. *The Return of the Native* is not only pre-commercialisation in terms of its temporal setting, it is also removed from the commercialisation of gambling spatially as the whole of the action is enclosed in a rural community. The Duke of St James in *The Young Duke* suffers his most catastrophic loss around a card table with other aristocrats. In the latter part of the century gambling wins and losses often occur in a commercialised framework, as happens to Will Dare in *A Laodicean* and William Latch in *Esther Waters*, even though Latch's commercial operation in the pub is outlawed. Gambling metaphors are more commonly employed in order to expose examples of the values of gambling inhering in the wider system. Gwendolen Harleth at the roulette table is a metaphor which demonstrates her powerlessness in society, confined to the fruitless pursuit of chance. While this is an implicitly political point relating to the position of women in Victorian society, gambling metaphors (and the language of gambling as a whole) are regularly used explicitly in relation to politics: a character is 'a beaten horse' in the race for Parliament (*Coningsby*), Napoleon is 'flinging his last stake' (*Vanity Fair*), Augustus Melmotte is 'down in the betting' (*The Way We Live Now*). Gambling metaphors, as this study has shown, also appear in relation to love, inheritances and commerce. The primary effect is to demonstrate the degradation of a plethora of human activities in the context of a society in which money was the major determinant. This threatened the aristocracy, which had traded previously with name and pedigree, and the middle class which proclaimed a very publically visible manifesto of thrift and industry, despite the fact that they were the frequent beneficiaries of new modes of social and economic living. The working class was drawn into wage labour but, for the overwhelming majority, a firm ceiling was placed on its income and realistic aspirations. Gambling metaphors in the nineteenth-century English novel thus articulate anxiety about the social consequences of newly dominant modes of economic behaviour.

One of the difficulties encountered in seeking to disentangle gambling as a literary theme in the nineteenth-century English novel is the extent to which gambling is entwined with other discourses. For example, gambling and love frequently inhabit the same space in the text. This may be a reflection of the level to which love and marriage represented a gamble in the nineteenth century. In a social context in which marriage was almost invariably for life, the decision to marry was the biggest gamble in many people's lives. Disraeli's Duke of St James is a fortunate gambler in this respect although, paradoxically, he has to renounce actual gambling in order to succeed in his marriage aspirations. Conversely, Eliot's Gwendolen Harleth is an unlucky gambler, although all the evidence suggests that the dice were loaded before she even sat down to play the game. This leads us on to another area upon which gambling trespasses; the representation of women. Gwendolen Harleth and Thackeray's Becky Sharp are lively and animated characters in a society which fixes them in a lowly or at best ornamental position. To gamble with money, with love, with life itself is what they have to do in order to escape their allotted roles. The only male character in this study to whom this applies is Moore's William Latch, and he is working-class with no real prospect of ever being otherwise.

Gambling thus appears to be a tool for the dispossessed, but all too frequently this is only an appearance. The game is rarely fair, the odds are rarely even. It takes all the tenacity and indomitability of a Becky Sharp to come out on top. Finally, we find a significant number of instances where representations of gambling overlap with trade and speculation. This exposes anxiety relating to the precarious nature of entrepreneurism. A large number of people depended upon the success of businessmen, as employers, for their livelihoods, and those individuals involved directly with Stock Exchange speculation were even more conscious of the vagaries of the market. The persistence in literature of the connection between speculation and gambling indicates the insecurity felt by many with regard to their own social and economic environment.

Benjamin Disraeli, Charles Dickens and William Makepeace Thackeray all use the figure of the debauched aristocrat in their representations of gambling. This was the main character type with which gambling was associated, until it became recognized as a more widespread social problem from around the mid-century. George Eliot's most developed gambling character is Gwendolen Harleth, who is located on a lower position in the social scale, although she marries an aristocrat. Almost none of Thomas Hardy's gamblers are from the upper class, and George Moore details gambling amongst the working class, especially servants. Anthony Trollope fits less comfortably into this pattern, as his gamblers are upper class. However, even in Trollope's case it is significant that the intervention of a lower-class gambling figure in *The Duke's Children* causes disruption. It is clear that the novelists considered in this study were influenced by the changing perception of gambling throughout the nineteenth century, as their gambling characters reflected the kinds of gambling and the kinds of gamblers who were being represented, and frequently attacked, in the wider society. There is, however, one social class which is conspicuously under-represented in the cast of gamblers in the Victorian novel. Cruikshank's *The Betting Shop* (1852) had stated that respectable, middle-class men were involved with gambling, but this is not reflected in literature. Instead, gamblers are wasteful aristocrats or irrational, lower-class people devoid of self-discipline; both types may be found in Dickens's *The Old Curiosity Shop*. Representations of gambling thus facilitate demarcations between an industrious middle class, the idle rich and the ignorant poor.

We cannot say with certainty that there was a significant increase in gambling in the nineteenth century. As people migrated to the towns and cities they brought their established modes of recreation with them, including gambling. As more people were drawn into an industrial wage economy, and as those who remained in steady employment saw their income level increase, it is not surprising that the amount of money spent on gambling increased, but it does not necessarily follow therefrom that there was any considerable growth in gambling itself. It may be significant that one of the most oft-quoted observers of mid-century England, Friedrich Engels, listed drink and sexual licence as the greatest social problems affecting the working class in England in the 1840s. He mentioned the working man's 'dependence upon all possible accidents and chances', but this mode of living is a state of involuntary gambling.[6]

If we are able to come to any conclusions at all about gambling in England in the nineteenth century, it must surely be to say that most gambling was controlled and recreational. This point was missed spec-tacularly by both right-wing and left-wing commentators. In literature, there is a correlation of sorts between representations of gambling and the way it was commonly perceived at the time. The debauched aristo-crat, the unscrupulous adventurer, the helpless addict, the gambling trap lying within every upper-class club or lower-class pub; one or more of these devices was used by all the novelists considered in this study. However, these representations of gambling have more in common with an ongoing and increasingly venomous anti-gambling polemic in the nineteenth century than with actual gambling itself. It can also be suggested that gambling in the nineteenth-century English novel both served and challenged dominant ideology, identifying gambling as a vice while simultaneously exposing its pervasiveness throughout so-called respectable society. In the post-Darwinian phase gambling situations in literature provide a forum for a lucid expression of the new world view. The descriptions of gambling in nineteenth-century literature cited in this study continue to engage the reader, but almost without exception they fail to confront the simple fact that gambling was a hobby, not a leprosy.

Glossary of Gambling Terms

All Fours   A card game for two players.

Ante   A bet placed in advance, e.g. prior to a horse race or before any cards have been dealt. In card games the ante stake is often raised as the game progresses.

Baccarat   A card game in which the player bets against a banker. The closest modern-day equivalent is the casino game of Punto Banco.

Bagatelle   'A game played on a table having a semi-circular end at which are nine holes. The balls used are struck from the opposite end of the table with a cue' (*OED*).

Blind Hookey   A card game in which the player is 'blind' in the sense that he bets before he sees his cards.

Chicken Hazard   A dice game which differs from normal hazard in the sense that the players compete directly with one another, rather than against a bank.

Écarté   A card game for two players, in which the cards from two to six inclusive are discarded.

Faro   'A gambling game at cards, in which the players bet on the order in which certain cards will appear when taken singly from the top of the pack' (*OED*).

Hazard   A dice game; the forerunner of the modern day casino game, 'Craps'.

Hombre   Otherwise known as 'Ombre'. A card game for three persons. The eights, nines and tens of the pack are removed. It was very popular in the seventeenth and eighteenth centuries.

Lansquenet   'A card game, of German origin' (*OED*).

Macao   A card game, the closest modern day equivalents being Vingt-et-Un and Blackjack.

Monte   A card game of Spanish origin, played with a deck of forty-five cards.

Pea-and-Thimble   A game which typically features three thimbles and one pea, with the player having to guess which thimble the pea is under, and with the operator using sleight of hand to confuse the player. Furthermore, an adhesive on the inside surface of the thimble allows the operator to convince the player that he has made a wrong guess, by moving the thimble against the pea before lifting the thimble to reveal nothing other than empty space beneath.

Pigeon   Colloquially, a gullible player in a gamble, who is generally exploited by the other participants.

Pitch-and-Toss   A game featuring a combination of skill and chance. Players take it in turn to toss a coin at a mark. The closest tosses all the coins, keeping those which land face-up. The next closest player tosses the remaining coins, and so on.

Poker Dice   A game played with anything up to five dice. Instead of numbers the dice feature ace, king, queen, jack, ten and nine. Five aces is the highest scoring combination.

Rouge-et-Noir   A more simple version of roulette, in which the alternative winning possibilities are red or black.

Speculation   'A round game of cards, the chief feature of which is the buying and selling of trump cards, the player who possesses the highest trump in a round winning the pool' (*OED*).

Trente-et-Quarante   This game is very similar to Rouge-et-Noir. In Trente-et-Quarante, the alternative winning possibilities are thirty or forty.

'A Leprosy is o'er the Land'

There follows the lyrics of a prize-winning entry in the National Anti-Gambling League's hymn-writing competition, 1905.

A Leprosy is o'er the Land
'But he was a leper' – 2 Kings v. 1.
Tune: 'Old Hundredth', Ancient and Modern, 166.

A LEPROSY is o'er the Land,
And calls for Thy redeeming aid;
O God of Britain, may we stand
True soldiers in this great crusade.
The war is long, hard is the fight,
The foes are many and are strong;
Uphold, O Lord, our feeble might;
As Thy poor servants face the wrong.

Thou knowest, Lord, the fell disease
Has smitten myriads, rich and poor;
The workman's hour, the wealth of ease
Are squandered for the gambler's store.
Palace and cottage, works and mart
Are suffering from the fatal bane;
Prison, asylum, refuge, home,
Are peopled with the victims slain.

May our weak efforts and our grief
Not vainly call upon Thy will;
Thou didst not ask the Syrian chief
For potent deeds or works of skill.
'Twas but to cast the warrior's pride,
To trust in Thy forgiving love,
To wash in narrow Jordan's tide,
And Thy forbearing mercy prove.

Lord of the forests and the kine
That wander on a thousand hills,
Look down upon this land of Thine
And heal it of these mighty ills.
The guilty nation wash, O Lord,
As Naaman was cleansed of yore;
Rescue it from the gambler's horde,
An honest, godly realm once more.

Notes

Introduction

1 The concern over the growth of gambling amongst the working class is mentioned in, D. M. Downes and others, *Gambling, Work and Leisure: a study across three areas* (London: Routledge and Kegan Paul, 1976), pp. 35–6, and J. M. Golby and A. W. Purdue, *The Civilisation of the Crowd: Popular Culture in England 1750–1900* (London: Batsford, 1984), p. 171. A contemporary article, 'A Fashionable Gaming-House: Confessions of a Croupier', *Bentley's Miscellany*, 15 (1844), 552–64, features a cautionary tale of a young man ruined in a gaming-house, and is discussed in the fourth section of chapter one.

2 George Cruikshank, *The Betting-Book* (London: W. & F. G. Cash, 1852), pp. 16–17.

3 Wray Vamplew, *The Turf: A Social and Economic History of Horse Racing* (London: Allen Lane, 1976).

4 Mark Clapson, *A Bit of a Flutter: Popular Gambling and English Society 1823–1961* (Manchester: Manchester University Press, 1992).

5 Roger Munting, *An Economic and Social History of Gambling in Britain and the USA* (Manchester: Manchester University Press, 1996).

6 J. Jeffrey Franklin, *Serious Play: The Cultural Form of the Nineteenth-Century Realist Novel* (Philadelphia: University of Philadelphia Press, 1999).

7 Andrew Steinmetz, *The Gaming Table: Its Votaries and Victims, in all Times and Countries, especially in England and in France* (Montclair, NJ: Patterson Smith, 1969). John Ashton, *The History of Gambling in England* (New York: Burt Franklin, 1968).

8 Gillian Beer, *Darwin's Plots: Evolutionary Narrative in Darwin, George Eliot and Nineteenth-Century Fiction* (London: Routledge and Kegan Paul, 1983). The impact of scientific discovery on the novels of George Eliot is also considered in, Sally Shuttleworth, *George Eliot and Nineteenth-Century Science: The Make-Believe of a Beginning* (Cambridge: Cambridge University Press, 1984). The intellectual landscape of Britain in the second half of the nineteenth century is discussed in, Stefan Collini, *Public Moralists: Political Thought and Intellectual Life in Britain, 1850–1930* (Oxford: Clarendon Press, 1991).

Chapter One
Gambling in Nineteenth-Century England
Gambling, Leisure and Crockford's Club, 1822–1844

1 Mark Clapson, *A Bit of a Flutter: Popular Gambling and English Society, 1823–1961* (Manchester: Manchester University Press, 1992), p. 16. See also, Roger Munting, *An Economic and Social History of Gambling in Britain and the USA* (Manchester: Manchester University Press, 1996), p. 15.

2 John Belchem, *Industrialization and the Working Class: The English Experience, 1750–1900* (Aldershot: Scolar Press, 1991), p. 175.

3 Peter Bailey, *Leisure and Class in Victorian England: Rational Recreation and the Contest for Control, 1830–1885* (London: Routledge and Kegan Paul, 1978), p. 24. The main contemporary record of pugilism was Pierce Egan's *Boxiana; or Sketches of Ancient and Modern Pugilism* (London: G. Smeeton, 1812).

4 Belchem, *Industrialization and the Working Class*, p. 50.

5 J. C. Reid, *Bucks and Bruisers: Pierce Egan and Regency England* (London: Routledge and Kegan Paul, 1978), p. 137.

6 An account of the contest is given in *Bell's Life in London*, 14 September 1845, cited in Kellow Chesney, *The Victorian Underworld* (London: Penguin, 1972, repr. 1991), pp. 314–28.

7 J. M. Golby and A. W. Purdue, *The Civilization of the Crowd – Popular Culture in England 1750–1900* (London: Batsford, 1984), p. 79.

8 D. M. Downes and others, *Gambling, Work and Leisure: a Study across Three Areas* (London: Routledge and Kegan Paul, 1976), p. 33.

9 Reuven Brenner and Gabrielle A. Brenner, *Gambling and Speculation: A Theory, a History and a Future of some Human Decisions* (New York: Cambridge University Press, 1990), p. 92.

10 The statistics on population are taken from Golby and Purdue, pp. 88–9.

11 Stella Margetson, *Leisure and Pleasure in the Nineteenth Century* (London: Cassell, 1969), pp. 6–7.

12 Belchem, *Industrialization and the Working Class*, p. 145.

13 Cited in, Robert W. Malcolmson, *Popular Recreations in English Society 1700–1850* (Cambridge: Cambridge University Press, 1979), p. 103.

14 Golby and Purdue, *The Civilization of the Crowd*, p. 144.

15 Henry Blyth, *Hell and Hazard: or, William Crockford versus the Gentlemen of England* (London: Weidenfeld and Nicolson, 1969), p. 44.

16 *The Reminiscences and Recollections of Captain Gronow, being anecdotes of the Camp, Court, Clubs and Society 1810–1860* (hereafter *Gronow*), ed. by John Raymond (London: Bodley Head, 1964), p. 255. Gronow wrote his memoirs for money and he may therefore have coloured his memories of incidents and characters in order to enhance the commercial appeal of his book. However, his account is still a valuable source of information concerning the gambling habits and ways of the upper classes in the early century.

17 A. L. Humphreys, *Crockford's, or the Goddess of Chance in St James's Street 1828–1844* (London: Hutchinson, 1953), pp. 26, 33.
18 Cited in ibid., pp. 50–1.
19 *Gronow*, p. 258.
20 J. Jeffrey Franklin, *Serious Play: The Cultural Form of the Nineteenth-Century Realist Novel* (Philadelphia: University of Philadelphia Press, 1999), p. 35.
21 *Gronow*, p. 58.
22 Andrew Steinmetz, *The Gaming Table: Its Votaries and Victims, In all Times and Countries, especially in England and in France* (Montclair, NJ: Patterson Smith, 1969), p. 131.
23 *Gronow*, p. 58.
24 Munting, *An Economic and Social History of Gambling in Britain and the USA,* p. 20.
25 Humphreys, *Crockford's*, p. 105. This process is described in more detail in chapter two.
26 Margetson, *Leisure and Pleasure in the Nineteenth Century,* p. 68.
27 Humphreys, *Crockford's*, p. 53.
28 John Ashton, *The History of Gambling in England* (New York: Burt Franklin, 1968), p. 134.
29 'Hell' was a popular generic name for a gaming-house. During its construction, Crockford's was also popularly known as 'Fishmonger's Hall', and 'The Pandemonium'.
30 Cited in Humphreys, *Crockford's*, pp. 16–17. See also Ashton, *The History of Gambling in England*, p. 122.
31 Reid, *Bucks and Bruisers*, p. 14.
32 *Gronow*, p. 256.
33 Humphreys, *Crockford's*, p. 201.
34 'The New Victorianism' is the title of the final chapter of Blyth's *Hell and Hazard* (see note 13).
35 *Gronow*, p. 18.
36 'Hells in London', *Fraser's Magazine*, 8 (1833), 191–206.
37 Downes, *Gambling, Work and Leisure,* pp. 34–5.
38 Michael R. Booth, *English Melodrama* (London: Herbert Jenkins, 1965). Booth asserts that melodrama was predominantly for the working class (p. 52). However, this is questioned by both Louis James and Douglas A. Reid in, *Performance and Politics in Popular Drama*, ed. by David Bradby, Louis James and Bernard Sharratt (Cambridge: Cambridge University Press, 1980, repr. 1981) who argue that melodrama was popular across a wide social range (see pp. 14, 78).
39 Wylie Sypher, 'Aesthetic of Revolution: The Marxist Melodrama', *Kenyon Review*, 10 (1968), 431–3 (p. 431).
40 Edward Moore, *The Gamester; A Tragedy in Five Acts*, in *The Select London Stage; A Collection of the most reputed Tragedies, Comedies, Operas, Melo-Dramas, Farces, and Interludes* (London: G. Balne, 183?).

41 'Hells in London', *Fraser's Magazine*, 8 (1833), 191–206 (p. 205).

42 H. M. Milner, *The Hut of the Red Mountain; or, Thirty Years of a Gambler's Life*, in Lacy's Acting Edition of Plays, Dramas, Farces, Extravaganzas, etc. etc., Volume 72 (London: Thomas Hailes Lacy, 1867).

43 'Ducange et Dinaux' were pseudonyms for Jacques Félix Bendin and Prosper Parfait Goubaux.

44 Edward Bulwer-Lytton, *Money: A Comedy in Five Acts* (London: Saunders and Otley, 1840); repr. in *Nineteenth Century Plays*, ed. by George Rowell (Oxford: Oxford University Press, 1972), pp. 45–120.

45 Juliet John, *Dickens's Villains: Melodrama, Character, Popular Culture* (Oxford: Oxford University Press, 2001), p. 61.

46 Frank Rahill, *The World of Melodrama* (Pennsylvania: Pennsylvania State University Press, 1967), pp. 1–28.

47 Edward Stirling, *The Old Curiosity Shop: or, One Hour from Humphrey's Clock* (London: Lacy, n.d.). Edward Stirling (1809–94) was an actor and stage manager as well as a playwright. In addition to writing a version of *The Old Curiosity Shop*, he also wrote a stage adaptation of Dickens's previous novel, *Nicholas Nickleby*. See, *The Revels History of Drama in English: Volume III, 1750–1880*, ed. by Michael R. Booth and others (London: Methuen, 1975), p. li.

48 *The Letters of Charles Dickens: Volume Two, 1840–41*, ed. by Madeline House and Graham Storey (Oxford: Clarendon Press, 1969), p. 147.

49 Cited in, Richard Paul Fulkerson, 'The Dickens Novel on the Victorian Stage' (unpublished doctoral dissertation, Ohio State University, 1970), p. 112.

50 H. Philip Bolton, *Dickens Dramatized* (London: Mansell, 1987). Bolton records 142 stage versions of *The Old Curiosity Shop*, pp. 189–209.

51 'Gambling', *Quarterly Review*, 168 (1889), 136–66 (p. 136).

52 A summary of gambling legislation up to 1710 is supplied in, Reuven Brenner with Gabrielle A. Brenner, *Gambling and Speculation: A Theory, A History and a Future of Some Human Decisions* (New York: Cambridge University Press, 1990).

53 John Ashton, *The History of Gambling in England* (New York: Burt Franklin, 1968), pp. 61–3.

54 The provisions of the Act of 1839 (The Police Act) which deal with gambling are detailed in Ashton, *The History of Gambling in England*, p. 140.

55 Peter Bailey, *Leisure and Class in Victorian England: Rational Recreation and the Contest for Control, 1830–1885* (London: Routledge and Kegan Paul, 1978), p. 25.

56 Roger Munting, *An Economic and Social History of Gambling in Britain and the USA* (Manchester: Manchester University Press, 1996), p. 21.

57 Cited in J. M. Golby and A. W. Purdue, *The Civilisation of the Crowd – Popular Culture in England 1750–1900* (London: Batsford, 1984), p. 85.

58 Brenner, *Gambling and Speculation*, pp. 62, 79, 121.

59 A sweepstake may be reasonably likened to a lottery, as both involve the

pooling of the stake money. There is a slight difference between the two, as the allocation of prizes in a sweepstake depends upon a sporting event rather than a blind draw. However, to the gambler (and especially to Esther Waters, who at this stage in the novel is wholly ignorant about horse racing) the process of gambling in a sweepstake is very similar to that involved in a lottery, in that a stake is deposited, in return for which the gambler receives one of a finite number of winning possibilities.

60 Cited in Ashton, *The History of Gambling in England,* p. 213.
61 Cited in Mark Clapson, *A Bit of a Flutter: Popular Gambling and English Society 1823–1961* (Manchester: Manchester University Press, 1992), p. 22
62 See ibid., p. 24.
63 Clapson states that the moral campaign against gambling was at its height between the 1880s and the 1930s (p. 209).
64 The enquiries were in 1808, 1844, 1901 and 1902.
65 British Parliamentary Papers, *Social Problems – Gambling 1, reports from Select Committees of the House of Commons and the House of Lords on Gaming with Minutes of Evidence, Appendix and Indices* 1844 (297) *Vol. I* (Shannon, Ireland: Irish University Press, 1968), p. 171.
66 Cited in Golby and Purdue, *The Civilisation of the Crowd,* p. 171.
67 See pp. 14–16.
68 Sir Llewellyn Woodward, *The Oxford History of England: The Age of Reform 1815–1870,* ed. by Sir George Clark, 2nd edn (Oxford: Oxford University Press, 1997), p. 605.
69 Wray Vamplew, *The Turf – A Social and Economic History of Horse Racing* (London: Allen Lane, 1976), p. 33.
70 Ibid., p. 77.
71 Charles C. F. Greville, *The Greville Memoirs: A Journal of the Reigns of King George IV and King William IV* (hereafter *Greville I*), ed. by Henry Reeve, 3 vols (London: Longmans, Green and co., 1875). Charles C. F. Greville, *The Greville Memoirs: A Journal of the Reign of Queen Victoria from 1837 to 1852* (hereafter *Greville II*), 3 vols (London: Longmans, Green and Co., 1885).
72 *Greville I,* 50 and 147.
73 *Greville II,* 403.
74 Cited in Vamplew, *The Turf,* pp. 90–1.
75 Ibid., p. 96.
76 'A Fashionable Gaming-House – Confessions of a Croupier', *Bentley's Miscellany,* 15 (1844), 552–64.
77 George Cruikshank, *The Betting Book* (London: W. & F. G. Cash, 1852).
78 'Betting-Offices', *Chambers's Edinburgh Journal,* 18 (1852), 57–8.
79 George Moore, *Confessions of a Young Man* (London: Heinemann, 1937), p. 4.
80 Charles Dickens, 'Betting-Shops', *Household Words,* 5 (1852), 333–6.
81 *Lectures to Young Men: Lectures Delivered before the Young Men's*

Christian Association, in Exeter Hall from November, 1857, to February, 1858 (London: Nisbet, 1858).

82 'The Demon of Homburg', *All the Year Round* (hereafter *AYR*), 2 (1860), 517–22 (p. 519).

83 Andrew Halliday, 'You Must Drink!', *AYR*, 11 (1864), 437–40.

84 Andrew Halliday, 'My Two Derbies', *AYR*, 13 (1865), 490–4.

85 Joseph Charles Parkinson, 'Against the Grain', *AYR*, 14 (1865), 442–5. Parkinson was a frequent contributor to *AYR* between 1860 and 1868. He submitted numerous articles on horse racing and/or gambling. In addition to the articles discussed in this chapter, he also published 'Extraordinary Horse-Dealing', 19 (1868), 252–5, and 'Pair of Horse Pictures', 19 (1868), 270–4.

86 Joseph Charles Parkinson, 'The Rough's Guide', *AYR*, 14 (1865), 493–6.

87 Joseph Charles Parkinson, 'Derby Dregs', *AYR*, 15 (1866), 487–9.

88 Joseph Charles Parkinson, 'Genii of the Ring', *AYR*, 15 (1866), 230–3; 'The Eve of the Battle', *AYR*, 15 (1866), 571–6.

89 Samuel Sidney (?), 'Clubs and Club-Men', *AYR*, 16 (1866), 283–8.

90 'Horse Racing in India', *AYR*, 15 (1866), 247–51.

91 'Royal Ascot', *AYR*, 18 (1867), 377–81.

92 'Old Stories Re-told: A Gambler's Life in the last Century', *AYR*, 18 (1867), 324–9.

93 'Far-Western Gamblers', *AYR*, 20 (1868), 489–93.

94 James Greenwood, 'Betting Gamblers', in *The Seven Curses of London* (London: Stanley Rivers, 1869), pp. 377–419.

95 Arguably the greatest chronicler of poverty and crime in Victorian London was Henry Mayhew, who describes the gambling of young men in 'Gambling of Costermongers'. However, as the form of gambling described therein is 'Heads or Tails' with coins, and as this form of gambling is not featured in any of the novels considered in subsequent chapters, Mayhew's account is not detailed here. It may be found in, *London Labour and the London Poor: The Condition and Earnings of Those that will work, cannot work, and will not work, vol. I, London Street-Folk* (London: Charles Griffin,1861), pp. 6–63.

96 Andrew Steinmetz, *The Gaming Table: Its Votaries and Victims, In all Times and Countries, especially in England and in France* (Montclair, NJ: Patterson Smith, 1969).

97 William Makepeace Thackeray, *Vanity Fair: A Novel without a Hero* (London: Oxford University Press, 1908), p. 823. Although *Vanity Fair* is set around the Napoleonic Wars, and *The Gaming Table* was published in 1870, the introduction of Becky Sharp at this stage of the discussion is valid because, like the courtesans mentioned by Steinmetz, Becky's conduct is sexually forward, having the ultimate goal of enhancing her own material welfare.

98 'Gambling', *Quarterly Review*, 168 (1889), 136–66.

99 See Ross McKibbin, 'Working-class Gambling in Britain 1880–1939', *Past and Present*, 82 (1979), 147–78 (p. 148).

100 *The Bulletin: The Occasional Record of the National Anti-Gambling League*, 1 (1893), p. 1. See also Clapson, p. 29.

101 John Hawke, *A Blot on the Queen's Reign: Betting and Gambling, Appeal to the Prince of Wales* (London: Elliot Stock, 1893).

102 R. C. K. Ensor, *The Oxford History of England: England 1870–1914* (Oxford: Oxford University Press, 1992), p. 142.

103 Roger Munting, *A Social and Economic History of Gambling in Britain and the USA* (Manchester: Manchester University Press, 1996), pp. 25–6.

104 'Shall I Bet?' can be found, for example, in *The Bulletin: The Occasional Record of the National Anti-Gambling League*, 2 (1900), p. 179.

105 David C. Itzkowitz, 'Victorian Bookmakers and their Customers', *Victorian Studies*, 32 (1988), 7–30 (pp. 18–19).

106 John Burns, *Brains Better than Bets or Beer* (London: Clarion Press, 1902).

107 J. Ramsay MacDonald, 'Gambling and Citizenship' in, B. Seebohm Rowntree, ed., *Betting and Gambling: A National Evil* (London: Macmillan, 1905), 117–34.

Chapter Two
'A Dissipated Career'
Benjamin Disraeli and a Failing Aristocracy

1 An account of Disraeli's visit to the casino in Frankfurt may be found in *Benjamin Disraeli Letters Volume I: 1815–1834* (hereafter *Letters* I), ed. by J. A. W. Gunn and others (Toronto: University of Toronto Press, 1982), p. 15.

2 Benjamin Disraeli, *The Young Duke: A Moral Tale, Though Gay*, 3 vols (London: Henry Colburn and Richard Bentley, 1831).

3 *Letters* I, p. 74.

4 Matthew Whiting Rosa, *The Silver-Fork School: Novels of Fashion Preceding Vanity Fair* (Port Washington, NY: Kennikat Press, 1964), p. 108.

5 Ibid., p. 109.

6 *The Reminiscences and Recollections of Captain Gronow, being Anecdotes of the Camp, Court, Clubs and Society 1810–1860*, ed. by John Raymond (London: Bodley Head, 1964), pp. 364–5.

7 Benjamin Disraeli, *The Young Duke: A Moral Tale, Though Gay*, 3 vols (London: Henry Colburn and Richard Bentley, 1853).

8 In *Coningsby* there is a minor character named Effie Crabbs, who is also a gaming-house proprietor.

9 *Letters* I, pp. 213–14. See also Robert Blake, *Disraeli* (London: Methuen, 1966, repr. 1984), pp. 71–2.

10 *Letters* I, pp. 418–19.

11 *Benjamin Disraeli Letters Volume II: 1835–1837*, ed. by J. A. W. Gunn and others (Toronto: University of Toronto Press, 1982), pp. 9, 14: 'I can say nothing certain about the Speaker: his fate depends upon negotiations in

train, but they bet at Crockford's 2 to 1 on Sutton' (p. 14).

12 *Benjamin Disraeli Letters Volume III: 1838–1841* (hereafter *Letters* III), ed. by J. A. W. Gunn and others (Toronto: University of Toronto Press, 1982), p. 280.

13 *Letters* III, p. 319.

14 *Benjamin Disraeli Letters Volume IV: 1842–1847* (hereafter *Letters IV*), ed. by J. A. W. Gunn and others (Toronto: University of Toronto Press, 1982), p. 83.

15 *Letters* IV, pp. 26, 29.

16 *Letters* IV, pp. 185–6.

17 Benjamin Disraeli, *Coningsby: or, The New Generation* (London: Longmans, 1881).

18 Blake, *Disraeli*, p. 215. Blake states that Disraeli's portrayal of the real-life debauched aristocrat is far more convincing than Thackeray's.

19 Richard A. Levine, *Benjamin Disraeli* (NY: Twayne, 1968), p. 67.

20 The 'Mr Hudson' referred to in the quote was George 'King' Hudson, a contemporary railway magnate. His career is also mentioned in chapter seven.

21 Benjamin Disraeli, *Sybil: or, The Two Nations* (London: Longmans, 1881).

22 Levine, *Benjamin Disraeli*, p. 68.

23 Louis Cazamian, *The Social Novel in England 1830–1850: Dickens, Disraeli, Mrs Gaskell, Kingsley*, trans. by Martin Fido (London: Routledge and Kegan Paul, 1973, first published 1903), p. 178.

24 Henry Blyth, *Hell and Hazard: or, William Crockford versus the Gentlemen of England* (London: Weidenfield and Nicolson, 1969), pp. 149–50. Paul Bloomfield, *Disraeli* (London: Longmans, 1961), p. 26. Barbara Dennis, *The Victorian Novel* (Cambridge: Cambridge University Press, 2000), p. 112. Blake, *Disraeli*, p. 212.

25 The compositional process of *Sybil* is outlined in Blake, *Disraeli*, pp. 196–7.

26 Benjamin Disraeli, *Tancred: or, The New Crusade* (London: Longmans, 1881).

27 *Letters* IV, p. 91ff.

28 *Benjamin Disraeli Letters Volume V: 1848–1851* (hereafter *Letters V*) ed. by J. A. W. Gunn and others (Toronto: University of Toronto Press, 1982), p. 31. Lord George Bentinck was a friend and political ally of Disraeli. He was also the man who conducted the investigation into the fraud perpetrated at the 1844 Derby.

29 *Letters V*, p. 57.

30 *Letters V*, p. 421.

31 There was a race horse called Coningsby, though it was not owned by Disraeli. He refers to the sale of the horse for six hundred guineas in a letter to his sister dated 25 November 1845. See *Letters IV*, p. 200.

32 *Hansard*, 3rd series, lxxxvi, 677. See also Blake, *Disraeli*, p. 236.

33 *Letters IV* , p. 229.

Chapter Three
'Tumult and Frenzy Reigned Supreme'
Charles Dickens's Gambling Characters

1 Charles Dickens, *Sketches by Boz: Illustrative of Every-day Life and Every-day People* (Oxford: Oxford University Press, 1957).

2 Charles Dickens, *The Life and Adventures of Nicholas Nickleby* (London: Oxford University Press, 1950).

3 *The Reminiscences and Recollections of Captain Gronow, being Anecdotes of the Camp, Court, Clubs and Society 1810–1860*, ed. by John Raymond (London: Bodley Head, 1964), p. 256.

4 Charles Dickens, *The Old Curiosity Shop* (Oxford: Oxford University Press, 1951).

5 *The Old Curiosity Shop* is set in a period between the 1820s and the mid-1830s. See Paul Schlike, *Dickens and Popular Entertainment* (London: Allen and Unwin, 1985), p. 105.

6 More recently, John Bowen has suggested that Nell's grandfather poses a sexual threat to her. See, John Bowen, *Other Dickens: Pickwick to Chuzzlewit* (Oxford: Oxford University Press, 2000), p. 139.

7 There is an interesting comparison to be made between the illustration of Nell's grandfather and Théodore Géricault's painting, *Monomanie du Jeu*. Géricault (1791–1824) included the painting as part of his series, *Portraits of the Insane*. It was probably painted in 1822. The female gambler of *Monomanie du Jeu* is, like Nell's grandfather, hunched and feeble. See, Lorenz E. A. Eitner, *Géricault: His Life and Work* (London: Orbis, 1982), pp. 242–9.

8 Gareth Cordery, 'The Gambling Grandfather in *The Old Curiosity Shop*', *Literature and Psychology*, 33 (1987), 42–61 (p. 51).

9 Schlike, *Dickens and Popular Entertainment*, p. 130.

10 Nell's grandfather's gambling mania may usefully be seen as a 'monomania'. This understanding of mental illness was originated by Philippe Pinel (1745–1826), and further developed by his pupil, Jean-Etienne-Dominique Esquirol (1772–1840). Monomania was used as a generic term for describing a delusional (yet inherently systematic) condition, obsessive and based on a false perception of reality. A further student of monomania was Etienne-Jean Georget (1795–1828) for whom, it is believed, Géricault painted his *Portraits of the Insane* (see note 7 above). See also, P. H. Pinel, *A Treatise* on *Insanity*, trans. by D. D. Davis (New York: Hafner, 1962). However, I have been unable to find any evidence to suggest that Dickens's portrayal of Nell's grandfather was consciously organized around the idea of monomania.

11 The recurrence of fever in Victorian novels is mentioned in, Michael Wheeler, *English Fiction of the Victorian Period 1830–1890* (London: Longman, 1985), p. 38. See also, Lewis Horne, '*The Old Curiosity Shop* and the Limits of Melodrama', *Dalhousie Review*, 72 (1992–3), 494–507 (p. 505).

12 Charles Dickens, *The Life and Adventures of Martin Chuzzlewit* (Oxford: Oxford University Press, 1951).

13 Charles Dickens, *Hard Times* (Oxford: Oxford University Press, 1955).

14 Charles Dickens, *Little Dorrit* (London: Oxford University Press, 1953).

15 *The Letters of Charles Dickens: Volume Eight, 1856–1858* (hereafter *Letters 8*), ed. by Graham Storey and Kathleen Tillotson (Oxford: Clarendon Press, 1995), p. 79.

16 This is not intended to date the action of *Little Dorrit*, which takes place in the 1820s. John R. Reed (1984) states that the timescale of the novel marks Merdle's suicide around 1825. My point is to show that Dickens may have been influenced by an event occurring around the time he wrote the novel, notwithstanding the fact that *Little Dorrit* is set in the previous generation. See John R. Reed, 'A Friend to Mammon: Speculation in Victorian Literature', *Victorian Studies*, 27 (1984), 179–202.

17 Sir Llewellyn Woodward, *The Oxford History of England: The Age of Reform 1815–1870*, ed. by Sir George Clark, 2nd edn (Oxford: Oxford University Press, 1997), p. 605.

18 On p. 220, John Chivery imagines his own tombstone which predicts that his demise will occur in 1826, following the rejection of his romantic advances by Little Dorrit.

19 *The Letters of Charles Dickens: Volume Three, 1842–1843*, ed. by Madeline House, Graham Storey and Kathleen Tillotson (Oxford: Clarendon Press, 1974), p. 325.

20 *Letters 8*, pp. 446–7.

21 Ibid., p. 450.

22 John Forster, *The Life of Charles Dickens*, 2 vols, rev. edn (London: Everyman, 1969, repr. 1980). Forster's concluding statement, with regard to Dickens's visit to Doncaster, reads as follows: 'Dickens might well believe, as he declared at the end of his letter, that if a boy with any good in him, but with a dawning propensity to sporting and betting, were but brought to the Doncaster races soon enough, it would cure him ', p. 192.

Chapter Four

'Gambler, Swindler, Murderer'
William Makepeace Thackeray's Losses and Gains

1 *The Letters and Private Papers of William Makepeace Thackeray: Volume I, 1817–1840* (hereafter *Letters I*), ed. by Gordon N. Ray (London: Oxford University Press, 1945), p. 86. Thackeray's letters to his mother are often confessional, a fact which may have arisen from the fact that he was separated from her at the age of five, when he returned from Anglo-India after the death of his father. He was therefore accustomed to corresponding at length with her by letter.

2 Ibid., p. 90.

3 Ibid., p. 91.
4 *The Reminiscences and Recollections of Captain Gronow, being Anecdotes of the Camp, Court, Clubs and Society 1810–1860*, ed. by John Raymond (London: Bodley Head, 1964), p. 365.
5 *Letters I*, p. 93.
6 Ibid., p. 95.
7 Ibid., p. 97.
8 Ibid., p. 98.
9 Gordon N. Ray, *Thackeray: The Uses of Adversity, 1811–1846* (London: Oxford University Press, 1955), p. 124.
10 Ibid., p. 134.
11 *Letters I*, p. 138ff.
12 Ibid., p. 186.
13 Ibid., p. 187.
14 Ibid., pp. 187, 191.
15 Ibid., pp. 197, 199.
16 Ibid., pp. 200–2. The diary entry quoted is prefaced 'S.18', i.e. Saturday 18. However, as the previous entries are headed 'Thursday. 17', and 'Fr.', and as the subsequent entries are headed, 'S.20', and 'M.21', it seems most likely that the entry actually referred to Saturday 19.
17 Ibid., p. 225.
18 Ibid., pp. 228–30, 237.
19 Ibid., pp. 225–6.
20 Charles C. F. Greville, *The Greville Memoirs: A Journal of the Reign of Queen Victoria from 1837 to 1852*, 3 vols (London: Longmans, Green & Co., 1885), II, 160–1.
21 William Makepeace Thackeray, 'A Gambler's Death', in *The Paris Sketch Book and Art Criticisms* (London: Oxford University Press, 1908), pp. 115–25.
22 William Makepeace Thackeray, 'The Amours of Mr Deuceace: Dimond Cut Dimond', in *The Yellowplush Papers and early Miscellanies* (London: Oxford University Press, 1908), pp. 190–206.
23 William Makepeace Thackeray, *The Memoirs of Barry Lyndon* (London: Oxford University Press, 1908).
24 William Makepeace Thackeray, *Vanity Fair* (London: Oxford University Press, 1908).
25 'A Fashionable Gaming-House – Confessions of a Croupier', *Bentley's Miscellany*, 15 (1844), 552–64 (p. 552). This article is considered in greater detail in chapter 1.
26 *The Letters and Private Papers of William Makepeace Thackeray: Volume II, 1841–1851* (London: Oxford University Press, 1945), p. 419.
27 Ibid., p. 421.
28 William Makepeace Thackeray, *The History of Pendennis* (London: Oxford University Press, 1908).

29 John Carey, *Thackeray – Prodigal Genius* (London: Faber and Faber, 1977), p. 30.

30 A. L. Humphreys, *Crockford's, or the Goddess of Chance in St James's Street 1828–1844* (London: Hutchinson, 1953), pp. 88, 163.

31 Cited in ibid., p. 217.

32 Cited in Geoffrey Tillotson and Donald Hawes (ed.), *Thackeray – The Critical Heritage* (London: Routledge and Kegan Paul, 1968), p. 92.

33 J. M. Golby and A. W. Purdue, *The Civilisation of the Crowd – Popular Culture in England 1750–1900* (London: Batsford, 1984), pp. 118, 121.

34 Ibid., pp. 122, 147.

35 Cited in Tillotson and Hawes, *Thackeray – The Critical Heritage*, pp. 101–2.

36 Michael Wheeler, *English Fiction of the Victorian Period 1830–1890* (London: Longman, 1985), p. 32.

37 *Letters I*, p. 507.

38 Gordon N. Ray, *Thackeray: The Age of Wisdom, 1847–1863* (London: Oxford University Press, 1958), p. 450.

39 See note 19 above.

Chapter Five
'Lose Strikingly'
Gambling with Life in George Eliot

1 *The George Eliot Letters: Volume V, 1869–1873* (hereafter *Letters V*), ed. by Gordon S. Haight (London: Oxford University Press, 1956), p. 312. Eliot's reference to the closure of the gambling-halls pertains to Bismarck's decision to shut them down in 1872, see Andrew Steinmetz, *The Gaming Table: its Votaries and Victims, in all Times and Countries, especially in England and in France* (Montclair, NJ: Patterson Smith, 1969), pp. 199–200.

2 *Letters V*, p. 436.

3 George Eliot, *Silas Marner* (Edinburgh and London: William Blackwood and Sons, 1878).

4 Sally Shuttleworth, *George Eliot and Nineteenth-Century Science: The Make-Believe of a Beginning* (Cambridge: Cambridge University Press, 1984), p. 80.

5 George Eliot, *Middlemarch*, 3 vols (Edinburgh and London: William Blackwood and Sons, 1878).

6 Gordon S. Haight, *George Eliot: A Biography* (Oxford: Clarendon Press, 1968), p. 420.

7 George Eliot, *Daniel Deronda*, 3 vols (Edinburgh and London: William Blackwood and Sons, 1878).

8 *Letters V*, p. 314.

9 Haight, *George Eliot*, p. 458, see also Gillian Beer, *Darwin's Plots: Evolutionary Narrative in Darwin, George Eliot and Nineteenth-Century Fiction* (London: Routledge and Kegan Paul, 1983), p. 186.

10 *The George Eliot Letters: Volume VI, 1874–1877* (hereafter *Letters VI*). ed. by Gordon S. Haight (London: Oxford University Press, 1956), p. 193.

11 Josephine McDonagh, *George Eliot* (Plymouth: Northcote House, 1997), p. 77.

12 *Letters VI*, p. 180.

13 Shuttleworth, *George Eliot and Nineteenth-Century Science*, p. 175.

14 Beer, *Darwin's Plots*, p. 149.

15 *Essays of George Eliot*, ed. by Thomas Pinney (London: Routledge and Kegan Paul, 1963), p. 445.

16 Alan Mintz, *George Eliot and the Novel of Vocation* (Harvard: Harvard University Press, 1978), p. 152.

17 Ibid., p. 152.

18 Beer, *Darwin's Plots*, pp. 185–6.

19 Shuttleworth, *George Eliot and Nineteenth-Century Science*, p. 184.

20 *Letters VI*, pp. 232–3.

21 D. M. Downes and others, *Gambling, Work and Leisure: a study across three areas* (London: Routledge and Kegan Paul, 1976), p. 13.

Chapter Six
'Doctrines of Chance'
Gambling as the Universal Trope in Thomas Hardy

1 *The Life of Thomas Hardy 1840–1928* (hereafter *Life*), by Florence Emily Hardy (London: Macmillan, 1962), p. 138.

2 Thomas Hardy, *Desperate Remedies* (London: Macmillan, 1912).

3 Thomas Hardy, *Far from the Madding Crowd* (London: Macmillan, 1912).

4 E. P. Thompson, *The Making of the English Working Class*, rev edn (London: Penguin, 1991), p. 444.

5 Thomas Hardy, *The Return of the Native* (London: Macmillan, 1912).

6 Carl J. Weber, *Hardy of Wessex: His Life and Literary Career* (New York: Columbia University Press, 1940), dates the action in 1842–3 (pp. 72–5). The same position is adopted by R. W. Stallman in, 'Hardy's Hour-Glass Novel', *Sewanee Review*, 55 (1947), 283–96. According to Pinion (see below), 'the period of the story was 1842–3 or 1847–8' (p. 31).

7 James Gindin, 'Hardy and Folklore', in *The Return of the Native* (hereafter *Return*, Norton Critical Edition), by Thomas Hardy (New York: W. W. Norton, Norton Critical Edition, 1969), p. 400.

8 See F. B. Pinion, *A Hardy Companion* (London: Macmillan, 1968), p. 32.

9 *The Collected Letters of Thomas Hardy: Volume 1, 1840–1892* (hereafter *Letters*), ed. by Richard Little Purdy and Michael Millgate (Oxford: Clarendon Press, 1978), p. 53.

10 In the strictest sense, the event is not a raffle, as the participants are not buying tickets for a draw. However, it is termed a raffle by the narrator (p. 262).

11 John Paterson, 'The Making of *The Return of the Native*', *English Studies*, 19 (1960), cited in, *Return*, Norton Critical Edition, p. 347.

12 Ibid., p. 339.

13 Ibid., p. 348.

14 *Letters*, p. 64.

15 This feature of gambling is discussed at length in, Erving Goffmann, *Where the Action is* (London: Allen Lane, 1969), pp. 105–206.

16 See Gillian Beer, *Darwin's Plots – Evolutionary Narrative in Darwin, George Eliot and Nineteenth-Century Fiction* (London: Routledge and Kegan Paul, 1983), p. 9. Beer notes the limitations of the individual existence within an evolutionary order. My statement that gambling 'pushes fate' is intended to underline the idea that gambling accelerates action. It is most likely that Venn and Wildeve would have come into direct conflict at some stage, given where they both stand in relation to Thomasin. However, without the gamble there is nothing in the text to suggest that their animosity could be focused in one dramatic incident. Strictly speaking, therefore, the gamble in *The Return of the Native* is neither a *part* of fate nor something that *changes* fate. Instead, the effect of the gamble is to hasten considerably a likely outcome.

17 Beer, *Darwin's Plots*, p. 254.

18 Thomas Hardy, *A Laodicean: A Story of To-day* (London: Macmillan, 1912). The Laodiceans feature in the Book of Revelation, chapter three, verses fourteen to sixteen. Laodicea was a prosperous city in Asia minor, the inhabitants of which were lukewarm in their faith. The non-committal nature of the Laodiceans ties-in with certain themes in the novel, namely Paula Power's reluctance to commit to a religious creed at the beginning of the novel, and the indeterminacy pervading Will Dare's entire being.

19 Cited in Paul Ward, '*A Laodicean*', *The Thomas Hardy Year Book*, 11 (1984), 28–30 (p. 29).

20 *Life*, pp. 145–6.

21 Peter Widdowson, *Thomas Hardy* (Plymouth: Northcote House, 1996).

22 Pinion, *A Hardy Companion*, p. 37.

23 Peter J. Casagrande, *Unity in Hardy's Novels: Repetitive Symmetries* (London: Macmillan, 1982), p. 175.

24 *The Literary Notebooks of Thomas Hardy: Volume 1*, ed. by Lennart A. Bjork (London: Macmillan, 1985), p. 92.

25 Ibid., p. 93. In the introduction to *Literary Notebooks 1*, attention is drawn to the significant connections between Hardy's notebook entries and *The Return of the Native* and *A Laodicean* (p. xxvi).

26 Abraham De Moivre, *The Doctrine of Chances, or a Method of Calculating the Probabilities of Events in Play* (London: Frank Cass, 1969).

27 F. N. David, *Games, Gods and Gambling* (London: Charles Griffin, 1962), pp. 163, 171.

28 'Meum and 'tuum' are Latin for 'mine' and 'yours'.

29 Thomas Hardy, *The Mayor of Casterbridge* (London: Macmillan, 1912).

30 Thomas Hardy, *Jude the Obscure* (London: Macmillan, 1912).
31 See Beer, *Darwins Plots,* p. 238.

Chapter Seven
'A Real Gentleman should never want the Money out of another Man's Pocket'
Anthony Trollope, Gambling and Class Contamination

1 See N. John Hall, *Trollope: A Biography* (Oxford: Clarendon Press, 1991), pp. 54–5.
2 Anthony Trollope, *An Autobiography* (hereafter *Autobiography*), (London: Oxford University Press, 1950), p. 53.
3 Anthony Trollope, 'On Horse Racing', in *British Sports and Pastimes* (London: Virtue, 1868), 9–69.
4 Anthony Trollope, *Sir Harry Hotspur of Humblethwaite* (London: Hurst & Blackett, 1871).
5 Anthony Trollope, *The Way We Live Now*, The World's Classics Series (London: Oxford University Press, 1951, repr., 1975).
6 Hall, *Trollope*, p. 385.
7 Michael Sadleir, *Trollope: A Commentary*, 3rd edn (London: Oxford University press, 1945, rcpr. 1961).
8 G. Kitson Clark, *The Making of Victorian England* (London: Methuen, 1962), p. 30.
9 Cited in Donald Smalley (ed.), *Trollope: The Critical Heritage* (London: Routledge and Kegan Paul, 1969), p. 398.
10 Andrew Sanders, amongst others, has noted a correspondence between Lady Carbury and Trollope's own mother: 'Lady Carbury has long been taken to be an oblique glance back at Frances Trollope.' See, Andrew Sanders, *Anthony Trollope* (Plymouth: Northcote House, 1998), p. 6.
11 The wider issue of Trollope's understanding of gentlemanly conduct is discussed in, Arthur Pollard, 'Trollope's Idea of the Gentleman', in John Halperin (ed.), *Trollope Centenary Essays* (Basingstoke: Macmillan, 1982, repr. 1985), 86–94.
12 *The Letters of Anthony Trollope* (hereafter *Letters*), ed. Bradford Allen Booth (London: Oxford University Press, 1951), p. 323.
13 *Autobiography*, p. 159.
14 Ibid., p. 160.
15 Ibid., p. 158.
16 Anthony Trollope, 'Whist at Our Club', *Blackwood's Edinburgh Magazine*, 121 (1877), 597–604.
17 Charles James Fox (1749–1806), a leading politician who became foreign secretary shortly before his death. He was also a renowned gambler.
18 Sir Llewellyn Woodward, *The Oxford History of England: The Age of*

Reform, 1815–1870, ed. Sir George Clark, 2nd edn (Oxford: Oxford University Press, 1997), p. 606.

19 Sadleir, *Trollope*, p. 398.

20 Anthony Trollope, *The Duke's Children*, The World's Classics Series (Oxford: Oxford University Press, 1983).

21 Sadleir, *Trollope*, p. 374n.

22 Joseph Charles Parkinson, 'Derby Dregs', *All the Year Round*, 15 (1866), 487–9.

23 Charles C. F. Greville, *The Greville Memoirs: A Journal of the Reigns of King George IV and King William IV*, ed. Henry Reeve, 3 vols (London: Longmans, Green and Co.), III, 139–40.

24 Charles C. F. Greville, *The Greville Memoirs: A Journal of the Reign of Queen Victoria from 1837 to 1852*, 3 vols (London: Longmans, Green and Co.), II, 396.

25 Ibid., I. 23.

26 *Letters*, p. 330.

27 Smalley, *Trollope: The Critical Heritage*, p. 468.

28 Ibid., p. 470.

Chapter Eight
'One Law for the Rich and another for the Poor'
George Moore's Working Gamblers

1   Cited in, Joseph Hone, *The Life of George Moore* (London: Gollancz, 1936), p. 195.

2   Ibid., pp. 18, 31.

3   Ibid., p. 32.

4   George Moore, *Confessions of a Young Man* (London: Heinemann, 1937).

5   Hone, *The Life of George Moore*, p. 43. See also *Confessions of a Young Man*, p. 8.

6   George Moore, *Spring Days* (London: Vizetelly, 1888). As *Spring Days* is not available in the Ebury edition of Moore's works, I have reverted to the first edition. The same also applies to *Mike Fletcher* (see below).

7   George Moore, *Mike Fletcher* (London: Ward and Downey, 1889).

8   George Moore, *Esther Waters* (London: Heinemann, 1937).

9   E. Bowen-Rowlands, 'A Glance at the History of Gambling', *Westminster Review*, 135 (1891), p. 659.

10 Cited in, Ross McKibbin, 'Working-Class Gambling in Britain 1880–1939', *Past and Present*, 82 (1979), 147–78 (p. 159).

11 The information on sweepstakes is taken from, David C. Itzkowitz, 'Victorian Bookmakers and their Customers', *Victorian Studies*, 32 (1988), pp. 7–30 (p. 14).

12 According to Hone, *The Life of George Moore*, the character of Mr Randal was based on Joseph Appley, the butler at Moore Hall in Ireland (pp. 21,

166).

13 In chapter twenty-five, mention is made of the Metropolitan Railway, thereby dating the action in or after 1862, the year in which the railway opened.

14 Itzkowitz, 'Victorian Bookmakers', p. 14: 'it was to the advantage of on-course bookmakers to be as noticeable as possible in order to attract the attention of potential customers'.

15 Gustave Doré and Blanchard Jerrold, *London: A Pilgrimage* (New York: Dover, 1970). There is no evidence to suggest that Moore's description is based directly on Doré's drawing. However, as an art critic of some reputation it is clear that Moore would have been aware of Doré's work and, furthermore, Moore mentions Doré in *Confessions of a Young Man* (ch. 1).

16 Hone, *The Life of George Moore*, p. 186.

17 Wray Vamplew, *The Turf: A Social and Economic History of Horse Racing* (London: Allen Lane, 1976), p. 203. The figures apply to a period before the time in which *Esther Waters* is set, but Vamplew's statistics give some indication of the number of outlets for working-class gambling on horse racing in Victorian London.

18 James Runciman, 'The Ethics of the Turf', *Contemporary Review*, 55 (1889), pp. 807–8.

19 The problems of enforcing the law regarding gambling were aired by Richard Mayne, Commissioner of the Metropolitan Police, in his evidence to the 1844 Select Committee on Gaming (see ch. 1).

20 I have been unable to locate any specific references to identify the nature of the gambling that went on at the Albert Club, though it was apparently patronised by members of Parliament.

21 J. M. Golby and A. W. Purdue, *The Civilisation of the Crowd: Popular Culture in England 1750–1900* (London: Batsford, 1984), pp. 118–22.

22 D. C. Pedder, 'The Tipster and his Trade', *Monthly Review*, 12 (1903), pp. 73–4.

23 The Cesarewitch is an alternative spelling of the Czarewitch, as mentioned in *Spring Days* (see p. 193).

24 Itzkowitz, 'Victorian Bookmakers', p. 18.

25 'Raising the ante' is a gambling term, most commonly used in Poker. It refers to an increase in the minimum stake which has the effect of making the pool of money larger and the gambling, therefore, more serious and consequential.

26 Moore's intentions with regard to *Esther Waters* are presented in Hone, *The Life of George Moore*, p. 165.

Conclusion

1 Hugh Cunningham, *Leisure in the Industrial Revolution* (London: Croom Helm, 1980), p. 140.

2 Reuven Brenner and Gabrielle A. Brenner, *Gambling and Speculation: A*

Theory, A History and a Future of some Human Decisions (New York: Cambridge University Press, 1990), p. 127: 'brewers had a strong political lobby, being linked with agricultural and industrial interests as well as with finance and retailing outlets. The alcohol industry was also a major employer of labour; sellers of drink were as numerous, for example, as sellers of food'.

3   It is acknowledged that the demarcation between active and passive is not entirely neat. For example, roulette contains active elements in the sense that the player is physically active in the course of the game and chooses the numbers on which he bets. Similarly, card games have a passive dimension in the sense that the player is dealt cards and therefore does not actively choose them. In identifying games and sports as active and passive, therefore, I am focusing on their primary qualities, seeing roulette as a fundamentally passive process and card playing as an active one.

4   *The Bulletin: The Occasional Record of the National Anti-Gambling League*, I, 1893, p. 1.

5   The idea that Wildeve's defeat in the dice game expresses a desired moral configuration is later undercut in *The Return of the Native* when he receives an inheritance. However, the dice game is essentially a contest between individuals, and the outcome confirms the moral and psychological supremacy of Venn over Wildeve.

6   Friedrich Engels, *The Condition of the Working Class in England* (Oxford: Oxford University Press, 1993), pp. 113, 139.

Bibliography

Primary Texts

Bulwer-Lytton, Edward, *Money: A Comedy in Five Acts* (London: Saunders and Otley, 1840); repr. in *Nineteenth-Century Plays*, ed. by George Powell (Oxford: Oxford University Press, 1972), 45–120.

Dickens, Charles, *Sketches by Boz: Illustrative of Every-day Life and Every-day People* (Oxford: Oxford University Press, 1957).

——, *The Life and Adventures of Nicholas Nickleby* (London: Oxford University Press, 1950).

——, *The Old Curiosity Shop* (Oxford: Oxford University Press, 1951).

——, *The Life and Adventures of Martin Chuzzlewit* (Oxford: Oxford University Press, 1951).

——, *Hard Times* (Oxford: Oxford University Press, 1955).

——, *Little Dorrit* (London: Oxford University Press, 1953).

Disraeli, Benjamin, *The Young Duke: A Moral Tale, Though Gay*, 3 vols (London: Henry Colburn and Richard Bentley, 1831).

——, *Coningsby: or The New Generation* (London: Longmans, 1881).

——, *Sybil: or The Two Nations* (London: Longmans, 1881).

——, *Tancred: or The New Crusade* (London: Longmans, 1881).

——, *The Young Duke*, rev. edn (London: Henry Colburn and Richard Bentley, 1853).

Eliot, George, *Silas Marner* (Edinburgh and London: William Blackwood and Sons, 1878).

——, *Middlemarch* (Edinburgh and London: William Blackwood and Sons, 1878).

——, *Daniel Deronda* (Edinburgh and London: William Blackwood and Sons, 1878).

Hardy, Thomas, *Desperate Remedies* (London: Macmillan, 1912).

——, *Far from the Madding Crowd* (London: Macmillan, 1912).

——, *The Return of the Native* (London: Macmillan, 1912).

——, *A Laodicean: A Story of To-Day* (London: Macmillan, 1912).

——, *The Mayor of Casterbridge* (London: Macmillan, 1912).

——, *Jude the Obscure* (London: Macmillan, 1912).

Milner, H. M., *The Hut of the Red Mountain; or, Thirty Years of a Gambler's*

Life, in *Lacy's Acting Edition of Plays, Dramas, Farces, Extravaganzas, etc. etc., Volume 72* (London: Thomas Hailes Lacy, [1867]).

Moore, George, *Spring Days: A Realistic Novel* (London: Vizetelly, 1888).

——, *Mike Fletcher* (London: Ward and Downey, 1889).

——, *Confessions of a Young Man* (London: Heinemann, 1937).

——, *Esther Waters* (London: Heinemann, 1937).

Stirling, Edward, *The Old Curiosity Shop: or, One Hour from Master Humphrey's Clock* (London: Lacy, n.d.).

Thackeray, William Makepeace, *The Memoirs of Barry Lyndon* (London: Oxford University Press, 1908).

——, *Vanity Fair: or, A Novel Without a Hero* (London: Oxford University Press, 1908).

——, *Pendennis* (London: Oxford University Press, 1908).

——, *The Paris Sketch Book and Art Criticisms* (London: Oxford University Press, 1908).

——, *The Yellowplush Papers and Early Miscellanies* (London: Oxford University Press, 1908).

Trollope, Anthony, *The Way We Live Now*, The World's Classics Series (London: Oxford University Press, 1951, repr. 1975).

——, *The Duke's Children*, The World's Classics Series (Oxford: Oxford University Press, 1983).

Parliamentary Proceedings

British Parliamentary Papers, *Social Problems – Gambling 1, Reports from Select Committees of the House of Commons and the House of Lords on Gaming with Minutes of Evidence, Appendix and Indices (297) Vol. VII* (Shannon, Ireland: Irish University Press, 1968).

Secondary Texts

Andrews, Malcolm, *Dickens and the Grown-up Child* (London: Macmillan, 1994).

Anonymous, 'Vanity Fair', *Fraser's Magazine*, Edinburgh, 38 (1848), 320–33.

Bailey, J. O., *British Plays of the Nineteenth Century* (New York: The Odyssey Press, 1966).

Barrett, Dorothea, *Vocation and Desire: George Eliot's Heroines* (London: Routledge, 1989).

Beer, Gillian, *Darwin's Plots: Evolutionary Narrative in Darwin, George Eliot and Nineteenth-Century Fiction* (London: Routledge and Kegan Paul, 1983).

——, *George Eliot*, Key Women Writers Series: I (Brighton: Harvester Press, 1986).

——, 'The Reader's Wager: Lots, Sorts, and Futures', *Essays in Criticism*, 40 (1990), 99–123.

Behrens, Robert, 'Benjamin Disraeli and the Triumph of Imagination', Politics Working Paper no. 43 (Warwick: University of Warwick, 1987).

Björk, Lennart A., ed., *The Literary Notebooks of Thomas Hardy*, 2 vols (London: Macmillan, 1985).

Blake, Robert, *Disraeli* (London: Methuen, 1966, repr. 1984).

Blake, Robert and Derek Beales, *Disraeli* (Devizes: Sussex Tapes, audio cassette tape).

Bloomfield, Paul, *Disraeli* (London: Longmans, Green & Co., 1961).

Bolton, H. Philip, *Dickens Dramatized* (London: Mansell, 1987).

Booth, Bradford Allen, ed., *The Letters of Anthony Trollope* (London: Oxford University Press, 1951).

Booth, Michael R., *English Melodrama* (London: Herbert Jenkins, 1965).

Booth, Michael R. *et al.*, ed., *The Revels History of Drama in English: Volume VI, 1750–1880* (London: Methuen, 1975).

Bowen, John, *Other Dickens: Pickwick to Chuzzlewit* (Oxford: Oxford University Pres, 2000).

Bradley, David, Louis James and Bernard Sharratt, ed., *Performance and Politics in Popular Drama* (Cambridge: Cambridge University Press, 1980, repr. 1981), pp. 1–16, 65–85.

Brightfield, Myron F., *Victorian England in its Novels (1840–1870)*, vol. 3 (Los Angeles: University of California Library, 1968), pp. 154–61.

Brown, Douglas, *Thomas Hardy* (Westport, Connecticut: Greenwood Press, 1954; repr. 1980).

Carey, John, *Thackeray: Prodigal Genius* (London: Faber and Faber, 1977).

Casagrande, Peter J., *Unity in Hardy's Novels: 'Repetitive Symmetries'* (London: Macmillan, 1982).

Cazamian, Louis, *The Social Novel in England 1830–1850: Dickens, Disraeli, Mrs Gaskell, Kingsley*, trans. by Martin Fido (London: Routledge and Kegan Paul, 1973).

Cordery, Gareth, 'The Gambling Grandfather in The Old Curiosity Shop', *Literature and Psychology*, 33 (1987), 42–61.

Corrigan, Robert W., ed., *Laurel British Drama: The Nineteenth Century* (New York: Dell, 1967), pp. 7–22.

Coveney, Peter, *Poor Monkey: The Child in Literature* (London: Rockliff, 1957), pp. 71–119.

Davies, Cecil W., 'Order and Chance – The Worlds of Wordsworth and Hardy', *The Thomas Hardy Year Book*, 8 (1978), 40–9.

Dennis, Barbara, *The Victorian Novel* (Cambridge: Cambridge University Press, 2001).

Eglington, John, ed., *Letters of George Moore* (Bournemouth: Sydenham, 1942).

Ellman, Richard, ed., *Edwardians and Late Victorians* (New York: Columbia University Press, 1959).

Flint, Kate, *Dickens* (Brighton: Harvester, 1986).

——, ed., *The Victorian Novelist: Social Problems and Social Change* (London: Croom Helm, 1987).

Forster, John, *The Life of Charles Dickens*, 2 vols, rev edn (London: Everyman, 1969, repr. 1980).

Franklin, J. Jeffrey, 'The Victorian Discourse of Gambling: Speculations on *Middlemarch* and *The Duke's Children*', *Essays in Literary History*, 61 (1994), 899–921.

Fulkerson, Richard Paul, 'The Dickens Novel on the Victorian Stage' (unpublished doctoral dissertation, Ohio State University, 1970).

Gallagher, Catherine, *The Industrial Reformation of English Fiction: Social Discourse and Narrative Form 1832–1867* (Chicago: University of Chicago Press, 1985).

Gettmann, Royal A., 'George Moore's Revisions of *The Lake*, *The Wild Goose*, and *Esther Waters*', *Publications of the Modern Language Association of America*, 59 (1944), 540–55.

Gilmour, Robin, *The Novel in the Victorian Age* (London: Arnold, 1986).

Gregor, Ian and David Lodge, *The Novels of Thomas Hardy* (Devizes: Sussex Tapes, 1972, audio-cassette tape).

Gregor, Ian, ed., *Reading the Victorian Novel: Detail into Form* (London: Vision Press, 1980).

Gunn, J. A. W., and others, eds, *Benjamin Disraeli Letters*, 5 vols (Toronto: Toronto University Press, 1982).

Haight, Gordon S., ed., *The George Eliot Letters: Volume III, 1859–1861* (London: Oxford University Press, 1954).

——, *The George Eliot Letters: Volume V, 1869–1873* (London: Oxford University Press, 1956).

——, *The George Eliot Letters: Volume VI, 1874–1877* (London: Oxford University Press, 1956).

——, *George Eliot: A Biography* (London: Oxford University Press, 1968).

Hall, N. John, *Trollope: A Biography* (Oxford: Clarendon Press, 1991).

Halperin, John, ed., *Trollope Centenary Essays* (Basingstoke: Macmillan, 1982, repr. 1985).

Hardy, Barbara, *The Exposure of Luxury: Radical Themes in Thackeray* (London: Peter Owen, 1972).

Hardy, Florence Emily, *The Life of Thomas Hardy 1840–1928* (London: Macmillan, 1962).

Hart-Davis, Rupert, ed., *George Moore: Letters to Lady Cunard* (London: Rupert Hart-Davis, 1957).

Hone, Joseph, *The Life of George Moore* (London: Gollancz, 1936).

Horne, Lewis, '*The Old Curiosity Shop* and the Limits of Melodrama', *Dalhousie Review*, 72 (1992–3), 494–507.

Horsman, Alan, *The Victorian Novel* (Oxford: Clarendon Press, 1990).

House, Madeline, Graham Storey, Kathleen Tillotson and others, ed., *The Letters of Charles Dickens*, 9 vols (Oxford: Clarendon Press, 1965–97).

Jeffares, A. Norman, *George Moore* (London: Longmans, 1965).

Levine, Richard A., *Benjamin Disraeli* (New York: Twayne, 1968).

Lohrli, Anne, compiler, *Household Words: A Weekly Journal 1850–59 Conducted by Charles Dickens – Table of Contents, List of Contributors and their Contributions* (Toronto: University of Toronto Press, 1973).

McDonagh, Josephine, *George Eliot* (Plymouth: Northcote House, 1997).

Melville, Lewis, *The Life of William Makepeace Thackeray*, 2 vols (London: Hutchinson, 1899).

Mintz, Alan, *George Eliot and the Novel of Vocation* (Harvard: Harvard University Press, 1978).

Morrell, Roy, 'Hardy in the Tropics', *A Review of English Literature*, 3 (1962), 7–21.

——, *Thomas Hardy: The Will and the Way* (Kuala Lumpur: University of Malaya Press, 1965).

Newey, Katherine Mary, 'Living Pictures: Topical and Contemporary Reference in English Melodrama, 1820–1848' (unpublished doctoral thesis, University of Sydney, 1990).

Oppenlander, Ella Ann, *Dickens's All the Year Round* (Troy, NY: Whitston, 1984).

Owens, Graham, ed., *George Moore's Mind and Art* (Edinburgh: Oliver and Boyd, 1968).

Pinion, F. B., *A Hardy Companion: A guide to the works of Thomas Hardy and their background* (London: Macmillan, 1968, repr. 1984).

Purdy, Richard Little, and Michael Millgate, ed., *The Collected Letters of Thomas Hardy: Volume I, 1840–1892* (Oxford: Clarendon, 1978).

Rahill, Frank, *The World of Melodrama* (Pennsylvania: Pennsylvania University Press, 1967).

Ray, Gordon R., ed., *The Letters and Private Papers of William Makepeace Thackeray*, 4 vols (London: Oxford University Press, 1945).

——, *Thackeray: The Uses of Adversity 1811–1846* (London: Oxford University Press, 1955).

——, *Thackeray: The Age of Wisdom 1847–1863* (London: Oxford University Press, 1958).

Reed, John R., 'A Friend to Mammon: Speculation in Victorian Literature', *Victorian Studies*, 27 (1984), 179–202.

Reynolds, Ernest, *Early Victorian Drama (1830–1870)* (Cambridge: Heffer, 1936; repr. New York: Benjamin Blom, 1965).

Rosa, Matthew Whiting, *The Silver-Fork School: Novels of Fashion Preceding Vanity Fair* (Port Washington, NY: Kennikat Press, 1964).

Sadleir, Michael, *Trollope: A Commentary*, 3rd edn (London: Oxford University Press, 1945, repr. 1961).

Sanders, Andrew, *Anthony Trollope* (Plymouth: Northcote House, 1998).

Schlike, Paul, *Dickens and Popular Entertainment* (London: Allen & Unwin, 1985).

Schwarz, Daniel R., *Disraeli's Fiction* (London: Macmillan, 1979).

Shelston, Alan, *A Lecture on William Thackeray: Vanity Fair* (Battle: Norwich Tapes, 1984, audio cassette tape).

Shuttleworth, Sally, *George Eliot and Nineteenth-Century Science: The Make-Believe of a Beginning* (Cambridge: Cambridge University Press, 1984).

Smalley, Donald, ed., *Trollope: The Critical Heritage* (London: Routledge and Kegan Paul, 1969).

Stallman, R. W., 'Hardy's Hour-Glass Novel', *Sewanee Review* 55 (1947), 283–96.

Sypher, Wylie, 'Aesthetic of Revolution: The Marxist Melodrama', *Kenyon Review*, 10 (1968), 431–3.

Terry, R. C., ed., *Oxford Reader's Companion to Trollope* (Oxford: Oxford University Press, 1999).

Tillotson, Geoffrey, and Donald Hawes, ed., *Thackeray: The Critical Heritage* (London: Routledge and Kegan Paul, 1968).

Tillotson, Kathleen, *Novels of the Eighteen-Forties* (London: Oxford University Press, 1961).

Trollope, Anthony, *Thackeray* (London: Macmillan, 1879, repr. 1887).

——, *An Autobiography* (London: Oxford University Press, 1950).

Walton, John K., *Disraeli* (London: Routledge, 1990).

Ward, Paul, 'A Laodicean', *The Thomas Hardy Year Book*, 11 (1984), 28–30.

Weber, Carl J., *Hardy of Wessex: His Life and Literary Career* (New York: Colombia University Press, 1940).

Wheeler, Michael, *English Fiction of the Victorian Period 1830 – 1890* (London: Longman, 1985).

Williams, Raymond, *The English Novel from Dickens to Lawrence* (London: Hogarth Press, 1984).

Worth, George J., *Dickensian Melodrama: A Reading of the Novels* (Lawrence: University of Kansas, 1978).

Background Material

Anonymous, 'The Demon of Homburg', *All the Year Round* (hereafter *AYR*), 2 (1860), 517–22.

——, 'A Board of Green Cloth', *AYR*, 12 (1864), 308–12.

——, 'Horse Racing in India', *AYR*, 15 (1866), 247–51.

——, 'Round the Roodee', *AYR*, 18 (1867), 253–9.

——, 'Old Stories Re-Told: A Gambler's Life in the Last Century', *AYR*, 18 (1867), 324–9.

——, 'Royal Ascot', *AYR*, 18 (1867), 377–81.

——, 'Far-Western Gamblers', *AYR*, 20 (1868), 489–93.

——, 'A Fashionable Gaming-House: Confessions of a Croupier', *Bentley's Miscellany*, 15 (1844), 552–64.

——, 'Betting-Offices', *Chambers's Edinburgh Journal*, 18 (1852), 57–8.

——, 'Hells in London', *Fraser's Magazine*, 8 (1833), 191–206.

——, 'Gambling', *Quarterly Review*, 168 (1889), 136–66.

Arnold, Matthew, *Culture and Anarchy*, ed. by J. Dover Wilson (Cambridge: Cambridge University Press, 1960. repr. 1988).

Ashton, John, *The History of Gambling in England* (New York: Burt Franklin, 1968).

Bailey, P. C., 'A Mingled Mass of Perfectly Legitimate Pleasures: The Victorian Middle Class and the Problem of Leisure', *Victorian Studies*, 21 (1977), 6–28.

Bailey, Peter, *Leisure and Class in Victorian England: Rational Recreation and the Contest for Control, 1830–1885* (London: Routledge and Kegan Paul, 1978).

Belchem, John, *Industrialization and the Working Class: The English Experience 1750–1900* (Aldershot: Scolar Press, 1991).

Best, Geoffrey, *Mid-Victorian Britain 1851–75* (London: Fontana, 1979, repr. 1985).

Blyth, Henry, *Hell and Hazard: or, William Crockford versus the Gentlemen of England* (London: Weidenfield and Nicolson, 1969).

Brenner, Reuven and Gabrielle A. Brenner, *Gambling and Speculation: A Theory, a History and a Future of some Human Decisions* (New York: Cambridge University Press, 1990).

Briggs, Asa, *A Social History of England* (London: Weidenfeld and Nicolson, 1994).

Buckingham, James Silk, *National Evils and Practical Remedies* (Clifton, NJ: Augustus M. Kelley, 1973).

Bulwer-Lytton, Edward, *England and the English*, 2 vols. (Shannon: Irish University Press, 1971).

Burns, John, *Brains Better than Bets or Beer* (London: Clarion Press, 1902).

Carlyle, Thomas, *Past and Present* (London: Ward, Lock and Bowden, 1897).

Chesney, Kellow, 'The Sporting Underworld', *The Victorian Underworld* (London: Temple Smith, 1970), pp. 267–306.

Clapson, Mark, *A Bit of a Flutter: Popular Gambling and English Society 1823–1961* (Manchester: Manchester University Press, 1992).

Collini, Stefan, *Public Moralists: Political Thought and Intellectual Life in Britain 1850–1930* (Oxford: Clarendon Press, 1991).

Cruikshank, George, *The Betting-Book* (London: W. & F. G. Cash, 1852).

Cunningham, Hugh, *Leisure in the Industrial Revolution* (London: Croom Helm, 1980).

David, F. N., *Games, Gods and Gambling* (London: Charles Griffin, 1962), 161–78.

Delgado, Alan, *Victorian Entertainment* (Newton Abbot: David & Charles, 1971).

De Moivre, Abraham, *The Doctrine of Chances: or a Method of Calculating the Probabilities of Events in Play* (London: Frank Cass, 1969).

Dickens, Charles, 'Betting Shops', *Household Words*, 5 (1852), 333–6.

Dickerson, Mark G., *Compulsive Gamblers* (London: Longman, 1984).

Doré, Gustave and Jerrold Blanchard, *London: A Pilgrimage* (New York: Dover, 1970, first published 1872).

Downes, D. M., B. P. Davies, M. E. David and P. Stone, *Gambling, Work and Leisure: a study across three areas* (London: Routledge and Kegan Paul, 1976).

Egan, Pierce, *Boxiana; or Sketches of Ancient and Modern Pugilism* (London: G. Smeeton, 1812).

——, *Pierce Egan's Book of Sports, and Mirror of Life* (London: T. T. and J. Tegg, 1832).

Eitner, Lorenz E. A., *Géricault: His Life and Work* (London: Orbis, 1982).

Engles, Friedrich, *The Condition of the Working Class in England* (Oxford: Oxford University Press, 1993).

Ensor, R. C. K., *The Oxford History of England: England 1870–1914* (Oxford: Oxford University press, 1992).

Franklin, J. Jeffrey, *Serious Play: The Cultural Form of the Nineteenth-Century Realist Novel* (Philadelphia: University of Philadelphia Press, 1999).

Fulford, Roger, ed., *The Greville Memoirs*, rev. edn (London: Batsford, 1963).

Goffman, Erving, *Where the Action is* (London: Allen Lane, 1969), pp. 105–206.

Golby, J. M and A. W Purdue, *The Civilisation of the Crowd: Popular Culture in England 1750–1900* (London: Batsford, 1984).

Grant, James, *The Great Metropolis* (London: Saunders and Otley, 1837).

Greenwood, James, 'Betting Gamblers', *The Seven Curses of London* (London: Stanley Rivers, [1869]), pp. 377–419.

Greville, Charles C. F., ed. Henry Reeve, *The Greville Memoirs: A Journal of the Reigns of King George IV and King William IV*, 3 vols (London: Longmans, Green and co., 1875).

——, *The Greville Memoirs: A Journal of the Reign of Queen Victoria from 1837 to 1852*, 3 vols (London: Longmans, Green and co., 1885).

Hadley, Elaine, *Melodramatic Tactics: Theatricalized Dissent in the English Marketplace 1800–1885* (Stanford: Stanford University Press, 1995).

Halliday, Andrew, 'You Must Drink', *AYR*, 11 (1864), 437–40.

——, 'My Two Derbies', *AYR*, 13 (1865), 490–4.

Halliday, Jon and Peter Fuller, ed., *The Psychology of Gambling* (London: Allen Lane, 1974).

Harrison, Brian, 'Religion and Recreation in Nineteenth-Century England', *Past and Present*, 38 (1967), 98–125.

Hawke, John, *A Blot on the Queen's Reign: Betting and Gambling, An Appeal to the Prince of Wales* (London: Elliot Stock, 1893).

Herman, Robert D., *Gamblers and Gambling: Motives, Institutions and Controls* (Lexington, Massachusetts: Lexington Books, 1976).

Hobsbawm, E. J., *Industry and Empire: From 1750 to the Present Day* (Harmondsworth: Penguin, 1968; repr. 1981).

Huizinga, Johan, *Homo Ludens: The Study of the Play Element in Culture* (London: Paladin, 1970).

Humphreys, A. L., *Crockford's, or The Goddess of Chance in St James Street 1828–1844* (London: Hutchinson, 1953).

Itzkowitz, David, 'Victorian Bookmakers and their Customers', *Victorian Studies*, 32 (1988), 7–30.

John, Juliet and Alice Jenkins, ed., *Rethinking Victorian Culture* (Basingstoke: Macmillan, 2000).

John, Juliet, *Dickens's Villains: Melodrama, Character, Popular Culture* (Oxford: Oxford University Press, 2001).

Kavanagh, Thomas M., *Enlightenment and the Shadows of Chance: The Novel and the Culture of Gambling in Eighteenth-Century France* (Baltimore: The John Hopkins Press, 1993).

Kitson Clark, G., *The Making of Victorian England* (London: Methuen, 1962).

Lectures to Young Men: Lectures Delivered Before the Young Men's Christian Association in Exeter Hall from November, 1857, to February, 1858 (London: Nisbet, 1858).

Lerner, Laurence, ed., *The Context of English Literature: The Victorians* (London: Methuen, 1978).

Lowerson, John and John Myerscough, *Time to Spare in Victorian England* (Hasocks, Sussex: Harvester, 1977).

Malcolmson, Robert W., *Popular Recreations in English Society 1700–1850* (Cambridge: Cambridge University Press, 1979).

Margetson, Stella, *Leisure and Pleasure in the Nineteenth Century* (London: Cassell, 1969).

Mayhew, Henry, 'Costermongers', *London Labour and the London Poor: The Condition and Earnings of Those that will work, cannot work, and will not work, vol. 1, London Street-Folk* (London: Charles Griffin [1861]), pp. 6–63.

McKibbin, Ross, 'Working-Class Gambling in Britain 1880–1939', *Past and Present*, 82 (1979), 147–78.

Meisel, Martin, *Realizations: Narrative, Pictorial, and Theatrical Arts in Nineteenth-Century England* (Princeton: Princeton University Press, 1983).

Munting, Roger, *An Economic and Social History of Gambling in Britain and the USA* (Manchester: Manchester University Press, 1996).

Parkinson, Joseph Charles, 'Slaves of the Ring', *AYR*, 3 (1860), 582–5.

——, 'Against the Grain', *AYR*, 14 (1865), 442–5.

——, 'The Rough's Guide', *AYR*, 14 (1865), 493–6.

——, 'Genii of the Ring', *AYR*, 15 (1866), 230–3.

——, 'Derby Dregs', *AYR*, 15 (1866), 487–9.

Pinel, P. H., *A Treatise on Insanity*, trans. by D. D. Davis (New York: Hafner, 1962).

Quinlan, Maurice J., *Victorian Prelude: A History of English Manners 1700–1830* (London: Frank Cass, 1941; repr. 1965).

Raymond, John, ed., *The Reminiscences and Recollections of Captain Gronow, being Anecdotes of the Camp, Court, Clubs and Society 1810–1860* (London: Bodley Head, 1964).

Read, Donald, *England 1868–1914: The Age of Urban Democracy* (London: Longman, 1979).

Reid, J. C., *Bucks and Bruisers: Pierce Egan and Regency England* (London: Routledge and Kegan Paul, 1971).

Royle, Edward, *Chartism* (Harlow: Longman, 1980, repr. 1984).

Sidney, Samuel (?), 'Clubs and Club-Men', *AYR*, 16 (1866), 283–8.

Statman, Daniel, ed., *Moral Luck* (Albany, NY: State University of New York Press), 1993.

Steinmetz, Andrew, *The Gaming Table: Its Votaries and Victims, in all Times and Countries, especially in England and in France* (Montclair, NJ: Patterson Smith, 1969).

Tawney, R. H., *Religion and the Rise of Capitalism* (London: John Murray, 1926; repr. 1943), pp. 197–287.

The Bulletin: The Occasional Record of the National Anti-Gambling League, November 1893.

——, May 1894.

——, November 1895.

——, November 1896.

——, May 1900.

——, May 1901.

Thomas, Keith, 'Work and Leisure in Pre-Industrial Society', *Past and Present*, 29 (1964), 50–63.

Thompson, E. P., *The making of the English Working Class* (London: Penguin, 1991).

Thompson, F. M. L., *The Rise of Respectable Society: A Social History of Victorian Britain 1830–1900* (London: Fontana, 1988).

Trollope, Anthony, ed., 'On Horse-Racing', *British Sports and Pastimes* (London: Virtue, 1868), pp. 9–69.

——, 'Whist at our Club', *Blackwood's Edinburgh Magazine*, 121 (1877), 597–604.

Vamplew, Wray, *The Turf: A Social and Economic History of Horse Racing* (London: Allen Lane, 1976).

Williams, Raymond, *Marxism and Literature* (Oxford: Oxford University Press, 1977).

Woodward, Sir Llewellyn, *The Oxford History of England: The Age of Reform 1815–1870*, 2nd edn (Oxford: Oxford University Press, 1997).

Index

Index